H.G. WELLS:

Six Scientific Romances
Adapted For Film

by

THOMAS C. RENZI

The Scarecrow Press, Inc.
Metuchen, N.J., & London
1992

Frontispiece: H. G. Wells. Photo courtesy of Anthony Slide. All other photographs are used by courtesy of the Museum of Modern Art/Film Stills Archive, New York City.

This book is based on the author's doctoral dissertation, State University of New York—Buffalo, 1989.

British Library Cataloguing-in-Publication data available

Library of Congress Cataloging-in-Publication Data

Renzi, Thomas C., 1948–
    H. G. Wells : six scientific romances adapted for film / by
Thomas C. Renzi.
       p.   cm.
    Includes bibliographical references and index.
    ISBN 0-8108-2549-X (acid-free paper)
    1. Wells, H. G. (Herbert George), 1866–1946—Film and video
adaptations.   2. Science fiction, English—Film and video adaptations.   I. Wells, H. G. (Herbert George), 1866–1946. II. Title.
PR5778.F55R46   1992
823'.912—dc20   92-19038

For my wife, Deb,
whose encouragement and support were boundless,

and for my newborn son, Matt,
who contributed to this work
with his extraordinary sleeping habits

CONTENTS

ACKNOWLEDGMENTS

I wish to thank Leslie Fiedler, Howard Wolf, and Brian Henderson for taking the time to review this work and make contributory comments. Especially, I would like to thank Alan Spiegel. His diligent guidance, his knowledge of film, science fiction, and H. G. Wells, and his thoughtful criticism and suggestions were invaluable to the completion of this project.

For the photograph of H. G. Wells appearing as the frontispiece of this book, I am indebted to Anthony Slide, who was kind enough to lend it to me. All other pictures are courtesy of the Museum of Modern Art/Film Stills Archive, New York City.

INTRODUCTION

A: Wells's Association with Film

On October 24, 1895, Robert W. Paul applied for a patent for a film project which would simulate a time journey from the Present to the Past and Future. His patent application describes in loose detail the complex and awkward mechanical contrivances he would use to effect the time trip. He would herd a limited number of spectators onto an enclosed platform which, rigged with gears and cranks, could be vibrated and rocked to mimic movement. Then he would flash slides and films depicting scenes from various time periods, their sequence creating the illusion of forward and backward passages through time.

Paul's inspiration for his invention came from H. G. Wells's *The Time Machine* (1895), a serialized magazine story which had gained instant and wide popularity. Paul wrote to Wells about his idea and the two met to discuss its feasibility. While the concept was insightful about the nature of film and admirably prophetic of the direction of filmmaking, nothing came of the project and the collaboration dissolved.

Although some critics imply that Wells's role in the invention was equally enthusiastic, Terry Ramsaye's account of the Paul-Wells effort suggests that Paul, a pioneer in film, initiated most of the ideas.[1] Yet Wells's involvement indicates his appreciation of this new medium and a number of his writings anticipate film as a powerful new influence on popular culture. As early as 1899, *When the Sleeper Wakes* considers its negative potential when Graham discovers that the kinetoscope, a type of television disparagingly called a Babble Machine,[2] has replaced books and writing. In *The Peace of the World* (1915) and *The Undying Fire* (1919), the

1

"cinematograph" bears mixed blessings as a tool of education and propaganda.[3]

In his *Experiment in Autobiography* (1934), Wells sees financial potential in the film adaptations of a number of his short stories: ". . . many have still undeveloped dramatic and film possibilities. I had no idea in those energetic needy days of these little tips I was putting aside for my declining years" (433). His concern with monetary residuals did not curb his outspokenness about the films which had been made of his works. He criticized Erle C. Kenton's *Island of Lost Souls* (1933) as "a travesty of his intent."[4] He praised James Whale's *The Invisible Man* (1933) because it revived the popularity (and sales) of his novel, but he "objected most strenuously to the device of making his scientist a helpless lunatic by way of the drug he took."[5]

In 1927, in one of a series of news articles under the general title *The Way the World Is Going* (published in book form in 1928),[6] he criticizes Fritz Lang's *Metropolis* at length, panning it as "the silliest film" he ever saw. His remark that he found "decaying fragments of my own juvenile work of thirty years ago, *The Sleeper Awakes,* floating about in it" and his other comparisons with his novel (written 1899, revised 1910) seem more a defensive excuse for his earlier naiveté than an objective analysis of Lang's film technique and style. He overlooks Lang's powerful use of visual metaphor and denounces what appear as scientific and sociological inaccuracies, an irony in that Jules Verne had underestimated Wells for similar reasons in 1903.[7]

In 1929, Wells made an antiwar statement in a work called *The King Who Was a King.* Subtitled "An Unconventional Novel," it is really an amateurish attempt at a screenplay which, in his introduction, he pretentiously offers to any filmmaker who might wish to produce it. While his introductory remarks dwell mainly on trying to justify his approach to the content and characters of the story, they reveal some of Wells's opinions on film, especially its usefulness as a tool of education and social influence.

Despite his early awareness of cinema's influential future and the fact that several of his books had contributed story material to the new industry almost from its inception,[8] Wells did not become actively involved in filmmaking until 1934 when producer Alexander Korda invited him to write the screenplay based on his sprawling "history of the future," *The Shape of Things to Come* (1933). *The King Who Was a King* was never made into a film, and Wells himself "regarded it as a 'prentice effort' preparatory to the scenario of *Things to Come*."[9]

Wells's venture into film writing was a brief, qualified effort, a disappointing irony because he seemed to have a natural approach to film method. His writing style occasionally incorporates descriptions which imitate filmmaking techniques, camera angles, and the use of special effects. However, the writer of novels does not automatically qualify as a capable scenarist. Wells's screenwriting proved less than adequate and needed substantial guidance and revision from the other production members, especially Korda, director William Cameron Menzies, and assistant screenwriter Lajos Biro. Wells admits his limitations:

> The task of putting my imaginative story into screen form was, however, far more difficult than I had imagined, and took much longer than I thought it would.
>
> It is only now that I realise how little I knew about the cinema when I wrote the scenario. Many of the sequences which slipped quite easily from my pen were extremely difficult to screen, and some were quite impossible. But that did not matter.
>
> The film has emerged spiritually correct, despite the fact that it now embodies many alterations suggested by Alexander Korda, William Cameron Menzies, and a score of other people.[10]

For *Things to Come,* Wells had written three scripts, the first totally unusable, the second unfilmable but providing the characters and basic plot of the third and final screenplay. Most Wellsian critics refer to this incident as proof of Wells's deficiency in film writing. However, Leon Stover's *The Prophetic Soul* (1987) presents a comprehensive analysis of the Wellsian philosophy embodied in *Things to Come* and contains, for the first time in publication, two key versions of

4   H. G. WELLS

the screenplay: *Whither Mankind?*—Wells's preliminary
script, and the finished shooting script of the film.

Whither Mankind? was Wells's preferred title. The pun
echoes the film's ending (and that of *The Time Machine*)
where Cabal's question to his friend is indirectly addressed to
Man: "It is this or that. All the universe or nothingness.
Which shall it be, Passworthy? Which shall it be?" A reading
of *Whither* shows that, at times, it bears out the widespread
accusation that Wells exaggerates the use of dialogue and
underestimates the power of action and imagery in furthering
his concepts. His scenario includes needless detailed descriptions laden with explanations of his symbolism, an approach
a dramatist might use in explaining the set designs for his
play. In contrast, *Things* presents a bare-bones screenplay,
with detailed but succinct descriptions of the sets and
instructions for character and camera movements.

The stories appear strikingly similar, the original dialogue
revised but followed closely, and the characters and structure
recognizable in the later draft. However, for Wells to say
"the film has emerged spiritually correct" suggests that,
despite the parallels and the admission that the film has
captured his intent, he has reservations about it. In another
comment, he appears dissatisfied with the dialogue. It strays
from his first conception of it, and he excuses it as not
entirely authored by him:

> . . . the Author, now almost through the toils of his
> apprenticeship, was in a state of fatigue towards the
> altered, revised and reconstructed text, and, although
> he had done his best to get it into tolerable film prose,
> he has an uneasy sense that many oddities and awk-
> wardnesses of expression that crept in during the
> scenario have become now so familiar to him that he
> has become blind to them and unable to get rid of
> them.[11]

Wells's argument is probably justified, yet when compared
with his other works, *Things to Come* clearly embodies his
ideas and presents a valid reflection of his vision for
mankind.

Wells assisted in a subsequent collaboration with Korda, *The Man Who Could Work Miracles* (1937), based on his short story about a man gifted with a "Midas touch," a supernatural power to make any wish come true. Wells was credited with the screenplay, but the consensus is that Korda had Wells's son Frank keep him from the production as much as possible while Lajos Biro (uncredited) did most of the scripting.

Wells's writing talent, exceptional in his novels, seems stymied when he attempts to translate his ideas for the visual medium:

> He wasn't a screenwriter; nor did he stop to consider that *ideas,* abstract thoughts, are almost impossible to present through a film—except by action, character, incident; certainly not through dialogue alone.[12]

The criticism of Wells's shortcomings in writing for film appears unanimous, yet his approach, which may have shown a lack of knowledge, did not exhibit a lack of skill. Maybe it was simply that his talent in this area needed more time for development. Still, despite his frustrating experience, he never lost his appreciation of the industry. He believed film the most efficient and effective method for reaching the widest audience. He remarked, perhaps half-seriously, that he would forsake novels for more screenwriting, an ambition which, of course, due to age and illness, did not materialize.[13]

B: The Adaptability of Wells's Works

Wells's earliest scientific romances, regardless of their classification, cross social and cultural boundaries, appealing to different people for different reasons. Jorge Luis Borges, in a famous eulogistic essay, accurately expresses the crux of Wells's universal mystique:

> Not only do [Wells's first novels] tell an ingenious story; but they tell a story symbolic of the processes that are

somehow inherent in all human destinies. The harassed
invisible man who has to sleep as though his eyes were
wide open because his eyelids do not exclude light is our
solitude and our terror; the conventicle of seated
monsters who mouth a servile creed in their night is the
Vatican and is Lhasa. Work that endures is always
capable of an infinite and plastic ambiguity; it is all
things for all men, like the Apostle; it is a mirror that
reflects the reader's own traits and it is also a map of the
world.[14]

These early works, especially, are layered with paradox
and ambiguity which incite speculative discussion and defy
conclusive arguments. Despite contradictions to credibility,
a reader not only accepts the willing suspension of disbelief
but craves it for the sake of traveling through time or meeting
an invisible man or discovering life inside the moon. In this
respect, Borges's comment suggests at least two reasons why
Wells's work appears suitable for film adaptation: popular
appeal and good storytelling.

From a commercial standpoint, Wells's popularity would
almost automatically insure interest in the cinematic version
of his work. As for the second reason, Wells's attractiveness
to filmmakers relates to several aspects of his storytelling
skills. First, as noted above, his descriptions often imitate
filmmaking techniques. Some famous examples occur in *The
Time Machine*, where the inventor's journey describes the
fast-forward and reverse-action modes of film. In his annotated *The Definitive Time Machine*, Harry M. Geduld
includes additional suggestions of sound dubbing and fade-in
and fade-out effects.[15] In "The New Accelerator" (1903),
two men, after taking a drug which speeds up their bodies'
systems, observe the retarded movements of people, animals, and vehicles, a mimicking of film's slow-motion effect.
And foreshadowing the camera's high-angle shot, the Narrator of *The War of the Worlds* describes the evacuation of
London as if seen from a balloonist's perspective (Bk.I:
Ch.17).

Secondly, Wells's central plots, which Borges notes may
merely serve as a "point of departure," are intriguing notions

in themselves. His inventiveness has conjured so many of these "what-if" premises that, between his novels and his short stories, he has formulated or touched on nearly all the major themes of 20th-century science fiction.[16] And they are more than mere fascinating conjectures. They press our primal buttons, manipulating and inspiring us with the chance belief that we might be able to become invisible, or grow into noble giants, or defy the barriers of time and gravity.

Thirdly, around his germinal idea, Wells deftly interweaves tone, style, and imagery to fabricate an engrossing tale. Serving as a kind of tension-release formula, a mysterious tone continuously alternates with surmise to create an aura of wonder and uncertainty. A pseudo-scientific "fact" may be at the core of the plot, but the story always floats in a nebulous sea of eeriness and the supernatural. Truth unfolds gradually while the Narrator leads, or misleads, his readers with speculations about his predicament. His theories, whether about the Eloi, Beast Men, or Selenites, bait curiosity, drawing the audience into a hazy realm of the bizarre.

Erle C. Kenton's *Island of Lost Souls* (1933) and George Pal's *Time Machine* (1960) imitate this alternate succession of mystery and speculation, capturing something of Wells's original tone and giving their stories a similar air of fascination. On the other hand, films which avoid or mishandle this sense of the mysterious lose that tonal quality. Don Taylor's *Island of Dr. Moreau* (1977), a fairly well-made film, lacks this trait (shot mostly in daylight, it relies more on horror than on mystery), and as a result, appears inferior as a remake of Kenton's earlier effort.

Wells's imagery is an important facet in the nature of his scientific romances and a key to their adaptability for film.[17] His clear, concrete descriptions impress the imagination with vivid, fantastic pictures. Moreau's Beast Men, the Time Traveller's view of buildings sprouting around him, and octopus-like Martians piloting gargantuan super-machines become incredible sights to consider for the visual medium. True, filmmakers often change the original images (the Time Traveller's journey is extended, the Martians appear anthro-

pomorphic), but Wells provides the initial visual concept
which they might adjust to suit their personal intentions.

Wells's imagery is also reflected in his treatment of
characterization. He creates interesting characters, such as
the Time Traveller or the Narrator, Curate, and Artilleryman of *The War of the Worlds,* but his stories are not
character studies. Instead, he concentrates on an external
conflict between an invader and the people who react against
the disruption of their routine lives: an Invisible Man upsets
a small, quiet village; Martians driving monstrous machines
ravage the London countryside; men fly to the moon and
antagonize the inhabitants.

Emphasis on external events contributes to the imagery
which gives Wells's early scientific romances their allegorical
nature and fills them with the mythical, protean quality
Borges mentions. Besides their richness in meaning and
substance, these "tangible" images give filmmakers something they can readily transfer to their visual medium.
Inventive plot ideas, mysterious tone, and allegorical style,
all contribute to the strength of Wells's storytelling technique
and make him a valuable source for film adaptation.

C: Wells as a Literary Source for SF Film

Wells explains in his preface to *Seven Famous Novels by
H. G. Wells* (1934) that for the inscrutability of magic he
substitutes the jargon of science, feigning a rational explanation for the fantastic technology at the center of his scientific
romances. Although he may not have originated his basic
concepts, such as invisibility or space travel, his incorpora-
tion of (pseudo-) science precurses the direction of modern
sf, and, as noted above, he proposes most of the major sf
themes. As a result, his works become foundational for the sf
which follows him, and his successors often borrow from
him, in part or in whole.[18] The six Wells novels examined in
this study contain primary themes which have repeatedly
appeared in twentieth century sf film.

Time travel is not an original idea for Wells, but his
approach to it is. Instead of a temporal transmission through

sleep or drug, *The Time Machine* offers a mechanical device constructed on scientific principles, a concept appropriate for the coming Age of Technology. *Planet of the Apes* (Franklin J. Schaffner, 1968), an absorbing sf film based on Pierre Boulle's novel, imitates Wells more than incidentally. With a spaceship acting as their Time Machine, three astronauts arrive in a future where apes (Wells's Morlocks) rule and humans (Eloi-figures) are suppressed. The fanciful *Time After Time* (Nicholas Meyer, 1979) bears an even more obvious connection by having Wells (Malcolm McDowell) use his invention to chase Jack the Ripper (David Warner) from Victorian England to 1979 San Francisco. And *Back to the Future* (Robert Zemeckis, 1985) contains some interesting twists in that the Time Machine is a DeLorean automobile and Michael J. Fox, sent into the past, must play matchmaker for his parents to ensure that he will eventually be born. The sequels, *Back to the Future, Parts II* and *III*, play even more heavily on the paradoxes and confusions inherent in time travel when one meets and interacts with the self in the past and future.

The man-as-creator motif in *The Island of Doctor Moreau* (1896) borrows from Mary Shelley's *Frankenstein* (1816), but Wells makes his science more explicit, convincing us of the feasibility of Moreau's creations. In George Pal's *Atlantis, the Lost Continent* (1961), a scientist (Berry Kroeger) reverses Moreau's experiments, using hypnosis and surgery to turn men into animals. Bela Lugosi in *The Ape Man* (William Beaudine, 1943), after injecting himself with spinal fluid from a gorilla, takes on the physical appearance and mannerisms of an ape.

Invisibility, once achieved with a magic ring or cloak, is attained when Wells's albino scientist combines chemistry and mechanics with optics. *The Invisible Man* (1897) was adapted into a fine film by James Whale in 1933 and followed by three mediocre-to-fair sequels (*The Invisible Man Returns*, 1940; *The Invisible Agent*, 1942; *The Invisible Man's Revenge*, 1944).

A plethora of imitations emerged, unrelated to the original except by the inclusion of an invisible character. All seemed to be trying to capitalize on the new kinds of special effects

created by John P. Fulton in Whale's film. In terms of
entertainment value, these elaborate illusions often succeed
even when the story fails, as in *The Body Disappears* (Ross
Lederman, 1941), a farcical mix-up about a student (Jeffrey
Lynn) who is presumed dead but has been turned invisible by
scientist Edward Everett Horton. One film, *The Invisible
Boy* (Herman Hoffman, 1957), is interesting in that Robby
the Robot (first seen in *Forbidden Planet,* 1956) copies
Wells, using a drug plus a machine to make a boy (Richard
Eyer) disappear. In general, these films, including *The
Invisible Man* and its sequels, rely only on a drug.

The War of the Worlds (1898) serves as the prototype for
the alien invasion films mass-produced in the fifties. Ironically, Pal's 1953 version of Wells's novel established a
standard for excellence, but only a few films could match it.
Most appear flat, clumsy, and unconvincing. Among the
better films, *Invaders from Mars* (William Cameron Menzies, 1953) contains a bland, flat tonal quality, one which
skillfully complements the innocent, simple perceptions of
the boy who tells the story. In *It Came from Outer Space*
(Jack Arnold, 1953), superior extraterrestrials land on earth,
with the twist that they have come not to conquer mankind
but only to repair their ship.

Space travel proposed in *The First Men in the Moon* (1901)
has many predecessors, ranging from Lucian's *A True Story,*
written around 170 A.D., to Jules Verne's 1865 and 1870
stories, *From the Earth to the Moon* and *Around the Moon.*
Wells's cavorite, however, as a scientifically created material
for launching a projectile, is an improvement over Verne's
idea of firing the spaceship from a colossal gun.[19] Space
travel reverses the alien invasion motif in that Man, entering
a strange environment, becomes the alien.

Georges Méliès's *A Trip to the Moon* (*La voyage dans la
lune,* 1902), based on the Verne and Wells novels, set the
precedent for space voyage films of the silent era. A number
of "A Trip to ———" titles appear, spaceships taking their
cargo to the moon, Mars, or Jupiter. In the late thirties, the
Flash Gordon and Buck Rogers serials preserved the interest
in galactic journeying. The fifties and sixties produced a

number of space travel sagas, some poor, some well-done. *Cat Women of the Moon* (Arthur Hilton, 1952), a classic clunker with bad script, phoney sets, and clumsy effects, borrows Wells's idea that the lunar beings inhabit the interior of the satellite. *Robinson Crusoe on Mars* (Byron Haskin, 1964) is an interesting film, with a well-drawn character study of a stranded astronaut (Paul Mantee).

The concept of scale in *The Food of the Gods* (1904) has its roots in Greek mythology (Prometheus and the Titans) and the Bible (Nimrod's race of giants). Wells uses increased size allegorically, to indicate how a few specially gifted individuals, by their exceptional contributions to mankind, represent the potential for progress and a greater society. Ironically, although they offer benefits, they must struggle against suppression by the common masses who view them as a threat to tradition and convention.

Most sf films based on the scale motif reverse Wells's intent and use the giant as an evil threat to society, not a benefactor. In films like *The Beast from 20,000 Fathoms* (Eugene Lourie, 1953) and *The Amazing Colossal Man* (Bert I. Gordon, 1957), an oversized monster personifies Science as an out-of-control menace to Nature and humankind. In a variation of the Frankenstein and Moreau stories, the giant revenges itself on those responsible for its creation (or reactivation), often killing innocent bystanders in the process.

Inverting the perspective of size, films such as *Doctor Cyclops* (Ernest B. Schoedsack, 1940), *The Incredible Shrinking Man* (Jack Arnold, 1957), and *Honey, I Shrunk the Kids* (Joe Johnston, 1989) miniaturize humans, turning familiar surroundings into an alien and threatening world. Ironically, this produces a theme more aligned with Wells's original intention. Man made small, like Man made gigantic, becomes eccentric to the world of common humanity and must struggle to survive on his own terms, by his own grit and determination. While the menacing giant monster signifies an antagonistic, alien entity, the miniaturized human relates to the audience personally and empathetically in a way similar to that suggested by Wells's innocent giants.

D: Intention of This Study

George Bluestone speaks for many critics when he refutes the validity of a comparison between film and literature, arguing that "the novel is a linguistic medium, the film essentially visual."[20] Yet, despite this obvious fundamental difference, Bluestone admits that "like the novel, it usually presents a narrative depicting characters in a series of conflicts" (vii). That is, films often tell stories and, like written or oral narratives, contain the same elements crucial to storytelling: plot, character, setting, voice, and theme. On that basis, although the nature of their presentations vary, the comparison between a film and its adapted novel is legitimate.

In *Fiction, Film, and Faulkner: The Art of Adaptation* (1988), Gene Phillips asserts a caution about scripting from a previous work:

> Although a work of fiction must undergo many superficial alterations in dialogue, characterization, and plot when it is transformed into a movie, these changes must not depart in any significant fashion from the fundamental conception and intent of the original author.[21]

Fidelity to the original becomes his standard for judging the film's merit. And since the adaptation claims association with a specific author and his work, this criterion appears justifiable.

However, Geoffrey Wagner, in *The Novel and the Cinema* (1975), takes a less stringent, more objective look at film adaptation. He examines the ways filmmakers approach novels as raw material for their own personal visions, and from this, classifies three methods of transferring an author's work to film: transposition, commentary, and analogy. Transposition occurs when "a novel is directly given on the screen, with the minimum of apparent interference." Commentary "is where an original is taken and either purposedly or inadvertently altered in some respect. It could also be called re-emphasis or re-structure." Analogy represents "a fairly considerable departure for the sake of making *another* work of art."

Of the films examined in this present study, none seems a clear transposition. Mostly, they tend to fit the area of commentary, clearly recognizable as Wells's stories but altered according to a "re-emphasized" central idea. On the other hand, Bert I. Gordon's two films and Nicholas Meyer's *Time After Time* belong to analogy. They borrow their basic plot ideas from Wells but greatly deviate from him.

In his book, *Filming Literature: The Art of Screen Adaptation* (1986), Neil Sinyard, like Wagner, discusses several ways of looking at the transference of the written word to the visual image. One consideration treats adaptation as a kind of literary criticism:

> When defining his approach to adapting a literary work for film, screenwriter Daniel Taradash said: "What I try to discover is the basic premise, the basic idea, the basic theme behind a particular piece of writing and to try to dramatise that without making it obvious" (Paul Mayersberg, *Hollywood: The Haunted House,* Penguin, 1969: 113). Two things are especially interesting and revealing there: the stress on "the basic theme"; and the implied emphasis on personal interpretation ("What I try to discover . . ."). There is no reference to the novelist's declared intention, nor to fidelity to the original, nor inclusiveness. Clearly, Taradash's conception of the role of the screenwriter is one of interpretation more than reproduction. . . .
>
> Taradash's comment underlines . . . the proposition that best adaptations of books for film can often best be approached as an activity of literary criticism, not of pictorialisation of the complete novel, but a critical essay which stresses what it sees as the main theme. Like a critical essay, the film adaptation selects some episodes, excludes others, offers preferred alternatives. It focuses on specific areas of the novel, expands or contracts detail, and has imaginative flights about some characters. In the process, like the best criticism, it can throw new light on the original. (117)

In conjunction with Sinyard's remarks, the following comparative analysis of H. G. Wells's earliest scientific romances and their film adaptations has a two-fold purpose.

First, organized according to the chronological order of Wells's publications, this book explores the progressive development of the writer and his predominant ideas. Of course, when examining an author, most critics use this method of organization, but here the added dimension of a comparison to film tends, as Sinyard claims, to "throw new light on the original." The author's material, viewed in relation to a filmmaker's treatment of it, results in a different attitude toward, and perspective on, his original work. Thus, much of the analysis of Wells proposed here, respective of the various film adaptations and interpretations, produces conclusions and ideas not readily seen when approaching his works directly and exclusively.

More specifically, Wells represents one man's vision of life and his attitude toward the forces which influence and manipulate it. The film adaptations serve as a counterpoint or foil, using his same basic material to present alternate visions created by different perspectives at different moments in history. Wells's scientific romances rely significantly on Darwinian theory which, in the late nineteenth century, proposed a bold, new outlook on humankind and its relation with its environment. Meanwhile, the films, made at different times during the twentieth century, adapt Wells's works to address and reflect the current issues as they have arisen: Science as a threat to humanity, the Cold War, Nuclear War, Providence and Religion, Ecology and Environment.

A second purpose arises automatically from a close comparison of the novel and film, namely, a consideration of the process of film adaptation. Examining the alterations, omissions, and inclusions of certain details reveals how filmmakers deliberately reshape the book to fit their cinematic conceptions.

In regard to this current study, two other adapted works of Wells need mentioning. The short story fantasy, *The Man Who Could Work Miracles,* and the utopian epic, *The Shape of Things to Come* (film title, *Things to Come*), not only became landmark films, but their author also had a direct hand in their production. Although not scientific romances, they bear some important relationships with the other works and a brief treatment of each appears in the appendices.

Notes

1. In "From 'Paul and *The Time Machine,*' " (in William Johnson, *Focus on the Science Fiction Film,* 1972), Ramsaye writes of the two men's enterprise. John Baxter (*Science Fiction in the Cinema,* 1970) and Garret Stewart ("The 'Videology' of Science Fiction" in George Slusser and Eric S. Rabkin, *Shadows of the Magic Lamp: Fantasy and Science Fiction in Film,* 1985), give sketchy versions of the relationship and suggest that Wells was deeply committed to the project when no proof exists that this was so.

2. This anticipates the monitor used in George Orwell's *Nineteen Eighty-Four* (1949).

3. Leon Stover, *The Prophetic Soul: A Reading of H. G. Wells's "Things to Come"* (Jefferson, NC: McFarland, 1987), p. 30, 105n.

4. Michael Benson, *Vintage Science Fiction Films: 1896-1949* (Jefferson, NC: McFarland, 1985), p. 47.

5. James Curtis, *James Whale* (Metuchen, NJ: Scarecrow, 1982), p. 107.

6. H. G. Wells, "Mr. Wells Reviews a Current Film," *The New York Times,* April 17, 1927, pp. 4, 22.

7. Robert H. Sherard, interview with Jules Verne in *T.P.'s Weekly,* extract in Patrick Parrinder, *H. G. Wells: The Critical Heritage* (London: Routledge and Kegan Paul, 1972), p. 101.

8. *La voyage dans la lune* (George Méliès, 1902) and *First Men in the Moon* (J. V. Leigh, 1919) are a couple of examples indicating Wells's influence on the earliest ideas for film stories.

9. J. R. Hammond, *Herbert George Wells: An Annotated Bibliography of His Works* (New York: Garland, 1977), p. 41.

10. Karol Kulik, *Alexander Korda: The Man Who Could Work Miracles* (London: W. H. Allen, 1975), p. 147; excerpt from J. Danvers Williams, " 'I Wrote This Film for Your Enjoyment,' says H. G. Wells," *Film Weekly,* February 29, 1936, p. 8.

11. *Two Film Stories: "Things to Come and "The Man Who Could Work Miracles"* (Cresset Press, 1940), in John Brosnan, *Future Tense: The Cinema of Science Fiction* (New York: St. Martin's, 1978), p. 58.

12. Paul Tabori, *Alexander Korda* (New York: Living Books, 1966), p. 159.

13. Frank McConnell, *The Science Fiction of H. G. Wells* (New York: Oxford, 1981), p. 213.

14. Jorge Luis Borges, "The First Wells" (1946), in Patrick Parrinder, *H. G. Wells: The Critical Heritage,* p. 331.

15. Harry M. Geduld, *The Definitive Time Machine* (Indianapolis: Indiana University Press, 1987), p. 100, Ch. 3, 3n.

16. McConnell, *The Science Fiction of H. G. Wells,* p. 7.

17. Imagery is also the key to his change in style in his later years. Books like *The Dream* (1924), *The Shape of Things to Come* (1933), and *Star-Begotten* (1937) forsake imagery for more didactic commentary and abstract theories, losing that special fascinating quality contained in his earlier works. The change was a conscious one, Wells crusading more overtly to waken mankind to social and political ills and hoping to inspire reform.

18. The object here is not to prove whether such borrowing is actual or deliberate, but merely to show that Wells's formulas have filtered into most sf. And although all sf writing deserves attention, especially those which have been adapted for the following films, the present study limits discussion to Wells's impact on the sf film.

19. Ironically, Wells borrows Verne's idea for his *Things to Come.* It seems hypocritical that he should have criticized Fritz Lang for incorporating "illogical" concepts in *Metropolis,* and then use an absurdity like a spaceship gun when science had progressed enough by 1936 to make clear the impracticality of such a device.

20. George Bluestone, *Novels into Film* (Berkeley: University of California, 1957).

21. Phillips's foreword, written by producer Jerry Wald (in "Fiction versus Film," *Films in Review 5,* no. 1, 1954, pp. 62–7), supports his claim, saying that, despite the changes in length and cutting, it is necessary to "keep the intent, the flavor, the theme, and the spirit of the original" (xii).

I: THE TIME MACHINE

A: George Pal's Reproduction of an Old Timepiece

In H. G. Wells's *The Time Machine* (1895), a turn-of-the-century inventor in Victorian England debates with his dinner guests the paradox of the fourth dimension. Certain that time comprises this elusive concept, he has built a machine for traveling through time and he embarks on it to prove his theories. He journeys ahead to the year 802,701 A.D. where he finds that the human race has evolved into two distinct species, the docile Eloi and the cannibalistic Morlocks. After several adventures, he leaves the Eloi to explore farther into the future. At one point, he discovers that earthly life has degenerated into a lower form of crab-like creatures. Traveling on, he ultimately witnesses the end of the world. He returns to the present to relate his experiences to his friends, then disappears in a final voyage on his machine.

Although their 1960 film excludes the trip beyond the world of the Eloi, director George Pal and writer David Duncan retain most of the chronology of the original narrative. However, they alter so many of the details of plot and character that they actually tell a different story. Deviating from Wells's concern with a natural demise of humankind, they incorporate images and ideas which emphasize the more immediate issue of their time, namely, the threat of humanity's self-annihilation through nuclear war.

In regard to narrative structure, one similarity of the two versions is the device of a story-within-a-story. In Wells's novel, the Frame Narrator[1] introduces the Time Traveller and lets him relate his adventure in an Inset Narrative. In Pal's film, David Filby (Alan Young) replaces the Frame Narrator and acts as a Frame Character, the person we see

18

first and last, at the beginning walking to the home of the inventor H. George Wells (Rod Taylor) and at the end leaving it after his friend disappears, supposedly to return to the year 802,701 A.D. Like Wells's time Traveller, George tells his story in an Inset Narrative.

The Frame Narrator and Frame Character serve at least two purposes. Their outside viewpoint carries a degree of objectivity and gives credibility to the inventor's Inset Narrative. Second, they ground the story in a reality with which the audience can identify before and after experiencing the wondrous trip in the Time Machine. This leads to an effect similar to the sensation the Time Traveller describes to his guests after his return:

> This room and you and the atmosphere of every day is too much for my memory. Did I ever make a Time Machine, or a model of a Time Machine? Or is it all only a dream? They say life is a dream, a precious poor dream at times—but I can't stand another that won't fit. (Ch. 12)

With the return to familiar surroundings, the reader, like the Time Traveller, might question the reality of such a strange experience, but then will have to conclude that, even if a fantasy, it subjected him to visions and events that affected him in some deep, emotional way. The thrill of being able to travel in time, the disgust toward cannibalism, the fear of a temporal finality, all elicit a strong emotional response. In this respect, the value of the dream experience is not whether it was real, but that it left an indelible impression. Both film and novel seem to do this.

The most obvious structural difference between Wells and the film occurs when the Time Traveller decides to journey beyond the era of the Eloi. The knowledge gained from his decision results in a central theme and tone different from the film, where George limits the extent of his trip to 802,701 A.D.

Wells's Time Traveller witnesses the end of the world, an apocalyptic vision which he carries back to the present. His revelation of finiteness implies that we can expect and must accept an end to life, an inevitable doomsday. In contrast, George, after battling the Morlocks to recover his Time Machine, heads by mistake into the future, but abruptly reverses direction without any new discoveries beyond the period of the Eloi. His truncated journey seems less disturbing than that of the novel because it does not quash belief in a perpetual future. It accommodates the reassuring concept of cycle, that after destruction comes rebirth and regeneration.

In each version, the Time Machine is devised for different reasons. Wells's inventor's interest in time-traveling seems primarily for the sake of scientific accomplishment, to gain knowledge for knowledge's sake. George, on the other hand, wants to leave the present because, as he tells Filby, "I don't care much for the time I was born into. It seems people aren't dying fast enough these days. They call upon science to invent new, more efficient weapons to depopulate the earth." George's motives are moralistic and reactionary. He seeks escape from a world in which affairs are so disastrously entangled that only an Armageddon could disentangle them. The Time Machine becomes his "deus ex machina." When George begins his journey, England is at war with the Boers in South Africa. Unlike the uninterrupted trip of Wells's Time Traveller (a brief description barely notes the physical discomfort of time travel and the changes in season, landscape, and architecture), he makes several stops coinciding with World Wars in 1917 and 1940, and with a projected World War III in 1966. War, a primary theme in Pal's film, is not an issue with Wells.

Among the Eloi, George befriends a young girl, Weena (Yvette Mimieux). Trying to answer his questions, she leads him to an abandoned museum and shows him the "talking rings," small flat rings which, when spun like a child's top, emit a recorded voice. From these he learns how humankind divided into two distinct species, the Upperworld Eloi and the Underworld Morlocks. After a 326-year war, nuclear fallout polluted the atmosphere and threatened extinction of life. Some people sought refuge underground, others took their chances "in the sunlight." In the voice-over, George says, "From the talking rings I learned that by some awful quirk of fate, the Morlocks had become the masters and the Eloi their servants."

Pal's film proposes a definite cause-effect explanation for the Eloi's futuristic society. George's time-stops during wars of the 20th century and information from the talking rings verify the social and biological evolution as the result of a nuclear holocaust. This kind of concrete information is not available to the Time Traveller, who makes no intermittent stops and lacks data on humanity's historical development. To shape his theories he relies on the scientific method, using empirical evidence to reach conclusions which he then reformulates with the discovery of new information. This reevaluation process continues throughout the story, and even when he proposes his final theory it appears inconclusive:

> So, as I see it, the Upper-world man had drifted towards his feeble prettiness, and the Underworld to mere mechanical industry. But that perfect state had lacked one thing even for mechanical perfection— absolute permanency. Apparently as time went on, the feeding of the Underworld, however it was effected, had become disjointed. Mother Necessity, who had been staved off for a few thousand years, came back again, and she began below. The Underworld being in contact with machinery, which, however perfect, still needs some little thought outside habit, had probably retained perforce rather more initiative, if less of every other human character, than the upper. And when other meat failed them, they turned to what old habit had hitherto forbidden. So I say I saw it in my last view of the world of Eight Hundred and Two Thousand Seven Hundred and One. It may be as wrong an explanation as mortal wit could invent. It is how the thing shaped itself to me, and as that I give it to you. (Ch. 10)

The Time Traveller bases his hypotheses on socio-economic conditions and theories (especially socialism) prevalent in his own period of the late 19th century, and on a metaphorical image of the Capitalist and Worker. Without

knowledge of some causal chain, he lacks concrete information to show what other variable elements may have affected
mankind to produce the bifurcation of the human species and
the predator-prey relationship of Morlock and Eloi. In many
respects, these ambiguities and unanswerable questions are
what make the novel so interesting.

In this difference between film and novel, it becomes
further apparent that Pal has not tried to mimic Wells. In
1960, the year of Pal's film, America and Russia co-existed in
the midst of a Cold War and an all-out nuclear confrontation
seemed imminent. Schoolchildren and office workers endured sporadic air-raid drills to prepare for such a catastrophe. Families built backyard bomb and fallout shelters or
stockpiled food in basement corners in the name of self-
preservation. Pal's *Time Machine,* with its special-effects
destruction of London by an atom bomb, the subsequent
volcanic response from Nature, and the hideous appearance
of the Morlocks as possible mutant casualties, seems to use
fear tactics to warn man to find alternatives to war before he
annihilates himself.

Yet the film contains ideas in addition to its serious
"message," giving it a timelessness beyond the limits of the
era it addresses. In alluding to the Boer War, the two World
Wars, and an extrapolated Third World War, it avoids a
specific statement about the prevailing Cold War and makes
a more universal anti-war statement. Secondly, many of the
captivating qualities of the novel appear in the film, such as
the wish fulfillment of a time-travel experience and the thrill
of possessing a power no one else has. The special effects by
Gene Warren and Wah Chang (which won Warren an
Oscar), with the time-lapse and stop-motion photography
creating the illusion of racing through the future and the
long-shot of the Eloi's decaying Great Hall seen from across
a brown expanse of desolate wasteland, are for the most part
of a high caliber and convince the audience that they share in
George's fantastic adventure.

After plot, a second major issue to consider is the
characters. In the novel, politicians, doctors, and newspaper-
men frequent the inventor's house in what seems an open
invitation every Thursday night.[2] With the exceptions of

Filby, Mrs. Watchett, Hillyer, and Weena, Wells uses no names, but designates the characters by professional title (Medical Man, Editor, Psychologist, etc.) or by descriptive trait (Very Young Man, Silent Man). This approach deprives the characters of individual identity and generalizes them as certain social types. Thus, when they reject his story, the impression is that their anonymous voices merge into a condemnation by the crowd.

At the same time, the occupational titles indicate that some of the guests comprise the professional middle class of society. As the controlling class, they would represent the ancestors of the Eloi, the "elite," the "God-people,"[3] who once lorded their power over the laboring Morlocks, only later to become their source of food. Despite the Time Traveller's speculations on human and social evolution, the guests vainly ignore his suggestion for social reforms. They condemn the tale as "a gaudy lie" and deny their implication in bringing about such a future. The Frame Narrator's final words sum up his friend's attitude, which the others vehemently denounce:

> He, I know—for the question had been discussed among us long before the Time Machine was made—thought but cheerlessly of the Advancement of Mankind, and saw in the growing pile of civilization only a foolish heaping that must inevitably fall back upon and destroy its makers in the end. If that is so, it remains for us to live as though it were not so.

What seems an optimistic view, shunning the Time Traveller's fatalistic doom in favor of a more hopeful outlook, may actually be a naive, indifferent response to a situation which could be changed by an effort of Will, if men would react positively and effectively to the warning.[4]

In the film, the inventor's guests deviate considerably from their original counterparts. They comprise a smaller group, four instead of the two varied and larger groups. And they all have names. Anthony Bridewell (Tom Helmore) and Walter Kemp[5] (Whit Bissell) are minor characters contributing to the skepticism toward time travel. Dr. Hillyer (Sebastian

Cabot) is a composite of Filby ("an argumentative person"), the Medical Man, and the Psychiatrist. He argues the most with George about the feasibility and practicality of a Time Machine and is loud, hostile, belligerent and prejudiced in his views. Cabot fits his role well, his large rotund figure creating an imposing physical presence which complements his overbearing attitude.

The fourth guest, David Filby, totally unlike the novel's Filby, more closely approximates Wells's Frame Narrator because of his role as a Frame Character and his having a closer relationship with George than the others do. If the warmth of their friendship touches the audience, it is mostly because of Alan Young's sensitive characterization. At times he sides with the guests and opposes George's theories, but by the use of subtle mannerisms he reveals his loving concern for George that is hidden behind his cold, logical advice. For instance, when he supports Dr. Hillyer's suggestion to contact the war office about his discovery, he turns away self-consciously, making it obvious that it pains him to have hurt George's feelings. After the others leave, he stays behind to comfort George. Their words become heated and Filby argues that some knowledge is better left alone, but he continues to show a tender concern for George's well-being and invites him to his house to bring in the new year. Then, at the film's end, as he explains in his Scottish accent[6] to Mrs. Watchett what must have happened to George and his machine, his expressions reveal a person who is genuinely thrilled over his friend's discovering love and life. His reaction to George's good fortune lacks envy and self-interest and reflects his nature as a truly kind soul.

The most important character to undergo alteration, however, is the Time Traveller. In the novel, Wells gives him no name, which suggests that he is Everyman, for we are all time travelers on a "journey" through life. The Time Traveller demonstrates this with a series of photographs of a progressively aging man, calling them "Three-Dimensional representations of his Four-Dimensioned being . . . " (Ch. 1). Also, as Everyman, he possesses the one power everyone has for escaping confinement in an eternal present: Imagination.

The Time Traveller explains how the imagination effects time-travel, and although it seems a trite explanation, it suggests one of the most subtle ironies of *The Time Machine*. For, while the Time Traveller himself may have traveled physically to the future, he proves his point in that his story transports his listeners mentally to a world different in time, though not in space, by exciting their imaginations with the images and experiences of events that happened to him at such a time. The idea that a story can displace time for an audience leads to an ambiguity within *The Time Machine*, and at the center of that ambiguity is the nature of Time Traveller himself.

The Time Traveller's friends already know him for a prankster: " 'Look here!' said the Medical Man, ' . . . is this a trick—like that ghost you showed us last Christmas?' " (Ch. 1). And the Narrator gives a lengthy analysis of his impish inclination to perpetrate hoaxes for his own amusement:

> I think that at that time none of us quite believed in the Time Machine. The fact is, the Time Traveller was one of those men who are too clever to be believed; you never felt that you saw all round him; you always suspected some subtle reserve, some ingenuity in ambush, behind his lucid frankness. Had Filby shown the model and explained the matter in the Time Traveller's words, we should have shown *him* far less scepticism. For we should have perceived his motives: a pork butcher could understand Filby. But the Time Traveller had more than a touch of whim among his elements, and we distrusted him. Things that would have made the fame of a less clever man seemed tricks in his hands. It is a mistake to do things too easily. The serious people who took him seriously never felt quite sure of his deportment: they were somehow aware that trusting their reputations for judgment with him was like furnishing a nursery with egg-shell china. (Ch. 2)

In his narrative, the Time Traveller confirms this assessment by revealing his penchant for playing the trickster, even if it means foolishly putting himself in danger. At one point, he nearly runs out of matches defending himself against the Morlocks because he has squandered them merely to make himself appear a magician or shaman to the Eloi: ". . . my store of matches had run low. . . . I had wasted almost half the box in astonishing the Upperworlders to whom fire was a novelty" (Ch. 6). In the Palace of Green Porcelain, the ruins of a gigantic museum, he takes time, with the threat of Morlocks around, to display a facetious, iconoclastic attitude toward religion: "In another place was a vast array of idols—Polynesian, Mexican, Grecian, Phoenician, every country on earth I should think. And here, yielding to an irresistible impulse, I wrote my name upon the nose of a steatite monster from South America that particularly took my fancy" (Ch. 8).

Later, he laughs after he first sets fire to the forest to repel the Morlocks (Ch. 9). His laugh may seem a displaced manifestation of fear, but it more likely reveals a personal enjoyment at his cleverness, for he laughs again when he deliberately walks through the lowered panels of the pedestal and into the Morlock trap, thinking smugly that he can outwit them. Instead, he nearly outsmarts himself when he cannot light his matches, and only brute force saves him from the Morlocks' clutching fingers.

The Time Traveller's story, therefore, because of his bent for practical jokes, carries the hint of deceit. And because of the Frame Narrator's estimate of the general attitude toward him, one entertains logical explanations to dismiss the three main things that may support his story: Weena's two flowers, his vanishing before the Narrator's eyes, and his failure to return.

In Chapter 12, the Frame Narrator resumes his story. After examining Weena's flowers, which the Time Traveller had placed on the table for all to see, the Medical Man says:

> "It's a curious thing . . . but I certainly don't know the natural order of these flowers. May I have them?"
> The Time Traveller hesitated. Then suddenly: "Certainly not."

The fact that the Medical Man cannot classify the flowers does not prove that they come from the future. It is doubtful he is an expert in that field, and even if he were, it does not guarantee his recognition of some rare species which the Time Traveller might have procured from anywhere to verify his story.[7] The Time Traveller's hesitation seems at once an innocent pause and a calculated silence to rethink his situation. His keeping the flowers may be out of sentiment, but it also suggests fear that if the Medical Man has enough time with them, the ruse may be discovered.

The Time Traveller's vanishing before the Narrator's eyes would seem a confirmation of his wondrous invention. Yet, when described as "a ghostly, indistinct figure sitting in a whirling mass of black and brass," he reminds us of the Medical Man's remark about his trick with the Christmas ghost and we realize he may be performing it here.

That the Time Traveller never returns from his final departure may give him credibility because of reasonable explanations for his disappearance (lost in time, frozen in a mountain, a Time Machine malfunction, etc.). However, his reputation raises enough contradictions to suggest him a jokester who might go to any great length, including losing himself, to have his friends believe he is time traveling. If so, he ironically repeats the episode when he had deliberately entered the Morlock trap thinking he could outwit them, but like Hawthorne's Wakefield, ends up gloating over a cleverness that may have actually led him to miserable circumstances in his self-exile from society.

The Time Traveller's character, then, affects his credibility, and in the larger sense contributes to the story's ambiguity. His tale sounds convincing, even if illogical and fantastic, because the idea of traveling in time appeals to the sense of wonder, to some unconscious wish for the possibility to free oneself from the restrictions of the present moment. Yet, however enticing the dream of time travel, the Time Traveller's reputation forces a reluctance to believe.

The character George, on the other hand, is more serious and does not have the reputation of a practical joker. The tale he brings back to his friends seems free of the Time

Traveller's ambiguity and, in the context of the story, appears believable. George's narrative begins with events of the previous Friday when the same four guests were present. Because he alone has experienced the time journey and witnessed the world of the Eloi, his story of the future could be as much a fabrication as the Time Traveller's. However, in this area, the film avoids the novel's ambiguities. The pictorial presentation which accompanies George's narration has the effect of concrete evidence verifying his story. We accept his tale as truth.

Wells's Time Traveller offers one particular bit of visual evidence which actually is not evidence at all. He says his whole experience could have been a dream, except that his Time Machine

> had started out from the south-east corner of the laboratory. It had come to rest again in the north-west, against the wall where you saw it. That gives you the exact distance from my little lawn to the pedestal of the White Sphinx, into which the Morlocks had carried my machine. (Ch. 12)

He takes them into the lab to see the battered machine resting where he said it was and where they had seen it last. Through verbal misdirection, however, he implies he had moved it since that last time, and now, even though it appears in that same location, it has actually "moved."

In George's case, an altered viewpoint near the end of the Frame Story makes his tale appear more credible. Filby leaves George's house with the other guests, but then returns, worried about his friend. The camera suddenly becomes an omniscient eye, cutting from Filby to George in his garden pulling his machine across the snow and through the open laboratory door. Obviously, the machine is too heavy to be moved easily. Moments later, as Filby breaks into the locked lab, a loud high-pitched whir from the Time Machine fades into a dying whine. After viewing the evidence, Filby explains to Mrs. Watchett George's disappearance. The single tracks in the snow, the cumbersomeness of the machine, the missing three books, and perhaps our romantic inclination to believe that he returns to Weena "right where he left her," make it easy to believe he has truly left on his invention.

Based on their characters, the Time Traveller's motivation appears more suspect than George's. The Time Traveller seems more prone to doing things with a flair for the sake of notoriety. Carrying a Kodak and knapsack and with the Narrator witnessing his departure, he makes a dramatic exit. In contrast, George leaves quietly and unassumingly, the only hint of his plan for departure suggested in a sentimental good-bye to Filby. When both of these men tell us they have invented a Time Machine, we might believe George, but will have reservations about the Time Traveller.

Besides contradictions created by the Time Traveller, other aspects contribute to ambiguities in the novel. The Narrator begins by calling time travel a "recondite matter," and the argument which follows results from its "paradoxical" nature. The underground world of the Morlocks and the sky at the end of the world are both a "rayless obscurity." The Time Traveller's proofs, the moved machine, Weena's flowers, and the Narrator's seeing him disappear may all be contradicted.

The Time Traveller tells his guests, "Say I dreamed it in the workshop," which can mean that he actually invented a Time Machine or that he concocted it out of his imagination. In fact, he tells his story in the smoking room, a place for "pipe-dreams," and the pipe is one of his props. After seeing the Time Machine for the first time, the Medical Man says, "It sounds plausible enough tonight . . . ; but wait until tomorrow. Wait for the common sense of the morning." They had been drinking, and what seemed a reality in an obscured state of mind might merely appear fantasy when perceived with a clear head.

Told from two perspectives the story's credibility is obscured even further. The Time Traveller may be an "Amateur Cadger," but the Narrator does not appear so, and his account, which tends to confirm his friend's, inclines us to believe him. The story becomes a counterpoint of certainty and doubt, clarity and vagueness, and for every argument to contradict the Time Traveller there seems another to support him. In the end, an unresolvable ambiguity exists between serious consideration of the reality of life's finiteness and amusement with the story as an elaborate fantasy.[8]

Another important association between the film and the novel involves the image of the Sphinx and its relation to the two inventors. Although it appears as a classic figure in Wells and a giant mouthless head in the film, it contains similar connotations for both stories. It alludes to the Theban monster which ate passersby who could not solve its riddle, and as such, symbolizes the cannibalistic Morlocks. Identified with Oedipus, who answered the riddle correctly and caused the Sphinx's suicide, George and the Time Traveller become riddle-solvers, but in different ways.

For George, little probing is needed. His questions are easily answered by the talking rings. He resembles Oedipus in his rash boldness and bravery, heroically descending into the Underworld to confront the Morlocks. Also like the foolhardy Oedipus, he fails to consider all the ramifications of his actions. He rescues the Eloi from one curse, but makes them vulnerable to another: independence from the Morlocks means return to the harsh struggle for survival.

The Time Traveller, unlike George, does not rescue the Eloi from the Morlocks, and the riddle he faces never seems quite thoroughly solved. As observer, he formulates and reformulates a number of theories about the Eloi-Morlock society until he arrives at one he believes best explains their relationship. However, his answer is mere speculation based partially on evidence and bias.

An interesting difference in their relation to Oedipus concerns their role as one who assumes a leadership position over the people. When Filby supposes George returns to the Eloi with his three books, we can imagine it is to lead them in rebuilding their society, but how much power he might wield is uncertain.

The Time Traveller becomes a figurative leader. He climbs to the crest of a hill where he discovers

> a seat of some yellow metal . . . , corroded in places, the arm rests cast and filed into the resemblance of griffins'

heads. I sat down on it, and I surveyed the broad view of
our old world under the sunset of that long day. (Ch. 4)

The golden seat contains ambiguous connotations. The
griffins' heads suggest that whoever sits in this seat sits on the
side of good and assumes the role of protector. The corrosion
and decay indicate the temporality of rule, or may imply, also
in accord with the griffin figures, that a corrupt authority, as
hoarders of wealth, once governed this land, a reflection on
the Eloi as the "elite" race.

When the Time Traveller assumes the throne, he becomes
master of all he surveys, except that the corroded seat, like
the eroded statue of Shelley's Ozymandias, suggests authority's vulnerability to time. The sunset view of "our old
world" signifies that he becomes ruler too late. Bernard
Bergonzi notes the recurrent apotheosis theme in Wells's
works, and here, as with Nunez in "The Country of the
Blind," the Time Traveller, with his unique power, might
have entertained ideas of becoming king but for the circumstances which prevented him.[9]

This image reflects the novel's larger implications about
humanity's vain assumption that it will forever dominate the
world. The Time Traveller's trip to the end of time reveals
that devolution will erase such self-inflated presumptions.
However, the Frame Narrator dismisses his friend's discovery with an optimist's attitude toward life: "If that is so, it
remains for us to live as though it were not so." And looking
at Weena's dried flowers, he declares: ". . . I have by me, for
my comfort, two strange white flowers . . . to witness that
even when mind and strength had gone, gratitude and a
mutual tenderness still lived on in the heart of man"
(Epilogue). Contradicting the Time Traveller's fatalism, he
proposes that the means are more important than the ends,
that people must live within the time given them, without
regard for things beyond their control. He clings to the belief
that even if the race of Eloi comes to exist, they will still
possess those qualities of compassion and appreciation which
are uniquely human.[10]

In the film, George's character embodies a similar contradiction between fatalism and hope. He tells Filby, "I don't

care much for the time I was born into." Critical of society, he uses war as the excuse for seeking a more agreeable era. Later, after defeating the Morlocks but still deprived of his machine, he sits by the river with Weena. His voice-over narrates: "I was imprisoned in a world in which I just did not belong." He tells Weena: "I wish we could go back to my time, or even to the time before that when the world was young. We could be so very happy." His future utopia has failed to materialize, and so he fantasizes about some former Edenic world that never really existed. What appears is a contradiction between the dream and reality.

George's vision of utopia does not exist and it seems unlikely that he will find happiness in any time period. Earlier, when he tells Filby he is disgusted with humanity's preoccupation with war, Filby says: "I agree with you. But here we are, and we have to make the best of it." At that moment, the irony is that George has invented a machine which can dispute Filby's cliché. By the end of the film, however, that irony becomes compounded, for George does find a society according to his specifications—free of war, free of collisions—but it proves a dissatisfying existence. If George were to find the utopia he seeks, it would require a human nature different from the one we now possess.

B: Pal's Film: Cyclical Renewal and the Illusion of Hope

The contradiction inherent in the inventor George's character embodies the final opposing views offered by Wells's Frame Narrator and Time Traveller. To reflect this more fully in his film, George Pal includes a number of interesting ambiguities which simultaneously suggest an optimistic outlook while portending doom. Using a variety of images, he contrasts the reassuring concept of cyclical renewal with the implication of a darker destiny for humanity.

In the film's opening scene, for example, the clocks float through the air before a black background, evoking negative connotations. They fly in straight lines, the only sound their ominous tickings. Their linear path across the black void

The Time Machine (1960, MGM/Turner Entertainment Co.): Inventor as Storyteller. George (Rod Taylor, center) displays Weena's flowers to his bewildered listeners. Filby (Alan Young, at Taylor's right), the loyal friend, counters the harsh criticism of the skeptic Hillyer (Sebastian Cabot, at Taylor's left). (Tom Helmore, far left, and Whit Bissell complete the group.)

implies that time's flight has morbid consequences: finality and death. When the clock tower rises out of the bottom of the frame, it slants left; that is, it suggests time is "out of joint," and the loud thunder crash and flash of lightning portend disaster and catastrophe. These images appear dreadfully foreboding rather than romantically optimistic.

Following the clock sequence, the credits appear against a blue-violet sky. Across this background drifts a series of images to indicate the change of seasons: first, a soft dusting of snow; next, petals from spring's cherry blossoms; then, an empty gap to imply summer; next, a fluttering of autumn leaves; and finally, another snowfall. The blue-violet hue comprises the end of the color spectrum and signifies the decay and finality of humanity's existence on earth. The change of seasons, with their stark representations, suggests bleakness and sadness, and Russell Garcia's grand but haunting orchestral music accompanying their change arouses feelings of meditative melancholy.

In the same way that the credits begin and end with a snowfall, the story itself begins and ends with Filby walking in a Courier-and-Ives setting, as if the present world were framed by an eternal winter. George's time-stops always occur in summer, suggesting that the Time Machine may be a way to escape the deep-freeze, but when he leaves, he, of course, takes the machine with him, and humanity is stranded without any fantastic deus ex machina.

As noted earlier, George, unlike Wells's Time Traveller, decides not to continue into the future beyond the era of the Eloi. This, together with Filby's romantic assumption that George has returned to Weena to help her people build a new world, contributes to the comforting and hopeful sense of cyclic renewal, that the world will go on, that no matter how deep and desolate a Dark Age might bury us, humanity, in time, will always emerge to rebuild civilization for itself. Connoting this optimistic idea is the repeated image of a death-rebirth cycle which George undergoes during his travel through time.

The first of these rebirth patterns occurs on George's journey to World War I. From his seat in his machine, he watches the effect of fleeting time on things outside his laboratory windows. Across the street in Filby's department store display window, a mannequin is repeatedly stripped and then dressed in changing clothing styles to reflect the passage of time. He is awed by the rapid opening and closing of flowers and the change of seasons, themselves indicative of cycle. Abruptly, a row of long vertical planks, one-by-one, plunk into place and seal up the windows. George, his face in shadow, narrates: "Then suddenly the light had gone. . . . In the year nineteen hundred and seventeen I stopped."

George "stopped" because "the light had gone," that is, he has figuratively died. The insertion of each plank is accompanied by a staccato rap, as if someone is hammering nails into the boards of George's "coffin."

The next scene begins with a long shot viewed from the

library through thick cobwebs hanging in the dining room doorway. In the background, George opens the kitchen door and steps into the dining room. It creaks loudly, like a door on a crypt. He walks forward to the open doorway and divides the cobwebs with his hands. As he steps through, the camera moves back to widen the view of the library where he had formerly conversed with his guests about the Time Machine. There is a pronounced silence, noticeable because of its contrast with earlier scenes in which his clocks on the walls and fireplace mantel had saturated the background with an interminable drone of clicks and pings. The once brightly lit room sits in a haze of gloom and shadow. Dustcovers drape the furniture. He lifts one small clock from the mantel, looks at it nostalgically, and blows off the thick layer of dust. A noise startles him. He turns. The camera cuts to several rats scurrying near the wall's rotted floor molding.

The image recalls a pyramid burial chamber where a royal personage lies interred with the artifacts dear to him in life and which he might need on his journey through death. In George's case, his journey into the future is a kind of death, because he has become dead to the people of his own time. Also, for him time has stopped and, like one dead, he finds time meaningless. Around him, his home succumbs to decay and turns to dust, yet like the mannequin in Filby's window, he never ages. Unfortunately, while he exists in his atemporal bubble, the only thing he can identify with is this non-living, inanimate replica of a woman.

Next, George walks behind the large round table on which he had demonstrated his model Time Machine. He steps to the chair where Filby had sat during the experiment and rests his hand on its back, but immediately he withdraws it, repelled by the touch of dust. Disgusted, he shakes his hand and swipes his sleeve.

Suddenly, from outside, the chimes of a tower clock sound a prelude to the hour. George walks to the front door and, opening it, finds boards across the threshold. As he kicks down the boards and steps out into the daylight, the clock chimes three times.

The image of George as a Christ-figure appears obvious by his "resurrection" and his removing the barrier at the mouth of his tomb. This identification fits his later role as redeemer of the Eloi. Ironically, however, George emerges from his "crypt" at three p.m., the time traditionally assigned to Christ's death. One possible implication is that, by leaving his machine, George returns to life, once more becoming subject to time and death.

George meets Filby's son, Jaimie, who tells him that his father was killed in the war, an event foreshadowed by the dust on Filby's chair. After removing the planks which block his view of the mannequin, George reseats himself in his Time Machine and continues his travels, entering a second birth-death cycle.

On this leg of his journey, a loud explosion buffets his machine from side to side. Curious, he stops again. The date on the control panel reads June 19, 1940. Through his skylight, George sees the night sky flashing with signs of warfare. Above London rooftops, searchlights crisscross in all directions, airplanes speed across the darkness, and balls of flame explode in the air. George does not leave the machine. The night scene reinforces the idea that George travels in the realm of death, but this time it also suggests a nightmare for him, another war only twenty-three years after the previous one.

George continues forward. An explosion and a burst of flames obliterate his house: "I found myself in the open air." When he reaches 1966, he hears a sudden high-pitched whining and slows down to investigate. The sound becomes recognizable as air-raid sirens. He lands in a park on a lawn surrounded by trees. His sundial stands in a flower bed and in front of it is a short square column bearing a square plaque with the inscription: "This park is dedicated by James Filby to his father's devotion to his friend George." Just then, the tower clock sounds the same four-note prelude as in 1917, but without the chimes to indicate the time.

This sequence mirrors a number of the film's images and motifs, the repetition itself suggesting a kind of cycle. The nighttime war scene followed by the explosive burst of flames suggests a descent into an underworld from which George makes a hasty escape into "the open air." This descent and ascent, a death and rebirth image, foreshadows two more he will make later, into and out of the Morlocks' lair. In addition, the sirens he hears and Filby's reference to the "all-clear" signal become the future devices of the Morlocks for controlling the Eloi. The park lawn becomes the lawn surrounding the Morlocks' Sphinx.

The tower clock, which sounded a death-hour before, now sounds no time at all, as if time has topped for all life. This seems so, for a nuclear bomb explodes, initiating a holocaust for humanity. George gets to his machine just as a wave of molten lava sweeps over him. He becomes entombed once more, this time in a mountain of rock: "Darkness . . . darkness for centuries. . . . I put my trust in time." And again time saves him when the rock eventually erodes away. In yet another image of rebirth, a circular hole of white light appears above him and opens wider as the rocks crumble away on all sides: "I was free again."

In the world of the Eloi, he repeats the cycle two more times. The first occurs when he descends into the throat of the Morlocks' well and then emerges after torching their labyrinth, turning it into an inferno (i.e., hell). The second occurs when he is lured into the Sphinx's pedestal to reclaim his stolen invention. His fires still burn as the Morlocks attack him, but he escapes their trap by clambering into his Time Machine.

Finally, after revisiting his own time, he leaves again to return to the Eloi period (if Filby's guess is correct), completing a double circle, from his present and back and from the Eloi's time and back, creating an overall outline of the recurring cycle of death, burial, and rebirth.

Already noted, the floating clocks which introduce the film forebode death and finality. Yet in another sense, with their circular faces and clockwise dial movement, they reinforce the antithetical idea of cyclical renewal. Associated with them, an almost infinite barrage of circle imagery reflects the concept of unending cycle: the sundial and mantel clock faces, the talking rings and the round table on which they are spun, the large round table on which George launches his model Time Machine, the dome of the Great Hall, among others.

The most prominent circle appears on the Time Machine

itself,[11] the large revolving disc that turns behind George. Its colorful cryptic patterns remind one of the Zodiac, the monthly cycle speeded up or slowed down at the traveler's whim. It also represents the Wheel of Fate, finally controlled by Man in that he can bypass the fixed segment of time allotted him and move freely into and out of his own chosen periods of existence.[12]

Related to the circle is the image of the arc. While the circle symbolizes an unbroken connection between cycles, the arc signifies connections between separate things. Through his skylight, George sees the sun and moon travel in an arched path across the sky, linking alternate light and darkness in the day-night cycle. Weena leads George through an arched doorway of the museum. He moves from ignorance to knowledge when the talking rings illuminate the connection between the past war and the present social condition.

The most significant arc seems to be the bridge which spans the road in front of George's house. It connects George's property with Filby's department store and symbolizes their bond of friendship. When the bridge rips apart in the cataclysmic World War III sequence, it appears to show the tremendous force it must take to sever their friendship. The destruction of the bridge and of Jaimie's park monument dedicated to "his father's devotion to his friend George" implies that nuclear warfare brings a catastrophic end to all traditional relationships. This foreshadows the future's more disastrous 326-Year War which splits the human species in two, producing the indifferent Eloi and the animalistic Morlocks.

The ruined dome on the Eloi's Great Hall, a great circle destroyed, relates to George's stopped clocks, and the collapse of the arched bridge in that cycle has ended for the Eloi. They live a monotonous routine existence. Weather and season remain unchanged. Stunted emotions prevent fluctuations in attitude. Every day is the same, until George, their Redeemer, "saves" them.

George's redemption of the Eloi, reviving their ambition for creativity and progress and awakening their emotions, appears an admirable quest. However, Pal injects a subtle paradox. George's attack on the Morlocks contradicts his pacifist position and his violent upheaval disrupts a contented, organized society which appears to be "running like clockwork."

This is a central paradox in the film and requires an examination of three particular images: the Warning signal, the Shelter, and the Collision. All three occur in the very first scene and reappear throughout the film in an interrelated way. The story opens with a long shot looking diagonally from George's front sidewalk across the street toward Filby's store. Filby opens his door, bundles up against the wintry night air, and walks forward diagonally across the street toward the camera. As he reaches the foreground, a bell sounds from outside the frame. Filby, startled, stops short and a bicycle passes in front of him, the rider waving apologetically.

When Filby left his house and stepped off the sidewalk into the street, he left his secure Shelter and entered an arena of risk. The bicycle bell provided a civilized Warning that alerted him in time to avoid a Collision. An almost identical scene occurs with George on his stop in 1917. After talking with Jaimie Filby, George, in a reverie, steps off the sidewalk. As he reaches the middle of the street, an automobile horn sounds from outside the frame and chugs past, causing him to halt momentarily. The same three related images appear, but a primary difference is in the nature of the Collision. A bicycle accident would probably result in minor injuries. An automobile accident, however, could result in death. Progress has increased the danger in humanity's arena of risk.

When George stops in 1966, again the three images appear, but this time, the Warning given by the sirens, although it prepares everyone to retire in time to their Shelter, is not enough. The Collision created by nuclear explosions and volcanic eruptions moves the danger directly into the Shelter. The fear associated with this catastrophe becomes ingrained in humanity to the point of producing a conditioned response. Later, when the Morlocks sound their sirens, the Eloi will act like automatons and enter the one Shelter which they assume represents security.

It is this automatic behavior which George resents. The books that are allowed to decompose on the shelves without being read, the lack of curiosity, the indifference toward life—to the point where they would have let Weena drown in the river,[13] all stem from a mental stagnation which has made them insensitive, unemotional robots, and which George hopes to reform.

His first night there, after the theft of his Time Machine, he spends with Weena in the forest near the Sphinx. He tells her:

> Man's past is mainly a grim struggle for survival, but there have been moments when a few voices have spoken out, and these rare moments have made the history of man, man's past, a glorious thing. I refuse to believe it's dead and gone. We've had our dark ages before and this is just another one of them. All it needs is for someone to show you the way out. I'm only a tinkering mechanic, but I'm sure there must be this hidden spark in one of your people. If only I can kindle that spark, my coming here would have some meaning.

George's wish to be crusader and redeemer comes true. However, an irony occurs between his words and his accomplishment. Life once faced "a grim struggle for survival," an arena of risk, a world full of Collisions. Now it has been reduced to the Warning and the Shelter. Both Morlock and Eloi accept this. George cannot. He is a product of a society that uses violence to secure and protect its rights, or what it believes are its rights. When he takes it upon himself to descend into the Underworld and fight the Morlocks, he fights for his property (his Time Machine) and his woman (Weena).

However, his invasion of the Morlock lair corresponds to the atomic bomb infiltrating the people's bomb shelters. He reintroduces Collision, the struggle for survival, when he singlehandedly punches, kicks, and bludgeons the Morlocks, until one Eloi, inspired to rebel, makes the first fist in centuries to save George from being choked to death. Others join the revolution, and after their escape and their destruction of the Morlock wells, George leads them to the river for a celebration. The civilization that has done away with war and violence has once more learned to fight and to revel in the exhilaration which comes from victory over a foe.

At the river, Weena questions George about the women of his time, how they look and how many he has known. She becomes coy and acts jealous. Weena exemplifies the change about to come over the Eloi. Caring and curiosity replace indifference and must almost inevitably lead to jealousy, rivalry, and competition, the negative side of ambition. In other words, George has rekindled a "hidden spark" in the Eloi, a passion for living, but he has also reawakened the negative emotions which must accompany that passion.[14]

A final implication is that, not having a Time Machine, humanity cannot travel through time in some protective bubble that excludes it from Nature's "struggle for survival." In the cyclic scheme of life, we must at times endure "dark ages," but we will at other times revel in moments that make our history "a glorious thing."

C: Two Asterisks: A Time Bomb and a Bio-fictional Analogy

Two additional films closely related to Wells's *The Time Machine* need consideration: a television movie of the same name, directed by Henning Schellerup in 1978, and *Time After Time*, scripted and directed by Nicholas Meyer in 1979 (from a story written by Karl Alexander and Steve Hayes). The first is less an adaptation than a remake of Pal's film, borrowing its theme and structure from its predecessor. The second, an analogy,[15] emerges out of Wells's story, but deviates dramatically from it.

Schellerup's *The Time Machine* stars John Beck as the new Time Traveller, Neil Perry. Unlike Pal's adaptation, which copies the novel by setting the Frame Story in Victorian England, the television movie begins in the present-day United States. NORAD tracks a Russian satellite orbiting the earth and detects a sudden malfunction. The capsule plummets into the atmosphere and NORAD projects it to hit

Los Angeles "dead center." ("The uranium on board could reach critical mass at impact," warns one official.) As a countermeasure, they alert Mega Corporation, the only facility with computers capable of guiding an untested antiballistic missile, the X-7B, to meet the satellite. Head scientist Ralph (Whit Bissell)[16] has trouble directing the missile, but Perry enters in time to recalculate the computers and destroy the rogue capsule.

Although assigned by Mega to develop a Deathray Laser and an Anti-Matter Bomb, Perry has been channeling his apportioned funds into his own project, a Time Machine. The situation implies that the corporate mind, influenced by government contracts, fosters the development of destructive weaponry, while the inventive individual, if left on his own, is inclined to create more beneficial devices for the world. Perry rebels against the corporate mindset. One Friday, he leaves on his machine for a journey through time.

In the next scene, J. R. Worthington (Andrew Duggan), head of Mega, visits the corporate office. Perry appears, his clothes dirtied, his face scratched. Trying to prove the value of his machine in warning humanity to reverse its self-destructive tendencies, he recounts in flashback his adventures in time travel.

Deviating from the novel and the earlier film, not only can his machine move in space as well as in time, but whereas the previous time-travelers report only on the future, part of Perry's adventures include visiting the past. He first stops in 17th-century Salem during the Puritan witch hunts. He is arrested, accused of being a sorcerer, and sentenced to be burned. However, he is conveniently tied in the seat of his machine and escapes before the fires singe his mustache. He next lands in California during the Gold Rush of 1849. This time taken for a claim jumper, he is imprisoned, but using a 20th-century paper clip he frees himself, regains his machine, and returns to his lab in the present.

In the hall, he meets a fellow scientist, Ed, who tells him how statistical projections of the effects of seepage from radioactive waste spell disaster for the environment and for man in the coming centuries. Ed cannot convince their boss, who believes such speculations are inaccurate. Perry realizes that this dilemma gives his Time Machine a purpose: he and the machine "were going into the future to prove the world was planting the seeds of its own destruction."

Setting out a second time, he and his machine are encircled by a broiling whirlpool of flame and smoke, obviously the result of a nuclear explosion. He stops in the year 2025 and finds the world a flattened, desolate wasteland. He continues forward, witnessing Nature's gradual reassertion of itself. Trees once more fill the landscape, but suddenly, metal segments clang into position, blocking his view. He stops his machine. (The computer screen is not shown to give us the date.)

What follows greatly parallels the adventures of Pal's time traveler, but in a more simplified and sterile way. Trapped in this time period after his machine is stolen, he befriends Weena (Priscilla Barnes) and the Eloi. In a similar way that George learned of the past from the "talking rings," Perry is shown a preserved museum, where a projecting device displays filmed footage of how the world came to destroy itself, preparing the way for the evolution of the bifurcated human species. Perry teaches the Eloi how to use plastic explosives to destroy the cannibalistic Morlocks. In the Morlocks' underground labyrinth, he regains his machine just as the final bomb explodes.

Perry's flashback tale dissolves into the present scene in the Mega office. Worthington sees military value in the Time Machine, and since Perry used Mega's funds to build it, he claims it as the property of the corporation. Perry feigns agreement, but then sneaks back into his lab to steal the machine. In a sentimental exchange between Ralph and Perry's secretary (Rosemary DeCamp), a scene akin to David Filby's final speculations with Mrs. Watchett, the scientist "eulogizes" Perry's disappearance as

> "the only chance of survival for the human race . . . because he'll be reshaping mankind, taking all the knowledge of thousands of years, creating a world based on the good things man has achieved. He'll be giving civilization the chance for a truly new beginning."

"That's a tough assignment, even for Neil."
"He'll do it, all right. After all, time is on his side."

The camera tracks in to a diagram of the Time Machine tacked on the wall. A dissolve takes us back to the world of the Eloi, where Weena, walking alone, spots Perry. In the final shot, they run to each other and lovingly embrace.

As with Pal's film, the thematic emphasis is on humanity destroying itself with weapons of war. Modernizing this idea further, the television movie suggests how the collaboration between industry and government perpetuates such folly. At times, Schellerup uses some interesting motifs and implications. For example, the "anti-matter bomb," which eventually annihilates civilization, is aptly named for its connotation as a suicidal weapon. Its deployment, for whatever reason, implies that humanity has a death wish, for it must no longer care about living. In other words, it is "anti-matter."

The references to military weaponry denote how Science is used for negative purposes, much as Pal's allusions to war suggest the same thing. In addition, Perry's encounter with the superstitious Puritans, who accuse him of using "a tool of the devil" while in fact he is experimenting with his machine to see what good it can contribute to humanity, reflects Wells's ambiguous suggestions about Science, its dual potential to help and to hurt mankind.

Overall, however, this television film, lacking any fascinating features which might engage the audience, does not hold together as a good cinematic work. First, while the story has merit, the storytelling is flawed. Trite, shallow dialogue prevents the characters from revealing themselves as more than stereotyped cardboard figures. Cliché situations, as in the opening scene with the renegade capsule about to explode on Los Angeles, are too predictable in their outcome. Such standard threats, coupled with the trite dialogue, make each of these harrowing moments a soft-sell crisis. In addition, occasional slow, plodding sequences deprive the film of any suspenseful pacing and show neglect for a careful balance between tension and release. Lingering close-ups on the characters, often used to display their ability at flexing facial muscles, and the absence of quick cutting to show a climactic scene from various angles, reduce the effectiveness of the critical situation by diluting its intensity.

Reduction of the ambiguities also lessens the depth of meaning of the story. Neil Perry, lacking the complexities of his two counterparts, mimics the flat characterization of a stereotyped hero. Defying Mega Corporation, he invents the Time Machine for the sake of humanity. This differs from George, whose quest is more selfish, but whose attitude and attachment to his machine make him more an Everyman with a mythic desire to live in eternity by breaking his bonds with time. Like George, Perry teaches the Eloi to defeat the Morlocks, but the situation does not define any contradiction in his character. George's violent disruption of the peaceful system accepted by both Morlock and Eloi contradicts his reasons for inventing the Time Machine in the first place. Perry's Eloi, however, have not abandoned the struggle for survival; they war against the Morlocks by wielding clubs and resisting their assault. Perry merely provides them with the advantage for ultimate victory over their enemies. In regard to the final trip on the Time Machine, the revelation of Perry's destination diminishes his potential as a time traveler. He seems again bounded by time while George, suspended in that mythic realm, retains some degree of mysterious omnipresence.

A second drawback to this film is the composition of many of its shots. Too often the framed images are sterile, two-dimensional pictures relating only to the narrative plane and not to the deeper underlying thematic issues. For example, the menacing Morlock sphinx in Pal's film is reduced to a blank pair of bronze doors in Schellerup's remake. And Pal's repeated use of a death-rebirth cycle and of the circle and arc motifs enhances the rich, ambiguous interplay between hope and doom, while Schellerup concentrates on moving Perry from one point to the next without including meaningful associated images in his shots. The result is a story which imitates its forerunner, but has refined its multiple layers into a simple, linear tale.

In respect to the invention itself, George's Time Machine beautifully captures the style of the Victorian period. More importantly, the wheel as its main mechanism provides it with a wealth of connotative meanings. Perry's machine, a streamlined version of George's, with its computer console and a triangular base and back, also captures the style of its era, but seems to lack the mystique of the earlier prototype. However, while this fails to contribute substantially to the story, it is not so much a flaw as are the mediocre and flimsy uses of the special effects.

In the time-traveling sequences, for example, Pal's film keeps George in touch with his environment. While he witnesses visible changes, his voice-over constantly remarks on what he sees and his facial expressions reflect his verbal comments. In Perry's case, the special effects become a dull, drawn-out affair, with him suspended in a void while bursts of light pass on either side of him and streaks of light pass above or below him. The voice-over is minimal and his depiction of faintness or thrill, without verbal accompaniment, seems moronic and silly. Other effects are worse. For the falling Russian satellite to appear on a screen in the Mega computer lab is ridiculous, as if some plane were following it and filming its gradual descent toward Los Angeles. And the Morlocks, in their blue coveralls and wooden, lifeless masks, look like maintenance men at a masquerade. Granted, on Pal's Morlocks, wrinkles in their nylon body-tights are sometimes visible, but their facial make-up gives them a vital horrifying expression absent in Schellerup's monsters. In another instance, when Perry arrives at the period of the Eloi, block-shaped segments from the image of the bronze doors clang into place, covering his view of the trees beyond. However, the segments are portions of the completed picture of the two solid doors, like pieces of a puzzle cut randomly through integral parts. The effect, in image and sound, makes no sense.

One excuse for the stunted quality of the film is that, as a television movie, its budget was probably limited, which means a curtailed allowance for special effects, props, sets, and extra shots needed to develop a more detailed and elaborate story. A second consideration is that the film claims affiliation with the Classics Library. Its purpose may have been to entertain a young audience and to acquaint it with Wells's story. On this basis, the film works well enough, but any higher aspirations seem difficult to justify.

The next film, Nicholas Meyer's commendable *Time After Time,* might be called a "bio-fictional analogy." As an analogy, it is not a strict adaptation of *The Time Machine,* but rather a film that borrows one or two of the original's central ideas to devise an entirely new and independent work. Unlike the analogies of Bert I. Gordon (see Chapter 6), Meyer's creation is a more serious and entertaining endeavor.

Time After Time is also a bio-fiction in that it romanticizes details from the life of H. G. Wells. However, instead of constructing the fiction to accommodate certain aspects of Wells's career, the film reconstructs Wells's career to accommodate the fiction. Wells's history is widely known and clearly established.[17] Its distortion, too blatant to ignore, hinders one's ability to maintain "a willing suspension of disbelief." If, however, this drawback can be tolerated, the film contains many features which make it a worthwhile and memorable accomplishment.

Briefly, the story depends on H. G. Wells and Jack the Ripper being contemporaries.[18] As in Pal's version, Wells does not merely write about the Time Machine, but actually invents one. The Ripper (David Warner) steals the machine and emerges in 1979 San Francisco. Having built the device, Wells (Malcolm McDowell) feels responsible for unleashing this fiend on some future utopia. He follows The Ripper to San Francisco, catches up with him, and destroys him.

The film's first few scenes establish all the primary motifs of the story. It begins in 1893 on a foggy London street where a prostitute emerges from a pub. She is solicited by a gentleman whom we cannot see. (The camera shoots subjectively from his viewpoint, initially looking at the woman from behind fence palings, then following her down the muddy street.) He offers her a gold coin and directs her to an alley. There, she entices him by lifting her skirts. In a close-up, his hand places an opened gold pocket watch on a nearby crate. A soft melody chimes from the mechanism and a photograph of a stern-faced woman appears inside the lid.

The prostitute is charmed by the music. She asks him his name. "John . . . but my friends call me Jack." Immediately, a soft tearing sound is heard and the woman's face freezes into a disbelieving stare. Thin spurts of blood graze the crate. A white-gloved hand drenched with blood closes the watch.

Jack the Ripper becomes identified with time (his watch), money (his coin), sentiment (music), and extreme irrational violence (his obsession to commit a repulsive, sexually perverted crime). The several isolated shots of his hands indicate that the main instrument of violence is not the weapon but the person who wields it.

The camera cuts from a long shot of a stream of blood flowing out of the alleyway, to a full shot of Big Ben against the night sky, and finally to the home of H. G. Wells. First seen through a lacy-curtained window, Wells sits at the head of a dinner table opposite an empty chair while he and four friends discuss his controversial positions on free love, socialism, and utopia. Awaiting the arrival of his closest and most admired friend, Dr. John Leslie Stevenson, he announces he has an invention to show them. Just then, his housekeeper, Mrs. Turner (Andonia Katsaros), slides open the foyer door and the absent guest (David Warner) appears behind it. Wells takes them into his basement to see his Time Machine. Afterwards, Stevenson, as he does routinely, beats him in a game of chess: "I know how (you) think." Wells answers, "Someday I shall win." Stevenson concludes, "Then you will learn how I think."

Stevenson's tardiness makes him a predictable candidate as the murderer. Yet the subsequent moments are filled with suspense because we still must dread what will happen when he turns out to be the Ripper. The Stevenson-Ripper character, the respectable gentleman-doctor masking the vicious social deviate, is obviously a Jekyll-Hyde facsimile.[19] More important, though, is a second image of the double suggested in the Wells-Stevenson friendship. First of all, they are linked by time (Stevenson's watch and Wells's machine), a motif strengthened by the shots of Big Ben mediating their two entrance scenes and of Wells sitting opposite the empty chair. Their relationship with time depends on how they *use* it: while The Ripper is bent on destruction (violence, murder), Wells works toward construction (writing on social reform, building the Time Machine). In addition, the issues discussed at the dinner table imply connections between the two characters in their attitudes toward women (equality vs. dominance), love (free love vs. perverted sex), socialism (communal sharing vs. monetary system), and hope for the future (peaceful utopia vs. violent anarchy).

Stevenson's first appearance, a tall imposing figure behind the sliding door, suggests his domination over the doorway. A symbol of passage, especially as the threshold of death, it tends to be under The Ripper's control, usually in that he dictates a violent end to life.[20]

Also important is the way the camera introduces us to The Ripper and Wells. Used subjectively in the initial scene, it identifies us with the murderer. We see the murder committed through his eyes, and we become intimate with him. Used objectively in the next scene, it acts as an observer viewing events from an external vantage point. The reason for the contrast seems that violence lies potentially within all of us (The Ripper) while the suppression of our violent tendencies must come from without (Wells). (One justification for the film's incorporating this idea is that in his later utopian writings, the real-life Wells switches from biological to social evolution. He assumes that human nature will not change, but predicts that external controls—especially through the educated guardians of his proposed utopias—will maintain order in society.) The chess game, in which Wells must learn how the deviate thinks before he can subdue him, forbodes this confrontation.

The police arrive, on the trail of the killer. Stevenson's black bag containing the bloodied knife and glove is discovered and he becomes a suspect. However, he has disappeared suddenly and without a trace. After the police leave, Wells realizes that his friend has escaped in his Time Machine. Fortunately, he has equipped the machine with a homing device so that unless a key, which he holds, is turned in the console, the machine, after completing a trip, automatically returns to its place and time of origin.

Expectedly, the machine reappears and Wells pursues the villain. He materializes in 1979 San Francisco in a museum exhibit dedicated, ironically, to "H. G. Wells: A Man Before His Time." He realizes that like himself, Stevenson needs to convert his English currency into American. He goes from bank to bank, questioning the exchange officers, until at the Chartered Bank of London he meets feminist Amy Robbins (Mary Steenburgen), who had dealt with the fugitive.

Amy had recommended a hotel to Stevenson. Wells follows the lead and confronts Stevenson in his room, demanding he return with him to their time period: "We don't belong here." Stevenson turns on the television. Changing channels, he shows how violence has pervaded every aspect of society, in real life (via the news), in sports, in cartoons, in movies, and in commercials. He retorts: "We don't belong here? I belong here completely and utterly. I'm home. It's you who do not belong here, you with your absurd notions of the perfect and harmonious society. It's drivel. The world has caught up with and surpassed me. . . . You know you can go into a store and purchase a rifle or a revolver—(Wells slaps him)—It's catching isn't it, violence?" Wells feels remorse. Stevenson demands the key that controls the Time Machine. Wells resists and they fight. Stevenson almost overpowers him, but a cleaning woman enters and scares him away. Wells chases him. Stevenson gets hit by a car but survives and escapes from the hospital before Wells can catch him.

As in Pal's version, the Time Machine has transferred the characters to a new temporal position where their conflict points to a flaw in our present society and suggests a need for reform. For Pal, the theme is that we must avert nuclear war. In *Time After Time,* The Ripper's comment on the state of society acts as a perverted endorsement from a twisted authority. Since it is obvious that he symbolizes the epitome of wanton, senseless violence, his remark suggests that we need to eliminate such pervasive barbarism.

Wells returns to the bank where Amy works. A self-proclaimed liberated woman, she asks him out to lunch. They eat in an upper-story revolving restaurant overlooking the bay. Next they see a movie, *Exorcist IV,* in which the violence is so frightening that Wells hides behind the seats. Afterwards, she invites him to dinner at her house. That night, while they make love, Stevenson prowls around a sleazy bar district, finally settling on a go-go dancer who catches his eye. The counterpoint between romantic love and calculated sexual violence once again contrasts Wells with Stevenson.

The next morning Wells hears a radio report of the two murders. He tells Amy about Stevenson, modifying the truth to make it believable. She suggests he notify the police. She goes to work and Stevenson returns to exchange more currency. He suddenly realizes it was she who led Wells to him at his hotel and he threatens her if she should interfere again. Wells is forced to go to the police. He claims he is Sherlock Holmes, sent here by Scotland Yard. The poor choice of an alias makes him appear a crackpot, and with no record of Stevenson from customs officials, the lieutenant (Charles Cioffi) refuses to believe him.

Wells finally tells Amy the truth, but she cannot believe such a fantastic story. He takes her to the museum where he shows her his machine. While they are busy at the museum, Stevenson murders his third victim, a salesgirl he picked up in a boutique. He opens his watch before slicing her throat. A drop of blood spatters near his eye, resembling a red tear and giving the impression that The Ripper feels remorse over the violence he is driven to commit.

Wells and Amy journey ahead three days (from Wednesday to Saturday). Amy still does not believe, until she accidentally finds a newspaper with Saturday's date. She also sees an article which says she has been the fifth victim of the killer, murdered Friday night in her apartment. She panics.

Wells cannot rescue the third victim, already slain, but he plans to rescue the fourth on Thursday night at the park noted in the paper. Amy suggests getting a gun, but he refuses: "The first man to raise a fist is the man who's run out of ideas." He sets out, with Amy driving, but a flat tire stalls them and they arrive only in time to see the body pulled from the lake.

Introduced here is the idea that fate cannot be thwarted, that Amy will die no matter what precautions they take. The Time Machine can move within temporal spheres, but the traveler cannot alter things which are meant to be. This is difficult to reconcile since Wells's and The Ripper's presence in the future has automatically affected events. Whether things can or cannot be changed is ever the paradox of time travel. In any case, the dread of Amy's certain, unpreventable death is a nice touch, heightening the intensity and suspense of the climax.

On Saturday, Amy takes a sedative while Wells goes out to purchase a gun. Obviously, he has become "the man who's run out of ideas." Violence appears an unavoidable disease which must inevitably infect the high-minded, no matter how much they try to stay aloof from it. However, by now, the police suspect him, and before he can return to Amy to awaken her, they arrest him for questioning.

In a suspenseful sequence of cuts, we see the simultaneous actions of Wells, Stevenson, and Amy. Wells, interrogated at police headquarters, pleads unsuccessfully for them to send protection for Amy. Stevenson selects his knife and heads for Amy's apartment. Amy sleeps the day away until she awakens nearly too late to escape. About to leave her apartment, she sees the knob on the door turn. (The door sits ajar. Earlier, Amy told Wells he had to slam it to close it securely.) Once again, The Ripper controls the threshold, the passage to life or death.

By the time Wells consents to confess if they will send a police car to Amy's apartment, it is too late. The police enter her apartment and find blood spattered on the walls and a severed hand on the floor. Wells is released. Despondent, he walks toward her apartment. While passing through the structural remains of the Pan-American Exhibition of 1914, he suddenly hears the musical chime of Stevenson's watch. Amy appears from behind a wall and explains that it was not she but her friend Carol (Geraldine Baron) who was murdered: "The newspaper was wrong." Stevenson steps behind her, puts a knife to her throat, and demands the key to the Time Machine. Wells tells him to release Amy first, but he retorts: "My mother was rather an atrocious woman in her way, but her many failings did not include mentally deficient sons." Wells agrees if he promises to free Amy. He says, "You have my word as a gentleman." Wells throws the key at his feet and Stevenson, with a smirk, says, "You should know by now that I'm no gentleman." He kidnaps Amy in a stolen car. Wells runs to Amy's garage. Vaguely familiar with the operation of her car, he fumbles with the ignition and gear shift, and races erratically after them.

The "gentleman" motif recurs several times in the film, appearing as early as the first scene when the prostitute remarks that his clothes suggest him a gentleman. The image of the "gentle man" is inherent in the concept of the double, Wells contrasted with Stevenson and the suave, sophisticated facade of the doctor contrasted with the underlying savage perversions of The Ripper.

Also important in this scene is Stevenson's reference to his mother. It may be her photograph in his watch, or it may be that of a sweetheart thwarted by her. In any case, his comment suggests that his mother is responsible for his obsession with violence. The implication, however, is vague and inconclusive—which is as it should be. Wanton violence lacks rationale and is too complex to afford a neat, simple explanation.

Wells catches up with Stevenson at the museum's Time Machine exhibit. He pleads for Amy's life, but Stevenson, visibly ambivalent, favors his darker impulses and refuses to give her up. He tries to force her into the cockpit, but as he turns, his watch chain hooks onto the handle of a second precautionary device Wells had put on the machine, a Vaporizing Equalizer. (Wells's watch chain had also caught on this handle when he first arrived in 1979, a further indication of their mutual link to time.) This device sends the traveler into time without the machine. ("And of course, without the machine," he had told his friends, "there is no coming back.") Stevenson's watch opens, the melody chimes, and the picture of the woman dangles on the chain. The distraction is enough for Amy to get away from him. He jumps into the machine and inserts the key. Wells steps forward and grabs the handle of the Vaporizing Equalizer. He pauses and stares at Stevenson. Stevenson turns, distraught, looks at Wells, and nods his head. Wells pulls out the rod. Stevenson screams in agonizing pain and disintegrates. Wells tells Amy, "I sent him where he belongs— Infinity."

Sending The Ripper into "infinity" has ambiguous implications. While his atoms may have been scattered into a
timeless realm, they may also have been planted into
forever. As the personification of violence, he is with all
people at all times.[21]

Wells says he will return to his own time: "I have to
dismantle the machine. . . . Until we master ourselves, we
have no proper use for time." He must return to write all
those books indicated by the exhibit: "Fiction, I hope. Every
age is the same. It's only love that makes any of them
bearable."

He enters the machine and starts to leave, but Amy calls
him back: "It's no life without you." She joins him in the
cockpit and as they kiss, the Time Machine dissolves.

As stated above, the primary weakness of the film
concerns its license with certain historical facts, especially in
regard to Wells's life and his relationship with Amy. In
reality, Wells met Amy Catherine Robbins in September
1892. Pursuing a B.Sc. degree at William Briggs's Tutorial
College, she was a student in Wells's biology class, an
ambition which may have earmarked her as a "liberated"
woman.

Wells, however, already had a wife. He had married his
cousin Isabel on October 31, 1891. Sexual incompatibility
(she was extremely priggish) and a general lack of common
interests (his worldliness, her isolated existence) led to their
marital breakdown within the year, although they were not
divorced until 1895. In the film, which begins in April 1893,
Wells tells Amy that he is not married ("Do you think I could
[make love to you] if I were?").

Wells's opinions on free love were probably not so defined
in 1893 as they were early in the next century. *The Food of
the Gods* (1904), *A Modern Utopia* (1905), *In the Days of the
Comet* (1906), and *Ann Veronica* (1909) are among the
earliest of his works which propose his stand on this
controversial issue. His extramarital affair with Robbins
(whom he nicknamed Jane) became a notorious scandal, but
was still not an example of free love. In *Experiment in
Autobiography,* he claims that he and his second wife

preferred the idea of living under common law, but to avoid social condemnation they decided to conform to society's dictates. They married in 1895.

Such trivia tends to distract from the "reality" of the fictional world. However, the film skillfully ties in enough relevant ideas to mask the distortions. By the time of the story's beginning in April 1893, the real Wells had written an early version of the Time Machine (*The Chronic Argonauts,* 1888), a project which might have prompted him to try to invent an actual working model. In addition, as early as 1885, he had become associated with the Fabian Society (he formally joined in 1903) where he became acquainted with socialism and Marxism, issues discussed at Wells's dinner table in Meyer's film. Ironically, the idea of free love caused the schism between him and the Fabians and he resigned in 1906.

All in all, the film is well constructed and well executed. The brief special effects used in the few time-travel scenes appear slight and unconvincing, but the actors give excellent performances and the story is captivating in its intrigue and suspense. Despite its distorted reality, the film works well and is highly entertaining.

Notes

1. Some discrepancy exists as to whether we can know the name of the Frame Narrator. Many recent critical works call him Hillyer, based on an event near the end of the story. On his return to "present-day" London from his trip in the future, the Time Traveller, just before stopping, says he "seemed to see Hillyer for a moment; but he passed like a flash" (Ch. 12). He is referring to the future event of the next day, when, just as he disappears on his second trip into time, the Narrator peeks into the room. However, the manservant walks into the room at the same time, and the question concerns which of the two men the Time Traveller had named. A case may be made for either, but because the most important characters remain nameless (Filby's brief appearance makes him a minor character) and the identity of his manservant complements the naming of his housekeeper, Mrs. Watchett, I prefer to consider the Narrator as anonymous.

2. In Chapter One, the Narrator says that if the Time Traveller's model machine had traveled into the past, "it would have been visible when we came first into this room, and last Thursday when we were here; and the Thursday before that; and so forth!" And in Chapter Two he notes that, of the guests from the previous week, only he, the Psychologist, and the Medical Man have returned. Together, these remarks suggest that the Time Traveller extends an open invitation to his acquaintances to have dinner with him every Thursday.

3. "Eloi," or "Elohim" in Hebrew, means God, while its plural form indicates the plurality of magnitude or majesty. Bernard Bergonzi, in *The Early H. G. Wells* (Manchester: Manchester University Press, 1961), suggests additional connotations of the name.

4. Something of the heroism of Oedipus is implied, Man defying an undeniable fate. However, Wells may not be that fatalistic. Of course, human devolution and the end of the world would be out of Man's control, but in this first of Wells's Utopian novels he forecasts the possible outcome of a present social structure and suggests that this is a condition Man can do something to change.

5. "Kemp" seems to be an allusion to the Wells character in *The Invisible Man* (1897), but beyond their name and their doubts about what science might achieve, the two characters have nothing in common. In other allusions, George wonders if man's ability to control time can alter "the shape of things to come." And on the control panel of his Time Machine are the words, "Manufactured by H. George Wells." Maybe Pal's intention was to borrow trivia from Wells to honor him by putting his broad stamp on the story.

6. Making Filby Scottish seems an interesting touch. As a red-headed owner of a department store, he bears the stereotyped image of the thrifty, hard-headed, argumentative Scot. And interviewed in the documentary *The Fantasy Film Worlds of George Pal,* Young admits that the ethnic choice depended in part on the traditional Scottish trait of extreme loyalty to friendships. The stock character works well here, especially in its clear defining of the sensitive bond which exists between him and George.

7. Wells's short story "The Flowering of the Strange Orchid" considers the infinite varieties of unnamed species existing in the world waiting to bring fame to each person who discovers them. The Time Traveller may have stumbled onto one such rare species and decided to use it as "proof" in his deception.

8. Of course, numerous arguments refuting physical movement through time have appeared ever since the first publication of *The Time Machine*. However, it seems more appropriate to approach the story as a realm which creates its own possibilities, and in that respect the Time Traveller deserves some credibility.

9. Bergonzi, *The Early H. G. Wells*, p. 73.

10. This, obviously, seems a contradiction of my earlier point that the Narrator's remark suggests a "naive, indifferent response" by him as spokesman for the inventor's guests. Wells's ambiguous implications require looking at the words in several contexts. See Frank McConnell's *The Science Fiction of H. G. Wells*, which elaborates on an optimistic interpretation of this passage.

11. The Time Machine itself resembles a sleigh, and considering that the story is set at Christmastime, it seems a deliberate and appropriate suggestion that Santa Claus's vehicle is a Time Machine. How else could he remain unaffected by time, looking like a perpetual father-image? How else could he defy the "laws" of time by making all his visits in a single night? And who else symbolizes cycle more than he, returning year after year at the same time, carrying out the same task?

12. With some discrepancy, the disc turns counterclockwise when George travels into the future, and continues that same rotation when, later, he reverses direction from future to past. Not knowing the science behind the machine, we cannot know how the machine operates, but if the disc relates to the passing of time, it seems its rotational direction should accompany changes in past-ward or future-ward movement. Along this line, another discrepancy involves the model Time Machine which George sends into the future. Its disc rotates clockwise, a direction which seems more appropriate to future-ward travel.

13. The image of the youths on the rock, staring indifferently at Weena's plight in the rushing current, suggests Narcissus's passive rejection of Echo for the sake of his own reflection in the water. Incidentally, this implies what the Eloi have become, a narcissistic society.

14. Pal's film does not incorporate Wells's idea of physical devolution, but it does consider an emotional degeneration which George reverses in Weena and the Eloi. This degeneration is symbolized in the Red Cross poster on the door of Filby's department store. When George meets Jaimie in 1917, the poster bears an elaborate painting of a Florence Nightingale/Madonna figure with hand extended in supplication. When he stops again in 1966, the poster simply pictures a red cross with the words "Give" and "Help" above and below it. Over time, the implied impassioned plea of a mother-figure has been reduced to a naked symbol and explicit words. The Eloi become identified with this kind of emotional sterilization.

15. This term comes from Geoffrey Wagner's three categories of adaptation—transposition, commentary, and analogy—each based on a film's degree of adherence to its source (see the Introduction, page 12).

16. The recasting of Whit Bissell in this remake is an obvious self-reflexive touch, much like the cameo appearance of Noel Neill in *Superman* (Richard Donner, 1978) after her regular role in the television series starring George Reeves.

17. Semi-biographical films, like *Agatha* (1979) and *Silkwood* (1983), which base their stories on a mysterious gap in an actual person's life, can often be intriguing because of the credibility of the proposed theory. Wells's life contains no such mystery to foster biographical speculation, but the film offers an interesting "what if" idea, even if that notion is impossible.

18. In a distortion of history, the film takes place in 1893 while the crimes associated with Jack the Ripper occurred between September and December, 1888. However, at least two doctors were suspected of the brutal murders, and the film coincidentally makes Wells's antagonist a doctor.

19. There seems an obvious allusion to *Dr. Jekyll and Mr. Hyde* (1886) in that the name of the author, Robert Louis Stevenson, is echoed in The Ripper's respectable identity, John Leslie Stevenson.

   At the same time, many of the real-life Wells stories contain references to *Jekyll and Hyde*. While convalescing from consumption in 1887, he read voraciously, Stevenson's books being among his fare. The influence appears evident in *The Time Machine,* where the Eloi and Morlocks are clear manifestations of the mild-mannered Jekyll and appetite-ridden Hyde.

20. The door motif also appears in Don Taylor's film version of *The Island of Dr. Moreau* (1977) but with broader implications (see Chapter 2).

21. In one of television's *Star Trek* episodes ("Wolf in the Fold," 1967, written by Robert Bloch), John Fiedler plays the incarnation of an evil essence which at one time lived in the person of Jack the Ripper. He is destroyed in a similar way that Stevenson is finally destroyed by Wells and with similar implications.

II: THE ISLAND OF DOCTOR MOREAU

A: A Triptych of *Genesis*

H. G. Wells's *The Island of Doctor Moreau* (1896) appears in two film adaptations, the first directed by Erle C. Kenton in 1933 and retitled *Island of Lost Souls,* and the second directed by Don Taylor in 1977, which retains the original title. Both films, imitative of Wells in many respects, contain variations in plot and character which give each its own individuality.

In terms of plot, the original presents a structure followed loosely by the two films. The protagonist, Edward Prendick,[1] surviving a shipwreck of the *Lady Vain* with two other men, spends several days adrift in a dinghy. On the point of starvation, they draw lots to see who will serve as food for the other two. The unfortunate winner resists. He fights with the second man and both fall overboard. Prendick, abandoned, collapses into a stupor until rescued by a cargo vessel.

Aboard the ship, Montgomery, Moreau's assistant, who is returning to the island with experimental animals, revives him. When Moreau's launch arrives to load the animals, the ship's drunk captain, angry after an altercation with Prendick, sets him adrift again in his water-logged dinghy. Reluctantly, Moreau yields to Prendick's pleas, accepts him as an uninvited guest, and grants him asylum in his walled compound which protects them from mysterious creatures that lurk on the island.

Prendick, without Moreau's knowledge, makes an excursion into the jungle, where he discovers strange Beast People living together in a kind of mock human society. Moreau explains that his research into a new field of surgical science has enabled him to shape these human-like creations out of common animals. Prendick, repulsed by the pain inflicted on the subjects, accuses Moreau of cruel indifference and criticizes his imprudent delving into knowledge that lacks practical applications.

Moreau restrains the base animal instincts of his Beast People by forcing them to adopt a contrived litany of Laws which they recite aloud in a pseudo-religious chant. However, frequent transgressions reveal the ineffectiveness of the Law, and the only thing that encourages true submission to Moreau's authority is the fear of a return to the House of Pain, the laboratory of creation.

In a final experiment, Moreau's victim, a puma, rebels and kills him. The other Beast People, witnessing the mortality of their "creator," become inundated with doubts and instincts too strong to contain. Their faithfulness to the Law weakens and they gradually return to their animal ways. Montgomery also falls prey to the most violent of the beasts. Prendick, alone for a time among the degenerate creatures, finally commandeers a dinghy to escape from the island and return to civilization.

Kenton alters Wells's introduction, omitting the cannibalism episode but including the ship's rescue. Taylor includes the plight of the three men, with a variation. One of them dies and the other two respectfully cast the body overboard, suggesting their adherence to civilized behavior by not eating human flesh despite their desperate circumstances. Leaving out the sea rescue, Taylor has Braddock (the Prendick-character played by Michael York) land directly on Moreau's island with the second survivor (who is immediately killed by the Beast People).

The most obvious deviation in the films is their inclusion of a love interest. In *Lost Souls,* Edward Parker (Richard Arlen) struggles to reconcile his attraction for two women, the island's seductive Lota (sensuously played by delicate, wide-eyed Kathleen Burke) and his attractive fiancée, Ruth (Leila Hyams), who relate to the polarized concepts of instinct and reason. Taylor reduces the romantic complication to one woman, Maria (Barbara Carrera, possessing Burke's lithe sensuality), making the similar point, but not as effectively or interestingly as Kenton.[2]

And finally, both films omit the novel's epilogue. The

outcome of Prendick's return to civilization is not necessary to an understanding of the story's main intentions (which is probably why the films dismissed it), but it gives Prendick, as Everyman, the chance to voice his new awareness that the evolution of humanity begins with bestiality, a trait which seems ingrained permanently and inescapably within us.

This becomes a general theme which can apply to all three works. Stated differently: Humanity possesses bestial instincts ("the mark of the beast"), traits refined through evolution but not eradicated, which solidify its kinship with the animal and diminish its claim to the lofty and noble position as the most intelligent, rational creation in the universe.[3] This idea incurs a conditional corollary. Although humans, by nature, cannot completely separate themselves from the Beast, their ability to feel pity raises them above the animal.

As the spokesman for humanity, each Prendick-character asserts this. Prendick is offended by Moreau's "indifference," Parker condemns Moreau for "cruelty," and Braddock appeals for some sense of "consideration." These sentiments echo the idea at the end of *The Time Machine* where the Frame Narrator looks at Weena's flowers and says: " . . . even when mind and strength had gone, gratitude and a mutual tenderness still lived on in the heart of man." Perhaps this—not intelligence or the ability to reason—is the saving grace by which humanity can claim some superiority to animals.

Prendick is not the only one concerned with compassion. In all three versions, Montgomery contributes to rescuing "Prendick" from death and shows disgust for Moreau's reckless experiments. In the films, the three women exhibit self-sacrifice for their love's sake. This ability of humans to extend themselves beyond the selfish animal instinct of self-preservation and to consider the needs of another at their own expense would seem to display their superiority to the animal who has no choice.

Directly related to these two issues is a third important concept, that scientific research becomes destructive and parasitic when it violates natural laws and lacks practical applications. Within the novel and the films, Moreau's science may differ in its procedure and motive, but it remains constant as a science hostile to the natural growth and development of living things.[4]

Wells's Moreau investigates "the plasticity of living forms," the flexible quality of living tissue which enables it to be stretched and contorted into any shape. With the exception of a few original creations, Moreau arbitrarily chooses man as his model and uses vivisection, blood transfusions, and transplants to mold creatures defined by his imagination. Kenton's Moreau (Charles Laughton) discovers a germ cell which accelerates evolution. On the premise, mistaken though it is, that according to the laws of evolution all living things tend toward the human form, he uses vivisection in stimulating that germ cell to turn animals into manlike creatures. Taylor's Moreau (Burt Lancaster, re-named Paul Moreau), like Kenton's, deals in cybernetics. However, his newfound germ cell controls, not evolutionary growth, but "biological destiny." By injecting a serum into this germ cell, and with some minor grafting and organ transplants, he can convert any animal into any other animal. Yet, from what we see of his Beast Men, instead of experimenting in a variety of creations, he seems, like Wells's Moreau, to have chosen man as his model.

Although, in Wells and Taylor, Moreau's choice of man as the model for his creations seems arbitrary, the coincidence is as necessary for their stories' themes as it is for Kenton's version with its more obviously stated intention. The Science appears plausible enough, Wells even going so far as to justify it in an afterword, explaining that the fictional Moreau's theories on vivisection have had some real-life, practical results.[5] And the fact that the Scientist experiments on animals, not humans, may seem morally acceptable. However, in a closer look, we see that Science, in its pursuit of knowledge, subordinates a concern for life. The pain inflicted on animals appears a cruel, senseless act by a heartless, indifferent Scientist. Taylor's Moreau echoes Wells's when he says, "To study Nature you have to be as remorseless as Nature" (Compare Ch. 14). If the Scientist adopts this philosophy, then his work must come into question. Blatant indifference to the pain of any living thing, even if animal, seems to show a disrespect for life in general.

Thus, in each instance, the point is that Moreau's localized Science has broader repercussions for humanity. In its attempt to re-create the paragon of creation, it merely mocks life by creating mutated, disfigured versions of humans. Science must know its limitations. It becomes irresponsible when researchers, like Moreau, put knowledge ahead of practical applications. Prendick condemns such an approach:

> Had Moreau had any intelligible object I could have sympathized at least a little with him. . . . I could have forgiven him a little even had his motive been hate. But he was so irresponsible, so utterly careless. (Ch. 16)

Moreau's search for theoretical knowledge without benefit of practical utility makes his quest completely egocentric and conceitedly ambitious.

Andrew Braddock, like Prendick, questions the scientist's motives. After giving an impassioned explanation about biological destiny, Moreau asks, "Can we control it?" Braddock responds, "Should we?" The doctor, disgusted, closes his cabinet of knowledge and walks away, but Braddock's question becomes the central issue of how far Science should go in learning certain truths. Perhaps some knowledge acts like a Pandora's box, subjecting humankind to more ill than good. As if to verify this, Moreau's Science in each story is thwarted by the problem of reversion of the flesh, the tendency of the surgically manipulated body to return to its original state. That the scientist's efforts have crossed into the realm of taboo is suggested by the fact that Nature undoes naturally what he has done artificially.

In regard to the characters, although the film personalities deviate from the respective originals, the reappearance of Moreau, Montgomery, M'ling, and "Prendick" contributes to the many parallels among the three works. Moreau remains the Scientist-Creator-Authority-Figure, who acts irresponsibly and cruelly in pursuit of a Forbidden Knowledge. Differences in the three Moreaus, however, lead to important differences in each version. These are discussed in greater detail below.

M'ling retains his role as deformed servant with some minor variations. As the first Beast Man Prendick sees, his strange, grotesque appearance establishes the mysterious tone connected with Moreau's island. Prendick analyzes him as primarily bear mixed with traits of dog and fox. In Kenton's film, M'ling (Joe Bonomo) is a Dog-man. Montgomery calls him "the faithful dog" when he bravely follows Moreau to confront the Beast Men and then sacrifices his life trying to protect him. In Taylor's film, M'ling (Nick Cravat) has the least active role. His main purpose is to turn Montgomery's body over to the Beast Men, who, after examining it, realize humanity's mortality and rebel against Moreau.

In a parallel to *The Tempest,*[6] Montgomery, as Moreau's assistant, has been compared to Prospero's Ariel, and like that "airy spirit" his faithfulness centers on a dependency to his master. For Taylor, he is a mercenary bound by money (played by a blustery, self-pitying Nigel Davenport in a limited but convincing role). For Wells and Kenton, he has been saved by Moreau from a legal indiscretion, giving him a closer resemblance to Ariel, who had been released from a cloven pine. (Arthur Hohl in the 1933 film plays the role with complete aloofness from beginning to end. At first it contributes to the mysteriousness, but later, when he offers to help Parker and Ruth escape, his betrayal of Moreau seems abrupt and inconsistent and fails to win the sympathy a more emotional performance might have gained.)

In every instance, Montgomery drinks heavily, apparently trying to dull his sensitivity to Moreau's hideous experiments. Originally, he may have been a decent, high-minded person, but his ideals have been corrupted. He finds Moreau's experiments repulsive, but due to his dependency, cannot leave him.

In both Kenton and Wells, Montgomery has a critical role. At the outset, after rescuing Prendick/Parker from the sea, he nurses him back to health. In addition, Kenton's Montgomery plays the savior a second time, helping Parker and Ruth escape from the island. Here, he sees the angel rescuing Lot from the fires of Sodom and Gomorrah, two cities destroyed by God's hand because of their unfaithfulness to His law. As Parker turns around to glance at the burning island, Montgomery delivers the caution: "Don't look back." Besides its literal directive, the statement also seems a warning against looking back into one's evolutionary heritage, into obscure knowledge that can lead to a fate like the one which has befallen Moreau.

Wells's Montgomery may begin as Ariel, but he turns into Stephano, who gains a position of authority by giving liquor to the Calibans of the island. Intoxication of their bestial instincts, however, lasts only temporarily, and when it wears off, they kill him.

Of the three Montgomerys, Taylor's seems least important, although, like Captain Donohue (Paul Hurst) in *Lost Souls,* his limited appearance has a bearing on the theme of the story. By their deaths, Montgomery and Donohue, both murdered by Moreau, reveal to the Beast Men the truth of human mortality and its relationship to lawmaking. That a self-proclaimed authority, mortal as the beasts, should prescribe the Law while considering itself above the Law, raises doubts about the validity of that Law and the credibility of the authority.

Edward Prendick is easily recognizable as Edward Parker in Kenton's *Island of Lost Souls* and as Andrew Braddock in Taylor's film.[7] In each version, he appears the primary character the audience follows throughout the story. His bewilderment and questions about Moreau's island become ours, and as the story builds in intensity and mystery we share his fears and dread. When the obscurity of the mystery clears for him, it clears at the same time for us. And when he tries to sort out the ethical questions involved, we do, too, and have just as much difficulty discovering concrete solutions.

Yet, the name change bears significance in relation to his different function in the films. In the novel, Prendick is a first-person narrator telling his story in flashback. He presents his experiences like an observer reporting events in the order they had occurred. Ironically, his viewpoint becomes coincidental with the word "eye," which appears numerous times throughout the story and reflects especially the nature or mood of various people and creatures who have "hard eyes," "glaring eyes," "eyes aflame," "roving eyes," etc. Prendick's eyes become the reader's single viewpoint for interpreting the events (except for the one chapter where Moreau expounds on his Science).[8] He cannot help but slant the story according to his limited viewpoint. He witnesses events from a restricted perspective and so draws imperfect conclusions, very much like the Time Traveller who constantly must revise his theories about future society and the relationship of the Eloi and Morlocks.

In this regard, the first-person narrator induces the reader to follow his line of thought, persuades him through reason to make the same erroneous conclusions that he makes while having the reader empathize with his alternate sensations of tension and release. Prendick is shipwrecked and saved, cast out of the *Ipecacuanha* and saved again. On the island, his first impression, that men are being mutilated and disfigured by Moreau, inverts the actual truth, that beasts are being transformed into pseudo-men, and on the basis of this false conclusion he is prepared to commit suicide rather than endure being a victim of Moreau's experiments. Moreau reveals the truth, however, and once more Prendick can feel secure. Then, in the end, after his anti-climactic ordeal living with the Beast Men, he returns to civilization where, expecting to find final security, he instead suffers paranoia, unable to dissociate aspects of the beast from humans in society. Through the first-person voice, the reader's empathy with the speaker remains strong and the vacillating emotions of the character become those of the reader.

The protagonists of the films differ from Prendick mainly because of two factors: a shift in the story's perspective from a first-person narrator to an omniscient point of view, and the introduction of a new character, a young woman of the island, manipulated by Moreau to seduce the protagonist.

By using an omniscient perspective, the films enable the audience to observe events from several angles and viewpoints and to know more about those events than any one character. In *Island of Lost Souls,* for example, we see Ruth planning to rescue Parker without his being aware of her effort. In Taylor's *Moreau,* Braddock explores the island while Charley, his co-survivor from the *Lady Vain,* remains resting at the edge of the jungle. Although Braddock fails to see what happens, we witness the sailor screaming, his body pulled through the grass by unseen attackers. Later, when Montgomery tells him that the mate died from thirst and exposure, we know Braddock is not getting the whole truth.

Primarily, though, the objective of the films in altering the perspective seems to be to give the story two central characters in clearer opposition to one another. In the novel, although Prendick disagrees with Moreau's ruthless philosophy and reckless experiments which endanger their lives, they are not actually adversaries. Prendick acts simply as an observer who later records his experiences in a book and presents it to the public for their own interpretation. In the films, Parker and Braddock share the central action with Moreau, who, in an expanded role, does become their antagonist, threatening their lives by making them part of his experiments. The brief theoretical, ideological altercation in the novel becomes a sustained physical conflict in the films.

In *Island of Lost Souls,* the adversarial relationship arises because Moreau plays God making an Edenic experiment. First, he tries to instigate sexual intercourse between Parker and his female creation, Lota. That failing, he encourages his Beast Man Ouran (Hans Steinke) to rape Ruth. Unlike in Wells's story, Moreau's actions directly threaten Parker's and Ruth's lives, and the conflict between Moreau and Parker becomes personal and physical.

Taylor imitates Kenton in establishing an open conflict between Moreau and Braddock, but with some differences. In Taylor's film, Moreau appears to use his ward Maria to seduce Braddock in the same way that Kenton's Moreau uses Lota, but the situation contains ambiguities which make this difficult to conclude with complete certainty. More obvious, however, is Moreau's subjecting Braddock to a regression experiment. The scientist begins slowly to turn Braddock into an animal, expecting him to cooperate in the experiment by describing for him the precise physiological changes he undergoes in the process. Moreau keeps him in a cage, and at one point offers him rats for food. As in *Lost Souls,* this monomaniacal quest for knowledge by a self-serving Scientist becomes a threat to the innocent, unsuspecting, common man.

B: Kenton's *Island of Lost Souls:* The Spirit of Wells's Original

In Rouben Mamoulian's 1932 film version of *Dr. Jekyll and Mr. Hyde,* the benevolent Jekyll (Fredric March) tries to distill the evil from human nature to purify it and make it wholly good. The attempt fails, and instead releases a doppelganger, the evil Hyde, who, inclined to sadistic violence, rebels against social proprieties and creates chaos.

A similar theme occurs in *Frankenstein,* James Whale's 1931 film. In a final climactic scene, the Monster (Boris Karloff) wrestles with Henry Frankenstein[9] (Colin Clive) on the top ledge of a windmill. Below, one of the townspeople points upward and shouts, "There's the murderer!" Supposedly he points to the Monster, but in fact he points to both combatants, for the Monster is really the manifestation of the doctor's "Hyde" nature. His evil alter ego has already killed a little girl and now destroys what remains of the good side by hurling it down to its death (a figurative death since, at the story's end, the doctor seems to be recuperating from his fall).

While using Wells as its source, Erle C. Kenton's *Island of Lost Souls* relates to these films by sharing with them at least two ideas: Science, despite its noble quest for knowledge, often creates "monsters" which harm, rather than help society; and humanity, considered basically good, actually possesses an ambiguous nature, with inclinations toward forbidden appetites which cannot be controlled by reason. *Dr. Jekyll and Mr. Hyde* and *Frankenstein* explore human nature as an innate moral contradiction. *Lost Souls* explores it as Wells does, as an evolutionary quality: human will has struggled, and continues to struggle, with its primordial bestial instincts.

In considering these contradictions in Science and human nature, Kenton's film echoes many of the thematic issues in Wells's original work, more so than does Taylor's version. An examination of the sequence leading into the horrible, frenzied finale uncovers many of these ideas.

Attempting to quell the threat of rebellion, Moreau appears at the edge of the pit where the Beast Men live. A high angle shot from behind Moreau shows him standing in

Island of Lost Souls (1933, Paramount/Universal Pictures): Authority's Illusion of Power. The human Trinity, Moreau (Charles Laughton, center), Parker (Richard Arlen, left), and Montgomery (Arthur Hohl, seated, right) may claim superiority over the dog-servant M'ling (Joe Bonomo), but he stands above them while the bar imagery shading the walls connotes a self-imprisonment that Moreau fails to realize.

the lower left corner, peering down on the riotous crowd running rampant around a bonfire and waving torches, their straw huts aflame. In his bright white duck suit, Moreau looms large in the foreground, while the Beast Men in the background appear small, subordinated by their creator's larger figure. The Sayer of the Law (Bela Lugosi, unrecognizable under his hairy make-up), in the center middle-ground, sits on a rock, his back to Moreau, and faces the bonfire burning directly in front of him. At Moreau's right, a gong hangs from the limb of a tree. He strikes it with a mallet in his ritual call to order. The Beast Men become silent momentarily, but then argue that Moreau has violated his own law "not to spill blood." Led by the Sayer and Ouran, they trudge defiantly up the pit's slope toward Moreau. In the next shot, at eye-level, Moreau, his gong behind him, retreats backward toward the left edge of the frame while he cracks his whip at the pitch blackness in the right half of the frame. Heads suddenly appear above the lip of the black pit. The Beast Men emerge, overrunning the very place Moreau stood while "holding court" and forcing him to retreat backwards. In the subsequent sequence of shots, the Sayer leads the horde of Beast Men and accuses Moreau: "You made us in the House of Pain. You made us—Things! Not men." (Chorus of Beast Men voices: "Things!") "Not beasts." (Chorus: "Things!") "Part men, part beasts. Things!"

The image of Moreau looming large at the edge of the pit exemplifies his significance as an authority figure. He is God the Creator, who has freed his "Chosen People" from the bondage of instinct. Here, he looks down from Mount Sinai, from where he has given them his Law, to find them in the midst of riotous revelry and instigating open rebellion against him. He has contradicted his own Law by having ordered Ouran to kill Captain Donohue, and ironically, the Beast Men use the reasoning power he has given them to infer his ability to die: All men are mortal; Moreau, like Donohue, is a man; therefore, Moreau is mortal.

If authority, the source of Law, violates its Law, then it negates the validity and legality of such Law. Moreau not only nullifies his Laws when he orders Donohue killed, but in a further irony, has already convicted himself because his vivisectional operations, by spilling blood, automatically violated the Law.

In Wells's novel, this same ironic self-condemnation occurs in regard to the image of Moreau's hand as a weapon of death. Prendick defies Moreau's restrictions and enters the lab while the doctor operates on the puma. Moreau grabs him by the shoulder to turn him out, and Prendick sees "a hand that was smeared red." Later, the puma escapes and turns on Moreau, killing him. When Prendick and Montgomery finally locate his body, they find that "one hand was almost severed at the wrist." This same poetic justice is implied by Kenton. The authority decreeing the Law cannot exclude itself from that Law, which becomes as binding on the authority as on its subjects.

Charles Laughton as Moreau deftly combines extremes of personality to reveal the madness that lurks beneath the scientist's inventiveness, ambitiousness, and genius. Slightly feminine in gesture and speech, he seems at first a silly, vain child. In his initial appearance, he displays a tantrum-like outburst, strutting up and down his launch and yelling at Captain Davis (Stanley Fields) for throwing Parker onto his boat. Later, that childlike quality turns into the sadism of a youth who enjoys pinching the legs off spiders. And this is part of his horribleness. He is the immature, mentally deranged scientist with power over life and death.

One particular scene exemplifies the grotesqueness and madness which make Laughton's Moreau a terrifying monster. Examining Lota's gnarled fingers, he laments despairingly on his failure to perfect his creations. He seems a sincerely dedicated scientist admitting defeat in his noble quest. Then, in the next moment, he notices Lota crying, the first of his creations to do so, and he realizes that her human reaction means his dream is still alive. His lethargic despondency switches to raving fanaticism, the abrupt mood change suggesting his emotional instability. At the same time, he ignores her sorrow, reveling in his own gleeful optimism. Telling Montgomery "This time I'll burn out all the animal in her," he intersperses his words with the snide laughs of a madman. Laughton's expressiveness in face and gesture, depicting the emotional fluctuations of the mad doctor, reveals his obvious relish for the part.[10]

In the climactic rebellion scene already described, Moreau, standing above the Beast Men, rules over a population of scientific mistakes. They are the results of his research in the acceleration of evolution. Earlier, while giving Parker a guided tour of the outcomes of his experiments with vegetable life—oversized orchids and lilies, a monstrously deformed asparagus—Moreau declares his premise: "Man is the present climax of a long process of organic evolution. All animal life is tending toward the human form." Parker does not argue the point, but Moreau's conclusion is wrong, and as the basis for the reckless pursuit of a mistaken objective it raises questions about scientific research in general, how practical and responsible it is.

In Moreau's lab, a lighted globe sits on the floor near the operating tables. While telling Parker he has "wiped out hundreds of thousands of years of evolution," Moreau leans against it. The globe signifies the goal of Science, to illuminate the world with the light of knowledge and to remove the shadows of ignorance. But then Moreau leads Parker to an operating table. He draws back the sheet and exposes the head of one of his victims, who begins to howl shrilly and painfully. With clinical indifference, Moreau fingers its face and examines it closely. There seems something logical and noble in Moreau's research, in his diligent, persistent search for knowledge, but his indifference toward the suffering of his subjects represents the sadism and cruelty of the inhumane Scientist who lacks compassion for the pain-stricken, who moves ahead relentlessly without regard for the discomfort of living things. In this respect, the Scientist is irresponsible. And in Moreau's case, his objective, to create men from beasts, raises questions of practicality which are never explained. What purpose could it serve other than to satisfy the monomaniacal dream of an imaginative scientist? There is no substantial end to justify the sadistic means. When Moreau shows Parker his "less successful experiments" turning a generator wheel with their feet, he asks, "Mr. Parker, do you know what it means to feel like God?" In his question, he reveals the egocentric, self-serving nature of the Scientist's ambition, which may underlie his supposed concern with bestowing the "light of knowledge" on the world.

Wells's Moreau is fundamentally similar to this. In Chapter 14, his long explanation to Prendick about his Science and philosophy implies an ambition to assume an authoritative role as a God-figure who expects to exercise absolute rule without compunction or restriction.

As Scientist, Wells's Moreau differs from Kenton's in that, while the latter pursues the acceleration of evolution by transforming beasts into men, the former wants "to find out the extreme limit of plasticity in a living shape." Despite this difference in objective, the critical issue concerns their numbed emotions toward the cruel, painful effects of their experiments on living creatures. They are ruthless and unpitying. They represent a flawed Science which, like Moreau isolated on his island, isolates itself from reality by pursuing knowledge without consideration of its effects on life and without clear, concrete applications for humanity. As Prendick says, this Science fails because it is "so irresponsible, so utterly careless."

As Creator, Wells's Moreau, unlike Kenton's, did not originally intend to approximate humans, but wanted to invent beings framed by his imagination. Prendick asks him

> why he had taken the human form as a model. . . . He confessed that he had chosen that form by chance. "I might just as well have worked to form sheep into llamas, and llamas into sheep. I suppose there is something in the human form that appeals to the artistic turn of mind more powerfully than any animal shape can. But I've not confined myself to man-making. Once or twice . . . " (Ch. 14)

Moreau trails off, letting the reader imagine for himself what inhuman forms he may have concocted. Later, when Moreau tells of his shaping "a limbless thing with a horrible face that writhed along the ground in a serpentine fashion," we see that the Creator has overstepped himself, creating an evil, murderous devil which invades and upsets the tranquillity of his controlled Edenic world.

Failures, however, do not deter him from further imaginative creating:

> . . . I have been going on, and there is still something in everything I do that defeats me, makes me dissatisfied, challenges me to further effort. Sometimes I rise above my level, sometimes I fall below it, but always I fall short of the things I dream. . . . But I will conquer yet. Each time I dip a living creature into the bath of burning pain, I say: this time I will burn out all the animal, this time I will make a rational creature of my own. (Ch. 14)

Ultimately, he wants to make a creature that is precisely as he imagines it, that meets his conception of an ideal, unique creation. This dream of "perfection" becomes frustrated, and like Kenton's Moreau, who sees hope in Lota's tears, he overcomes personal despair with the determination to succeed.

Returning to the film's climactic sequence, we find a number of additional elements which relate to the novel. Moreau's whip, for instance, as a symbol of authority, is established early as a literal weapon of control. Leading Parker through the jungle to his compound, he slashes his whip at inquisitive creatures to keep them at bay. Then, in the scene where Parker first encounters the Beast Men in their pit, Moreau stands in his usual place of authority, and while the Beast Men chant the Law, he holds his whip horizontally with both hands and gradually raises it from thigh to chest level. The whip takes on significance as his ruler's staff or scepter.

In Wells's story also, by inflicting pain, the whip gives Moreau physical control, while it symbolizes the authority of the man whose hand wields it. There is a difference, however, in that he, Montgomery, and Prendick all have whips, authority appearing to be dispersed among them. They represent the Holy Trinity, a self-elected authoritative clique whose members, though separated by a hierarchical structure, have power over inferior beings outside their circle.

At the climax of the film, as Moreau retreats from the Beast Men, he feverishly snaps his whip at them. Several medium-close shots show his whip striking the heads and faces of the Sayer, Ouran, and a third Beast Man, all of them moving forward relentlessly and unflinchingly, impervious to its sting. His whip can no longer inflict pain, and so it dissipates as a symbol of authority.

Wells implies a similar loss of authoritative power. In both novel and film, part of the Beast Men's litany of the Law says: "His is the Hand that makes. His is the Hand that wounds. His is the Hand that heals." When the puma kills Moreau and nearly severs his hand, the implication is that the loss of his hand is the loss of his power to wield the whip of authority.

Kenton's Moreau also loses authoritative control. Retreating from the edge of the pit, he cracks his whip at the dark void on the right side of the frame. Suddenly, the blackness becomes filled with the Beast Men emerging from the pit and we see a man overwhelmed by the hideous, ugly, monstrous creations of a warped imagination. Moreau, suffering from the phantasmagoria of Poe's Roderick Usher or from the delusions of the narrator in "The Tell-Tale Heart," has entertained perverted imaginings too long, and now they are about to engulf and destroy him. Less dramatically, in Wells, the puma represents the one perverted creation which Moreau can no longer contain. It rebels and kills him.

The Sayer's lament to Moreau, that "you made us— Things! Not men, not beasts . . . Things," alludes to Kenton's title. The Beast Men, being both and neither man or beast, are "lost souls." This suggests the enormity of the crime committed by Moreau: He has destroyed the integrity of living creatures.

Ironically, the humans on the island also appear to be "lost souls." Moreau came here, forced to perform his experiments in exile after being exposed for his mutilations of research animals. Montgomery, who escapes reality through drink, accompanied Moreau to the island after Moreau helped him escape a prison term for a "professional indiscretion." Parker starts the story as a castaway from a sunken ship, and becomes one again when Captain Davis throws him overboard into Moreau's launch. On the island, these men, this Trinity, can claim superiority due to their supposed intelligence and free will, but they are virtually prisoners. What's more, for safety's sake, they must stay confined inside Moreau's locked enclosure. Within the compound, the tangled vines, slatted partitions, and mazes of bars are reminders of their natural and self-imposed restrictions. Man is "lost" in his mistaken belief that he is freer than the beast.

A final consideration of Kenton's film concerns his most obvious alteration in the story, the introduction of the female characters, Ruth and Lota.[11] Ruth's importance is that she brings to the island Captain Donohue, whose death provokes the Beast Men to rebel, and she plays an unwitting part in Moreau's experiment in sexual reproduction between a human and one of his creatures. Her love for Parker is evident, especially in her extreme perseverance to rescue him after his shipwreck. She represents the human female who can give him a natural human love, as opposed to Lota, whose role in Moreau's experiment suggests an unnatural love between man and beast. Yet it is Lota's love, more passionate and sensual, which appears more attractive.

Lota, like Eve, is a gift to man from the Creator (or like Miranda, a gift from Prospero). She is to be Parker's helpmate, his companion, fulfilling the Creator's wish that "It is not good that the man should be alone" (Gen. 1:18). But she is also a Siren or Circe, who means to seduce man from his desire to return home and to detain him for her own ends. For Parker, Lota represents the occasion to yield to animalistic instincts, while Ruth relates to his human conscience, his reason for remaining nobly celibate.

In an important scene, Parker sits by a pool reading a book. Lota's reflection appears upside down in the water behind him. Playfully, she circles the pool, the camera tracking gradually upward to show her in a full shot. She sneaks up on Parker, startling him. "Talk to me," she says. He shows her the book, which tells how to make a short-wave radio transmitter. She does not understand fully, but when she realizes the book is the means to his leaving her, she snatches it from him.

The next shot shows the smooth glassy water in the pool reflecting the inverted image of Lota approaching it from above, head to body to legs. She tosses the book into the water. Ripples move outward in semi-circles from the stone barrier surrounding the pool just as Parker's inverted image appears alongside her. The ripples distort their images. The book contains a knowledge which excites opposite responses in the two people. For Parker the knowledge is practical and desirable; for Lota the knowledge is destructive and taboo. The situation relates to Moreau's pursuit of knowledge for its intrinsic value versus the condemnation of that pursuit by men who want to see practical results from scientific research. At the same time, Lota's and Parker's reflections, distorted by the disrupted water, signify how individual lives are disrupted by controversial knowledge which causes upheavals in the routine of everyday life.

In the next scene, the ripples having subsided, Parker sits next to Lota on the stone wall above the pool. She leans backward against his chest and rubs up and down, purring like a kitten. He turns her around and kisses her passionately. Immediately he feels remorse for his unfaithfulness to Ruth. He pushes Lota aside and walks away. She follows and tries to revive that passionate moment. She faces him, puts her arms around his shoulders, and tries to kiss him. An ambiguous pause gives the illusion that Parker is submitting to her. Instead, he slowly reaches back for her hands, holds them in front and examines them. They appear gnarled. He suddenly realizes that Lota, too, is a Moreau creation.

Parker's remorse and self-control separate him from the beast. Will power and the love of another keep him from yielding to instinctive sexual appetite. Yet the realization in the garden about the nature of his "Eve" stirs angry emotions and he turns against the Creator. He climbs up the spiral stairway leading to Moreau's upper quarters and enters the doctor's room. Moreau at that moment is preparing tea and laying out all the proper china and silver, the proper custom for a civilized man. He confesses the truth about Lota's origin. Parker punches him. He crashes into his silver salver, knocking it over, then falls backward against the wall and onto the floor. The man of Science, the intellectual torch-bearer of progress, has his own life upset when a layman resorts to brute force to express dislike for his disruptive inventions. In this way, both innovative Science and the reaction against its implementation work to create chaos within an ordered society.

Also in this scene, before Parker hits Moreau they stand in the foreground in medium-full profile, eye to eye. After being struck, Moreau falls backward to a sitting position in the lower right background. Parker remains standing in the foreground, a large figure on the left side of the frame, while Moreau, a moment ago just as large, has shrunk to a small insignificant figure. This shot mirrors the one at the pit where the large figure of Moreau dwarfed the riotous Beast Men. Here, the omnipotent god Science meets violent opposition at the hands of an unappreciative society and must accept rejection.

Following Parker's altercation with Moreau, the next scene shows Moreau's altercation with Lota. He demands to know how Parker discovered his secret. Lota shows her hands. Moreau grabs them and drags her to her bed where a barred rectangular window above it gives him better light. She kneels on the bed while he stands examining her fingers. Again, the image is of a dominant authority figure intimidating an inferior being.

Even when Montgomery enters the frame, left, a similar relativity among the positioned characters occurs. Moreau has dropped forlornly to the bed, sitting on the edge, while Lota, still on her knees, has fallen forward on the sheets, burying her hands in her hair. Montgomery appears large in the left foreground, and the other two appear as dwarfed, imprisoned figures, constrained by the limits of the perimeter of the bed, with the barred window overhead and the large stone blocks in the wall behind them. Their sharing the bed suggests a consummated relationship, a shared doom.

Montgomery asks Moreau what is wrong, and Moreau echoes Wells's lines: "The stubborn beast flesh creeping back . . . day by day, it creeps back." Moreau seems ready to surrender to despair, but then he hears Lota crying. He grabs her by the hair and turns her face upward, saying, "See this. First of them all to shed tears. She IS human. I'm not beaten. . . . This time I'll burn out all the animal in her. . . . Get everything ready." Lota cowers, lays her head back against the wall, and extends her arms horizontally along the headboard, while her feet point together toward the foot of the bed. She has assumed the posture of one crucified and the image foreshadows her role as a Christ-figure.

Indeed, she plays the savior when, later, she ambushes and kills Ouran to protect Parker, who is fleeing with Ruth and Montgomery. In her attack she sustains fatal wounds, so that her attempt to save her loved one becomes an act of self-sacrifice. Coincidentally, she saves Ruth, her rival, and her gesture seems even more selfless and loving. Her tears of sorrow, her special tenderness toward Parker, and now her self-sacrifice establish her as the image of humanity that rises above the animal contained within it and makes it worthy of the phrase, "superior creature."

C: Taylor's *The Island of Dr. Moreau:* A Revised Spirit

John Brosnan speaks for many critics when he says that, compared to the 1977 remake, Kenton's *Island of Lost Souls* (1933) "was far superior to this dull travesty directed by Don Taylor. . . . "[12] His reasons:

> *Lost Souls* . . . has style, atmosphere, and moved at a fast pace. More importantly, it retained Wells's original idea of Moreau achieving his humanoid-animal creations by means of vivisection and the literal grafting of flesh and bone onto his tortured subjects. Thus the description of his laboratory as the dreaded "House of Pain" has a powerful relevance, and the beast men understandably regarded him with a mixture of terrible fear and awe. But in the new film the makers brought the Doctor's methods up-to-date and made him a genetic engineer (in 1911!) who creates his "humani-mals" by means of injecting his subjects with chromosomes; thus the references to the House of Pain lose all meaning and Moreau himself is diminished as a symbol of godlike power and cruelty (246–7).

Brosnan's estimate has merit, but is not completely fair to Taylor's version. True, as a black-and-white film, *Lost Souls* contains a more mysterious and haunting atmosphere than the color remake. The murky chiaroscuro of Moreau's island, with its tangled vines and gigantic vegetation, intensifies the eeriness. Also many scenes in Kenton's film take place at night, while Taylor's occur mostly during the day.

Yet Brosnan's conception of the "House of Pain," although accurate in regard to Wells, does not do Taylor justice. The film Moreau's explanation of his treatment accounts for more than simple injections: " . . . some surgery, implants of various organs, and he should grow to resemble any creature we please." Later, when Moreau subjects Braddock to a regression process to turn him into a beast, Braddock's screams and grimaces verify the mental and physical torment of a painful operation.

Michael York portrays Andrew Braddock as a likable, congenial character. His sincere compassion for the plight of

The Island of Doctor Moreau (1977, American International Pictures):
Nature in Rebellion. Braddock (Michael York) cannot control the pet serval
Maria (Barbara Carrera) hands him. Similarly, Moreau cannot prevent
Nature from reversing his Science, animal instinct always overriding the
humanity he instills in his creatures.

the Beast People earns him the audience's empathy. Such
identification is important to the film, since he, like
Prendick, represents Everyman, who has been buffeted asea
until he arrives by chance at Moreau's island to gain a new
insight into Humanity's relationship with Nature. At critical
moments, as when he discovers the lair of the Beast Men or
when he finds himself being transformed into a beast, his
emotions rise to a crescendo. His passionate outbursts
counter Moreau's more sedate, composed manner.

Burt Lancaster's Moreau appears dignified, serious, and
totally humorless, and although his is in marked contrast to
Laughton's portrayal, which is more charismatic and interesting, he comes closer to the character of the original
scientist. Like Wells's Moreau, he is completely immersed in
his science and abstains from all diversions and light banter.[13]

Despite this strong parallel in characterization, Taylor's film deviates more from Wells than does the 1933 film because of its refined tonal quality and the omission of some interrelated motifs retained in the earlier adaptation. Yet, although Taylor borrows some ideas from *Lost Souls,* such as the bar-imagery to suggest entrapment and constriction, and while his film lacks Kenton's moodiness and complexity, it is original enough to appear interesting in its own right.

Taylor's technical and literary approach, his use of camera angles and symbolism, reveal his artistic capabilities. As an example, he alters Kenton's climax where Moreau sets out alone in his final confrontation with the rebelling Beast Men. The scene occurs in daytime and Moreau rides on horseback, meeting the creatures just outside one wall of the enclosure. A sequence of high-angle subjective shots from Moreau's viewpoint looking down on the group of Beast Men, and low-angle subjective shots of the Beast Men looking up at Moreau on his horse, mirror earlier shots when he had visited their cave and addressed them from a high ledge. In both cases, this establishes the relationship between authority and subjects.

When the Beast Men attack Moreau, upending his horse and throwing him to the ground, the throne, the seat of authority, is violated, as it was in Kenton's film when the Beast Men overran Moreau's sacred ground. Moreau, brought down to the same level as the Beast Men, loses his status as deity, and so, as an equal, becomes subject to their law of the jungle where prey can also turn predator.

Moreau fends off his attackers with his last vestige of power, his whip. The whip has lost its figurative property as symbol of Authority, but it retains its literal power to inflict pain. Moreau must rely now on brute force since he has lost his ability to control through fear. Kenton's Moreau suffered a similar dethronement and an identical reduction in the power of his whip.

As Moreau retreats from his rebellious creatures, two other Beast Men, searching for a way to enter the compound, stumble onto the open, unguarded gateway. Coincidentally, Moreau backs up toward the gate, then turns and runs into the unplanned ambush. Circling him on all sides, the Beast

Men trap him, knock off his hat and take away his whip, thus violating his crown and usurping his Authority.

The altercation in the gateway, where the scientist is finally mauled to death by his Beast Men, is appropriate because of Moreau's association with doorways. He is the guardian of the threshold of change, of the doorway to transformation, of the boundary between good and evil, knowledge and ignorance, humanity and bestiality. In many scenes, he either steps into a doorway or opens a door, or else appears in situations involving doors.

His initial entrance occurs at the gate tower with the sun directly behind him. As Keeper of the Gate, he forms an image which could signify two things. First, the sun creates a halo around him and suggests a deified aspect, indicating his god-like status as Creator of the Beast Men. At the same time, his dark figure blocks out the sun, and the Scientist, the man who supposedly pursues and expounds knowledge, like Kenton's Moreau with his luminous globe, in fact obscures the "light of knowledge."

Immediately preceding Moreau's entrance, Braddock, running from unknown bestial pursuers, falls into a pit below the gate tower. A trap door closes on the opening, sealing him inside. Moreau also controls this door, and Braddock, having been snared by the scientist, becomes no more than a laboratory animal subjected to the doctor's powers of transformation. When Moreau appears to Braddock for the first time, he stands in the doorway, wearing a white suit and holding a book under his arm. The image connotes a missionary priest, an ordained minister on a quest to convert souls, which is what Moreau, in his way, does. Later, as Braddock tries to escape the island with Maria, Moreau intercepts him in her doorway, injects him with a sedative, and begins his process of Transubstantiation on him.

This image of Moreau as priest occurs also in Kenton's film. One scene shows Moreau lighting candles for dinner, that is, for the communion ritual, and at dinner he makes a toast with Donohue which consecrates an ironic bond with the ill-fated captain. More obviously, Moreau's operating table is his "altar" where he "sacrifices" victims in a ritual of Transubstantiation. This same priest-image occurs in Wells when Moreau offers Prendick brandy and biscuits (Ch. 6), and when Prendick sees the puma being changed into a human on Moreau's "framework" (Ch. 10).

The irony of the Beast Men killing Moreau in his gateway, the threshold that up to now he has controlled, parallels Kenton's version where the Beast Men torture Moreau on his own "altar." In true poetic justice, the uncompassionate Scientist becomes the victim of the deformed products of his reckless experiments.

Moreau had killed Montgomery (as Kenton's Moreau had ordered Ouran to kill Donohue), violating his own Law and thus nullifying it. An Authority of ambiguous laws cannot justify itself and brings its own destruction. What is left is Chaos: the Sayer (Richard Basehart) pleads with the Beast Men to respect the Law despite Moreau's violation, for without the Authority figure, there is no Authority. The Beast Men free Moreau's caged beasts, and in a symbolic merging with the animals, wrestle with, or ride them, crashing through walls, unable to find the proper threshold over which Moreau, in spite of his perverted use of it, had some control.

Taylor's film, like Kenton's, introduces a Miranda-figure in the person of Maria.[14] And as in the earlier film, Moreau plays the matchmaker. In a love scene which at first appears innocent and spontaneous, Braddock caresses Maria who has turned her back to him. As he strokes her hair, she purrs contentedly, much as Lota had done with Parker. From a medium close-up of the two lovers, the camera tracks left across the room until it stops at the window shutters. It peers between the slats, and in an extreme high-angle shot shows Moreau standing below, looking up, the image of a degenerate Peeping Tom. The implication is that Maria's sexual interlude with Braddock is not spontaneous but planned in a similar way to Moreau's plan, in Kenton's film, for Lota to seduce Parker. In *The Tempest*, Prospero's manipulation of the relationship between Miranda and Ferdinand seems to make it a contrived love affair. However, the manipulation by both Moreaus of a natural, emotional sexual union perverts the affair even more because in their sinister, selfish intent they have no concern for the lovers' feelings, but reduce love to a calculated scientific experiment.

In Taylor's film, Maria ostensibly seems a human female. However, evidence in the story makes her true nature ambiguous, in one way making her mysterious (Is she or isn't she human?) and, in another, suggesting that the ending of the film differs from the original intention of the filmmakers.

With a few exceptions, we see Maria only when Braddock sees her, so that our estimate of her is nearly limited to his subjective perception of her. She first appears in a long, high-angle shot, Braddock's viewpoint from the second-floor balcony. The scene is quiet and peaceful in the half-light of dusk. With her are Montgomery, standing, and Moreau, sitting on a small park bench beneath a young sapling. Maria stands, holding a leash tied to a small serval pacing on the bench next to Moreau. Behind and to the right of the threesome is a greensward, semi-circular in shape. Maria is literally connected to the cat and must be identified with it. The dusky half-light obscures a clear view of the scene, and the semicircular sward suggests that what Braddock sees can be perceived as no more than a half-truth. Only Moreau, the Creator-Scientist sitting beneath the combined Trees of Life and Knowledge, has access to the whole truth of the island.

Moreau explains to Braddock that he "found her in a crib in Panama City. . . . Any man could have had her for the price of a dozen eggs. Still find her attractive?" Braddock answers, "I'm an amoralist," a variation of the accusation by Wells's Moreau that Prendick is a "materialist" because he worries about pain and pleasure. Braddock's self-complacent admission becomes ironic when, after seeing the lab animals and Beast Men treated cruelly, he is forced to make a determination about right and wrong. His argument later with Moreau in the garden on the subject of "consideration" becomes a moralistic position. And when he finally undergoes the transformation ordeal himself, his moral position becomes solidified.

Following the evening scene in front of the house, the four people go in to dinner. The camera tracks in and around the circular table, beginning with Maria sitting left and Braddock

right. A huge, dark, open window against the rear wall fills
the gap between their heads. Varied camera angles emphasize this square, black void, suggesting that some dark,
mysterious gulf exists between them. This gulf, whatever it
might be, is transcended physically by their becoming lovers,
despite the implication, by her association with the serval,
that her nature is not originally human.

After her initial appearance with the serval, Maria later
walks the pet on the beach, holding it by a leash and waving
a red scarf. She encounters Braddock, who is surveying the
damage done to his dinghy. While they converse, she
transfers the cat from her arms to his, and in the exchange it
breaks free. It runs into the jungle, the red scarf caught in its
leash and fluttering behind it like a bright flag. The fact that
she, and not Braddock, finds the serval reinforces the idea
that she shares some affinity with the animal.

Later, Maria and Braddock return to examine the boat
and he talks of her returning with him to England. She states
her reluctance to leave the island: "I'm afraid . . . I couldn't
live anywhere else but here . . . This is the only place I
know." Again, her human origins seem suspect. As a human
female, she should prefer to go with Braddock to England,
but like the serval, she rejects what appear to be the
restraints of civilization and feels more at ease in the natural
setting of the jungle.

In a subsequent scene, Braddock walks into Moreau's lab
while the doctor is absent. While exploring the room he finds
a red scarf on the floor. He looks puzzled, but the implication
is that this is Maria's red scarf and that she dropped it on a
visit here, possibly for sporadic treatments to maintain her
humanness.

In the climactic finale where Braddock fends off a Beast
Man while he and Maria make their escape in the dinghy,
Maria helps him defeat the creature. She proves, like Lota,
that she is capable of fighting for her mate. The Beast Man
seems nearly indestructible, until Braddock at last rams a
broken oar into its mouth, killing it. The act suggests a sexual
union of the two, Beast-man with Man-beast, a fusion of the
two natures, one inextricably linked with the other.

The film's conclusion presents an outcome contrary to the

previous suggestions that Maria is other than human. As it is, Braddock looks at his hands and feels his face, amazed that the effects of Moreau's serum have worn off and he has returned to his human state. Suddenly, he hears the blare of a horn from a steamship. He jumps up and yells, signaling.

Maria, meanwhile, seen from Braddock's viewpoint, sits in the bottom of the boat with her back to him, her long black tresses tangled about her head. The scene arouses the expectation that, while Braddock has reverted to his original human appearance, Maria will have reverted to some former beastly appearance, exposing herself with a disfigured face or holding up gnarled hands like Lota's. The camera cuts to a medium close-up of her face. She appears distraught and pathetic and her lips move feebly without sound. However, instead of a horrible discovery, this tense moment with its dark forebodings is suddenly thrust aside to allow for the suggestion of a happy romantic end. A more logical conclusion would have been the revelation that Braddock's figurative union with the Beast Man is paralleled by his literal union with a Beast Woman, a further erasing of the thin line that separates human aspirations from bestial tendencies.[15]

Notes

1. Prendick is renamed Edward Parker in *Island of Lost Souls* and Andrew Braddock in Taylor's film. The reason for the change is unclear since the other important names, Moreau, Montgomery, and M'ling, are retained. Possible implications of the revision are discussed below.

2. A primary deficiency in Taylor's version is the general simplification of both Wells's and Kenton's layered motifs. Otherwise, it appears a well-made film.

3. This motif recurs in many of Wells's works, such as *The War of the Worlds* (1898), *The First Men in the Moon* (1901), "In the Abyss" (1897), "The Sea-Raiders" (1897), "The Star" (1899), "The Crystal Egg" (1899), and "The Empire of the Ants" (1911).

4. Another important motif in Wells's scientific romances is the ambiguity of Science's effects on humankind. Benefits are too often attained at the expense of suffering and lives. In his later utopian writings, Wells downplays the ambiguity and champions Science as a necessity for progress and the betterment of the human condition. *The Food of the Gods* (1904) marks an important change in his attitude.

5. In an 1895 essay, Wells speculates that artificial reshaping of living tissue through vivisection could produce new, distinct species of creatures. ("The Limits of Individual Plasticity," in Robert M. Philmus and David Y. Hughes, eds., *H. G. Wells: Early Writings in Science and Science Fiction,* Berkeley: University of California, 1975.)

6. In *The Early H. G. Wells,* Bergonzi calls *The Island of Doctor Moreau* a "demonic parody of another and older island story, *The Tempest . . .* " (100). He points out the parallels of Moreau as Prospero, Montgomery as Ariel, and M'ling as Caliban.

7. Both Richard Arlen as Parker and Michael York as Braddock give fine performances. Arlen displays a sensitive, vulnerable quality which makes him perfect as the innocent, impressionable man used by Moreau for his experiment with Lota. York gives a more high-strung and emotional portrayal, suitable as a man arguing for "consideration" for the Beast People and contrasting Moreau's remote, indifferent air.

8. This becomes a common device in the scientific romances. A Frame Narrator, ignorant of scientific details, allows the scientist in an inset narrative to describe his experiences or explain the "logic" behind his Science. In *The Time Machine,* the inventor dominates the story, but in subsequent works, a layman (a first-person or third-person narrator) tells most of the story and lets the scientist speak only briefly. Wells already experimented with this structural method in the *The Chronic Argonauts,* labeling his sections "exoteric" and "esoteric" viewpoints.

9. This is another example of an unaccountable name change. Mary Shelley's scientist was Victor Frankenstein. In the film, a character named Victor Morris (John Boles) appears as Henry's rival for Elizabeth (Mae Clark).

10. Laughton's Moreau differs from Wells's in personality, yet the implications of their irresponsible scientific research appear strikingly similar. Burt Lancaster's Moreau in Taylor's film more closely resembles the original character in his serious, dignified demeanor.

11. Both films introduce a female character, which, as a Miranda-figure, strengthens the parallel to *The Tempest*. In Kenton's film, Lota plays this part.

12. *Future Tense: The Cinema of Science Fiction* (New York: St. Martin's, 1978), p. 246.

13. Compare Laughton's hearty amusement at his own joke when he tells Prendick how difficult it is to teach his Beast Men speech, but "someday I will create a woman and it will be easier."

14. Taylor's change from two women to one is an example of his simplifying Kenton's film with the effect of diminishing the potentialities in his own. The eternal triangle of Parker, Lota, and Ruth enriches Kenton's film with various layered meanings, from the conventional device of the test of a lover's faithfulness to the implication of the human caught between instinct and reason, desire and conscience. Although such ideas are suggested, Taylor's omission of the triangle makes it more difficult to realize Braddock's relationship with Maria as a man struggling with his animal nature.

15. In another scene confirming this implication, the Bullman (Bob Ozman) attacks and wrestles a tiger to satisfy an irrepressible hunger for flesh. Maria's identification with the serval means that Braddock has also been "wrestling" with a cat to satisfy a parallel and equally demanding appetite.

III: THE INVISIBLE MAN

A: The Invisible Men: Griffin and Jack Griffin

H. G. Wells's *The Invisible Man* (1897), when adapted to James Whale's 1933 film, undergoes little variation in the narrative structure. The sequence of events and many of the key images and symbols, such as rooms and windows, remain fairly intact. The significant differences center on the Invisible Man himself, his personality, his relationship with the other characters, and his scientific process for invisibility.

Both stories begin with the Invisible Man arriving at Iping, a small country village, where he rents a room at an inn and hopes to continue experimenting to find an antidote to his condition. He wears gloves and keeps his head bandaged to hide his transparency, but his violent temper, eccentric behavior, and shortage of money soon lead to a confrontation with Mr. and Mrs. Hall, his landlords. When they demand the rent, he flies into a rage, tearing off his bandages and exposing his invisibility. The shock sends the villagers into a panic and creates havoc across the countryside.

In Wells's story, the Invisible Man, Griffin, next enlists the help of a tramp. He needs him to recover his notebooks from the inn and to carry the money he steals. Soon, however, the tramp, Thomas Marvel, runs away, and Griffin, pursuing him, is shot by an American. Seeking refuge, he stumbles into a house which coincidentally belongs to an old school-mate, Dr. Kemp. He confides in Kemp, telling him the story of his life and how he became invisible. He expects Kemp to be his visible confederate.

Whale's story omits the tramp episode, but Kemp (William Harrigan), now a fellow scientist and co-worker, partially absorbs Marvel's role by helping the Invisible Man, renamed Jack Griffin (Claude Rains), recover his note-books. Jack sneaks into Kemp's house, explains how he discovered the secret of invisibility, and threatens him with death if he does not become a partner to his plans.

In both versions, Kemp feigns support and then "betrays" the Invisible Man by informing authorities of his whereabouts. Wells's Griffin, in a vengeful rage, pursues Kemp across the countryside. He catches up with him in a town, but while they grapple, a navvy strikes Griffin down with a shovel and the townspeople beat him to death. As he dies, his naked, battered body materializes on the ground before them.

In Whale's film, the Invisible Man promises to kill Kemp at ten o'clock the following night. The police want to use Kemp as bait, but he fearfully refuses. Jack evades Kemp's precautions and catches him alone in his car. He ties him up and sends him over a cliff to his death. The next morning a farmer discovers Jack asleep in his barn. He informs the police and they set fire to the barn. Spotting his footprints in the freshly fallen snow, they pinpoint his position and shoot him down. He dies in a hospital bed, materializing before his weeping lover, Flora (Gloria Stuart).

The film ends here, but the novel contains an epilogue. Money stolen by the Invisible Man has been left to the tramp Marvel because no one knows who else can claim it. Marvel buys an inn with his "inheritance." He still has Griffin's notebooks, filled with their strange cyphers. At night he reads them and dreams of how, if he could decode their mysteries, he would not make the same mistakes made by the Invisible Man.

Griffin and Jack Griffin, scientists seeking fame by making a new discovery, fall under the curse of the man overtaken by the monster within him. In the film, Jack's ambition parallels Dr. Henry Jekyll's, repeating the myths of Eden and Pandora where meddling with Forbidden Knowledge results in disaster. The situation in the novel, however, differs because of Griffin's unique circumstances.

The single most important thing about Wells's Griffin is that he is an albino. Before he becomes invisible, he is already an anomaly, a "monster," which presents certain personal and social ramifications. However, when he first reveals his abnormality to Kemp, he does not dwell on its implications. Instead, he glosses over it, and his unwavering "fixed idea"[1] to achieve scientific success, not his albinism, becomes the scapegoat for the dulling of his human sympathies. Emphasis on the causes of his perverted behavior is shifted from the albinism to the monomaniacal drive of an obsessed scientist.

Griffin's albinism appears a minor coincidental factor in determining his motivation, but when seen in relation to one of Wells's earlier works, the albino, as a freak, becomes the manifestation of a special kind of mental freak, the genius. In *The Chronic Argonauts* (1888), written as a serial for Wells's school newspaper, the inventor of a Time Machine, Dr. Moses Nebogipfel, explains to Rev. Cook how in his boyhood he had identified with the story of the Ugly Duckling:

> Even when I read that simple narrative for the first time, a thousand bitter experiences had begun the teaching of my isolation among the people of my birth—I knew the story was for me. The ugly duckling that proved to be a swan, that lived through all contempt and bitterness, to float at last sublime. . . . In short, Mr. Cook, I discovered that I was one of those superior Cagots called a genius—a man born out of my time—a man thinking the thoughts of a wiser age, doing things and believing things that men now cannot understand, and in the years ordained to me there was nothing but silence and suffering for my soul—unbroken solitude, man's bitterest pain.

It is difficult to read Nebogipfel's words without feeling them attributed to Griffin as well. The difference occurs in how the two men react to these conscious sensations and how they use Science to overcome their dilemma. Nebogipfel, seeking escape, invents a machine to take him into the future where his ideas can be appreciated in a "wiser age." Griffin, seeking fame and then power, becomes invisible so that he can move undetected among men, controlling them by acting as an unseen force of fear and terror.

Whale's Jack Griffin, unlike the freak Griffin, appears more representative of universal humanity. He does not have Griffin's physical stigma to separate him from humankind, and his added first name makes him a more generic figure. "Jack" carries the commonality of the likes of Hawthorne's Young Goodman Brown, another Everyman who, coincidentally, uncovers a Forbidden Knowledge which leads to misery.

Both Invisible Men share the delusion of attaining world domination, but the origin of that delusion differs, producing a basic contrast in the motivation of the characters. Griffin's delusion is born out of an innate selfishness which exists even before his transformation. He tells Kemp:

> I had to do my work under frightful disadvantages. Oliver, my professor, was a scientific bounder, a journalist by instinct, a thief of ideas—he was always prying! And you know the knavish system of the scientific world. I simply would not publish and let him share my credit. I went on working, I got nearer and nearer making my formula into an experiment, a reality. I told no living soul, because I meant to flash my work upon the world with a crushing effect—to become famous at a blow. (Ch. 19)

His secretiveness borders on paranoia and his selfishness shows him excessively conceited and possessive. Fame motivates him, and after the discovery of invisibility, that ambition grows into the overblown dream of an aspiring tyrant:

> To do such a thing would be to transcend magic. And I beheld, unclouded by doubt, a magnificent vision of all that invisibility might mean to a man—the mystery, the power, the freedom. Drawbacks I saw none. You have only to think! (Ch. 19)

Fundamentally, Griffin does not change after the experiment. Prior to his transformation, his albinism makes him a physical monster and his scientific genius makes him a mental monster. Afterwards, invisibility only exaggerates his monstrousness by giving him the illusion of a power which he believes he can use to subdue society.

By contrast, Jack, before becoming invisible, seems an ordinary human being. His friends talk of him as a normal, sound person with warm emotions. His love for Flora and her love for him suggest how strong his ambition must have been to make him forsake her for his private quest.[2] The attractive Stuart plays her role well as the fervently anxious lover and helps win the audience's sympathy for Jack.

Jack works for her father, Dr. Cranley (Henry Travers), in a steady, lackluster job researching food preservatives. As close friends, Flora and Cranley display their loyalty and respect by protecting him from the police and by defending him when Kemp criticizes his secretive experiments. (Harrigan, as Kemp, expertly portrays the sneaky, sleazy coward who tries unsuccessfully to seduce Flora after Jack has disappeared. His lack of compassion shifts the designation of "villain" from Jack to himself.) The concern of Jack's two friends before and after his transformation prove that he is not totally isolated from the community of humankind as the albino Griffin is.

Jack's delusion results from his taking the drug monocaine, which, while making him transparent, gradually induces madness. Like Griffin, he exhibits a monomania for world domination, but this obsession takes hold only after he has swallowed the mind-warping drug. Griffin's calculated plan to use invisibility to conquer the world makes him a more detestable villain than Jack, who, because of the inadvertent side effect, appears a victim.

It becomes ironic that Griffin, who kills only one man (and that not conclusively proven), should appear more evil than Jack, who kills over a hundred people. In the end, however, despite the contrast between their innate and induced villainy, the Invisible Men manage to elicit a feeling of tragedy. To achieve this, the novel and film use some similar approaches.

Both Invisible Men are extremely ruthless and savage, but humor mitigates their violence. The revelation of their invisibility to the villagers instigates a kind of slapstick, Mack-Sennett melee in which everyone stumbling over one another in a futile effort to apprehend them nullifies the painful reality of bumped heads and bruised bodies.[3]

In the film, Jack hurls proprietor George Hall (Forrester Harvey) down the stairs, producing exaggerated strident screams from his wife Jenny (Una O'Connor). Jack's white shirt floats and weaves about the furniture, leading Constable Jaffers (E. E. Clive) and others in a farcical romp around the room when they try to arrest him. Outside, he throws a rock through the window of a tobacconist's shop and says, "We do our part" (i.e., to help stop smoking). He steals a bicycle out of the hands of a man (Walter Brennan) and the bicycle appears to pedal off by itself. The remarkable special effects devised by John P. Fulton, such as the floating shirt, the self-propelled bicycle, and an old man's hat plucked off his head and thrown into a puddle, entrance us in their surrealism and undercut the reality of the violence.

Wells compounds the farce when the Invisible Man enlists a simple-minded tramp as his ally and then bungles his attempt to punish him for desertion. After telling Kemp of his nonsensical experiences, he admits, "Every conceivable sort of silly creature that has ever been created has been sent to cross me" (Ch. 23). It seems so, and the humor, which emerges from the juxtaposition of ridiculous situations with his serious, grandiose designs, tends to minimize the horror of his evil.

Using irony, the film and the novel produce a similar kind of black comedy in the comparable scenes where the Invisible Men reveal to Kemp their plan to inflict a Reign of Terror on humankind. Wells's Griffin delivers a cold, calculating speech which intensifies the horror of his motives:

> This invisibility, in fact, is only good in two cases: It's useful in getting away, it's useful in approaching. It's particularly useful, therefore, in killing. . . . And it is killing we must do, Kemp. . . . Not wanton killing, but a judicious slaying. The point is, they know there is an Invisible Man—as well as we know there is an Invisible Man. And that Invisible Man, Kemp, must now establish a Reign of Terror. Yes, no doubt it's startling. But I mean it. A Reign of Terror. He must take some

> town like your Burdock and terrify and dominate it. He
> must issue his orders. He can do that in a thousand
> ways—scraps of papers thrust under doors would
> suffice. And all who disobey his orders he must kill, and
> kill all who would defend them. (Ch. 24)

The casualness with which he can talk of killing makes him an
object of dread and terror. Yet the trivialities accompanying
the enormity of his conspiracy, world domination dwindling
to the take-over of a small local village and the "thousand
ways" to issue commands reduced to paper slips slid under
doors, become dramatic irony turning him into a buffoon. He
may incite fear, but he also appears a fool who must be
momentarily tolerated.

Jack, too, exposes a comical side to his monstrousness, but
is deliberately facetious. His mixture of terrifying threats and
dark sarcasm makes him at once more sinister and more
humorous. He tells Kemp, in a calm, gleeful tone:

> We'll begin with a Reign of Terror. A few murders here
> and there. Murders of great men, murders of little men,
> just to show we make no distinction. We might even
> wreck a train or two.

To Kemp's dismay, Jack coolly demonstrates how he might
strangle a switchman to cause the train accident. As with
Griffin, his eager willingness to kill makes him a dreadful
creature, and his delight in conceiving his evil plan contrasts
with Kemp's horror, creating the effect of black comedy. In
addition, Jack revels in his maliciousness, coupling his sadism
with a sense of humor, a trait not apparent in Griffin.
Because of this, Jack seems the more attractive, if not more
likable monster.

In the events immediately preceding the albino Griffin's
death, continued contrasts between violence and humor
obscure the foreboding of a tragic outcome. Griffin sends
Kemp a letter with a death threat, but it is written in pencil
on a greasy sheet of paper and on the reverse side is "the
prosaic detail, '2d. to pay.' " Attacking the two police in
Kemp's house, Griffin nearly kills one with an axe, while

Kemp, deserting, leaves the police to defend it and earns the sarcastic praise from one of them: "Doctor Kemp's a hero." Mr. Heelas's casual remark about the damage done to Kemp's house (" 'I could have sworn it was all right'—he looked at his watch—'twenty minutes ago' ") and his frantic effort to fortify his house against the Invisible Man contrast with his callous refusal to let Kemp inside. Following this, in the long chase after Kemp across the countryside, Griffin's vehement tenacity appears laughable.

The farce diminishes the seriousness of the desperate situations and is probably what contributes most to the shock and horror of Griffin's abrupt death at the hands of the villagers. The description of his battered, naked, stark white body lying crumpled on the ground produces the incisive horror of tragedy, making the Invisible Man seem, if only at this particular moment, a martyr. The pathetic image of his corpse surrounded by the milling crowd that has just killed him represents the conflict of the individual against the masses. He could be Shakespeare's exiled Coriolanus slain by the common rabble that misjudged him, or Ayn Rand's "creator," Howard Roarke, persecuted by the "collective" that envied him.

Of course, his martyrdom is ambiguous. He is, first of all, the Irresponsible Scientist who tampers with Forbidden Knowledge and endangers society with the results of a monstrous experiment. Yet, at the same time, he is the individual who dared use his imagination to create something innovative, regardless of the sacrifice.[4]

Jack's death also suggests tragedy, despite his greater success as a terrorist. He kills a police inspector for not believing in his existence. He robs a bank and throws two men over a cliff. He reroutes a train, sending it over an embankment and killing a hundred and twenty people. He murders Kemp in what seems the most horrible of his crimes because it is the most sadistic. After tying Kemp up and placing him in his car, Jack describes in detail how he will roll over the precipice and break arms and legs before he falls to his death. Then he releases the brake, and Kemp goes over the edge, his scream suddenly cut off as his car bursts into flames.

Yet all the time, we are aware that this is not Jack the Man committing these crimes, but Jack the Monster. As in the film version of *Dr. Jekyll and Mr. Hyde*,[5] he is a benevolent scientist whose miscalculation makes him as much a victim as the people he kills. When he lies on his death bed, and Flora, weeping, comes to him, we cannot feel righteous that justice finally prevails. Rather, unlike with Wells's Griffin, whose behavior seems a matter of choice, we sympathize with the man who unwittingly has fallen into a trap of his own making.

The scene which becomes the most poignant for making the audience aware of Jack's crisis occurs when Flora meets him at Kemp's house. His unexpected tenderness toward her shocks us into realizing that he is not the ogre we have supposed but a man worthy of the devotion she has been showing. Especially touching is the moment when he takes her by the hands, seats her on the window box, and says, "That funny little hat. I've always liked it." The incongruity between this trivial sentimentality and his ruthless ambition reveals the instability of his temperament and how a cruel disposition has replaced his capability for showing gentleness.

As Jack, Claude Rains, his face covered completely by bandages, cannot rely on facial expressions to complement his words. Gestures help, but nearly all his emotion and personality depend on voice inflection and rhythm.[6] This he executes superbly, as here, where the initial romantic tone of his speech gradually yields to mad vindictiveness. At one moment Jack speaks softly to Flora, telling her his experiment was for her. The next, he talks quickly and scornfully, ridiculing her father: "He's got the brain of a worm, a maggot, beside mine." And finally he raises his voice loudly, in frenzied triumph: "Don't you see what it means? Power. Power to rule, to make the world grovel at my feet. . . . Even the moon's frightened of me, frightened to death!" The extremes of tenderness and fanaticism clearly reflect the pitiful plight of a man whose humanity is being overtaken by baser emotions.

Regarding the nature of the Science, the film does not refer to any principles from physics or use any scientific jargon to explain Jack's invisibility, which seems a flaw in an otherwise tightly constructed movie. The knowledge for achieving invisibility becomes nothing more than the pseudo-science of *Dr. Jekyll and Mr. Hyde.* Dr. Cranley's explanation to Kemp about monocaine's effects fails to clarify the natural or scientific laws involved in the transformation. Lack of some elaborate, even if vague scientific explanation tends to qualify the film more as Horror than as Science Fiction, although its connection with Wells's story gives it scientific relevance. There appears no clear reason why Wells's more "realistic" scientific explanation could not have been incorporated into the film.

Wells, on the other hand, replaces the flimsy Science of Stevenson's *Dr. Jekyll* and Shelley's *Frankenstein* with "an ingenious use of scientific patter."[7] The Science behind Griffin's invisibility merges fact with fancy. His explanation of refraction and reflection, and his description of a two-step process using a drug and a mechanical device, make his achievement seem "logical."

As in *The Time Machine,* Griffin's Science involves the fourth dimension, with Light replacing Time as the additional factor in physical geometry. His research with pigments and "optical density," the property which determines the degree of visibility of things, leads him to his fantastic discovery.

He tells Kemp of his initial ecstatic feelings:

> "One could make an animal—a tissue—transparent! One could make it invisible! All except the pigments—I could be invisible!" I said, suddenly realizing what it meant to be an albino with such knowledge. It was overwhelming. I left the filtering I was doing and went and stared out of the great window at the stars. "I could be invisible!" I repeated. (Ch. 19)

Griffin staring out of his window into the heavens presents an image contrasting with Prendick's final words in *The Island of Doctor Moreau:*

> There is . . . a sense of infinite peace and protection in the infinite hosts of heaven. There it must be . . . that

whatever is more than animal within us must find its
solace and its hope.

Prendick's vision can be shared by all men. Griffin's vision
relates to himself alone, and in the strictest sense, since the
application of that knowledge can only be used on himself. It
becomes a kind of "selfish Science," and Griffin, like a
miser, hoards his knowledge, destroying the machine he built
and leaving "gaps" in his notes as a safeguard against
thievery. The result is that he succeeds in his research, but at
the price of divorcing himself from human relationships.

Jack shares Griffin's inclination for secrecy. Kemp remarks how he became reclusive, working in his lab with
locked doors and drawn blinds. Flora says that lately he had
not been "so keen to tell me about his experiments."
Originally, however, Jack's motives for his research must
have included Flora. When she meets him at Kemp's house,
she asks him why he became invisible. He tells her that he did
it for her, that he "was so pitifully poor" and "had nothing to
offer" her. Then he adds:

> I wanted to do something tremendous, to achieve what
> men of science have dreamt of since the world began, to
> gain wealth and fame and honor, to write my name
> above the greatest scientists of all time.

Obviously, his concern for Flora did not exclude motives
which were also self-serving. He possesses Griffin's ambitious nature as a scientist with self-gratifying goals. Still,
unlike Griffin, whose resentment alienates him from society,
Jack reveals traces of human sensitivity. His feelings for
Flora counter the gravity of his scientific myopia and
contribute to his being a more sympathetic character.

Despite their alienation from society, the Invisible Men
establish one relationship which becomes singularly important, that with Doctor Kemp. Kemp represents their antithesis, and the contrast between him and them produces a
central motif which appears similar for the two versions of
the story.

For the albino Griffin, this antithesis is epitomized in the scene where he enters Kemp's house after suffering a gunshot wound. For several minutes, Griffin, a disembodied voice, converses with Kemp and uses physical force to contain him. Kemp expresses disbelief, "I demonstrated conclusively this morning . . . that invisibility—," but is cut off by Griffin's retort: "Never mind what you've demonstrated!" (Ch. 17).

Griffin's apparent achievement contrasted with Kemp's persistent but absurd disbelief signifies their extreme positions in approaching scientific research. Griffin is the practical scientist who uses experiments to uncover concrete evidence which will prove or disprove his hypotheses. Such experiments may contribute to progress and to the good of humanity, but often, as in the case of invisibility, the outcome can be disruptive and disastrous. In contrast, Kemp is a theoretician, a kind of "armchair scientist" who bases the feasibility of his hypotheses on abstract reasoning. His Science is socially "safe" because it is abstract. It remains within the bounds of conservatism by not threatening society with anything radically new to disrupt its routine existence. However, influenced by propriety and not by imagination, his passive approach may overlook valuable, useful ideas. Both methods are purposeful, but neither is wholly desirable.

The confrontation between Kemp's theoretical science and Griffin's practical science becomes integrated with the images of Kemp's house and Griffin's being exiled to the outside. When Kemp first appears to us, he

> was sitting in his study in the belvedere. . . . It was a pleasant little room with windows north, west, and south, and bookshelves covered with books and scientific publications, and a broad writing table, and, under the north window, a microscope, glass slips, minute instruments, some cultures, and scattered bottles of reagents. Doctor Kemp's solar lamp was lit, albeit the sky was still bright with the sunset light, and his blinds were up because there was no offence of peering outsiders to require them pulled down . . . the work he was upon would earn him, he hoped, the fellowship of the Royal Society, so highly did he think of it. (Ch. 15)

Although Kemp's study contains minor scientific apparatus, such equipment appears subordinate to his interest in the written word of "books and scientific publications" and his own theorizings. Unlike the secretive Griffin, he keeps his windows open. This signifies his candor and his willingness to share his discoveries, but it also carries a motive no more selfless than Griffin's, for in revealing his work, he, too, expects to gain fame. In addition, the windows provide him a perspective on the outside world, but they make him an observer, not a participant, which means he shares figuratively in Griffin's "crime" of isolation. As a result, his light of knowledge, like Moreau's in *Island of Lost Souls*, comes from a limited artificial source, and his failure to derive his ideas from the more important genuine light of reality means that his vision lacks relevance to the actual outside world.

In Whale's film, the contrast between Kemp and Jack presents a similar ambiguity in the nature of scientific investigation. Early in the film, the conniving, back-stabbing Kemp uses Jack's absence as an opportunity to win Flora's love for himself. He tells her that Jack "meddled in things men should leave alone." Working for her father, he defends their dull, ordinary research with food preservatives: "It's a plain, straightforward job. It's not romantic, but it saves hundreds of deaths and thousands of stomach aches." Then he criticizes Jack for working secretively behind locked doors and closed blinds. (In the very next scene, we see Jack tortured by his reckless mistake, trying to find "a way back" to Flora, and we sense the treachery in Kemp's scheming.) In this, Kemp mirrors his original counterpart with his conservative approach to Science and his concern for social propriety. When his methods are contrasted with Jack's radical, ambitious experimentation, they resemble the extreme approaches to Science used in the novel.

The central motif emerging from this contrast iterates the one contained in Wells's *Island of Doctor Moreau* and *The Time Machine*, namely, that Science has ambiguous value in its contribution to knowledge and progress. The good it sometimes achieves is often at the expense of lives and ethics, its useful innovations disruptive to social conventions and traditional beliefs.

B: Science vs. Humanity and Nature: Imagery and Symbolism in *The Invisible Man*

In the early 1930s, filmmakers produced Mad-Doctor films as rampantly as their scientists created monsters. Films like *Doctor X* (Michael Curtiz, 1932), *Dr. Jekyll and Mr. Hyde* (Rouben Mamoulian, 1932), *Island of Lost Souls* (Erle C. Kenton, 1933), and *Mad Love* (Karl Freund, 1935) exploit the Edenic curse that self-destruction comes from tampering with Forbidden Knowledge. A doctor or scientist, driven by his search for knowledge, creates a monster which goes out of control. After causing chaos and panic, the monster kills

The Invisible Man (1933, Universal Pictures): Science versus Humanity. Entering the inn, The Invisible Man (Claude Rains, left) interrupts the common folk in their game of darts. The scene foreshadows his disruption of their daily routines when he reveals to them the effects of his reckless experiment.

or brings about the death of its creator before it is finally destroyed.

The scenario of these films becomes an allegory for their historical context, the Great Depression. The monster Economic Chaos, created by some obscure, unidentifiable source, disrupts the lives of ordinary, innocent people without justifiable cause. Government, represented by Science, loses its credibility as benefactor and now acts as a source of society's problems.

James Whale, a major theatrical and film director of the 1930s and '40s, made three important sf-horror films in this period. *Frankenstein* (1931), *The Invisible Man* (1933), and *The Bride of Frankenstein* (1935) share the idea that humanity plays a double role governed by an uncontrollable fate. As the obsessed Scientist, Man has only the illusion of command over his self-made circumstances, and as the tormented Monster, he is subject to the failings instilled in him by his Creator. The Monster, personifying Irresponsible Science or Science-Gone-Wrong, is his evil nature set free to wreak havoc on humanity without the restriction of conscience, remorse, or moral law.

Jack Griffin is Whale's embodiment of the Scientist-Monster duality, the Creator merged with his uncontrollable Creation. Although Jack may blame the drug monocaine for his irrational behavior, he is no less tyrannical than the novel's Griffin, who appears a deranged malcontent even before his transformation. Unaware that their Science has merely given them a false sense of absolute power, both propose a direct assault on humanity and nature, their ambition to use their invisibility "to make the world grovel at my feet."

First of all, as personifications of a Science which threatens humanity, both Griffins share an irony in the significance of their name. As already noted in the chapter on *The Time Machine,* griffins, mythological beasts with the body of a lion and the wings and head of an eagle, build their nests of gold which they defend against invaders. Generally depicted on the side of good, they signify the role of protectors.

Jack and Griffin, as scientists, automatically assume a position as protectors of the public good. Their research has the potential for discoveries that could help or harm the community, and they, in their capacity to defend or destroy, are expected to be especially conscious of contributing to the welfare of the community. Instead, they pervert their eponymous role and become monsters of death and destruction.

Other ironies in the mythological allusion relate to the griffins' efforts to protect their gold from the Arimaspi, a race of one-eyed horsemen. In Wells, Griffin fails to prevent Thomas Marvel from stealing his money, proving further that invisibility does not give him the power or control over men which he believes it does.

Jack, meanwhile, steals a cash drawer from a bank and flings the money to passersby on the street. He sings, "Up and down the city roads/In and out the eagle/That's the way the money goes/Pop goes the Weasel!" Then he drops the drawer on the head of a policeman and madly yells, "Moneymoneymoneymoneymoney!" This "griffin" steals instead of defends, and his striking the policeman shows disrespect for the authority that acts more as the protector than he. Like the eagle-headed griffin, he is "the eagle" that can go at will "up and down the city roads, in and out." Contrary to the griffin, he displays a contempt for money. The results are humorous, but if money represents the economy, and a correct, prudent use of it implies economic stability, Jack's abuse of it invites economic chaos and financial ruin for the country.[8]

Because their obsessive ambition to conquer humanity blinds their sense of logic, the Invisible Men believe they control their situations, when in fact they are subject to various natural and man-made laws which limit their power and mobility. This becomes apparent in the various images connoting restriction and conformity.

In the film's opening scene, the wind whistles across an open, snow-swept landscape. It appears all the more stark and desolate because a lone figure, Jack Griffin, trudges forward on the snow-covered road outlined by bare fence railings. The swirling snow alternately blurs and uncovers him, suggesting that his scientifically induced invisibility is overridden by Nature's whim to show or hide him at her discretion.

For the film, the fence becomes an important recurring image of restriction. Man-made, it represents the conventions devised to restrain society's members along a designated path of conformity. In this scene, Jack wipes off the road sign which says, "To Iping 1/2 m." This means that if he walks the route outlined by the fences, he will follow the safest route to the village. The road winds and does not appear the shortest, most direct line to the buildings in the background. He could step outside the fencing and try a different, shorter path, but to do this is to stray beyond the safe, marked road toward society. Also, taking an independent road shows rebellion against conformity, which carries an automatic punishment of alienation from the community. However, in experimenting with monocaine, Jack has already chosen his own different path.

Later, when Jack escapes from Kemp's house, he breaks through another "fence," a police cordon. Yet he is not content merely to get away. First, he slaps one policeman, tweaks another's nose, then knocks off the captain's hat and kicks him in the seat when he bends over. High overhead shots of Kemp's house and yard show the police cordon converging to entrap him. Suddenly, one policeman in line is lifted backwards by his feet. Jack swings him around in a circle, then strips off his pants as he releases him. The pants drag along the ground, up onto a garden bench, and over a high wall. The police chase the pants as far as the wall and stop. In the next cut, an old woman runs screaming up a country road. She disappears out of the frame and the pair of pants come skipping up the road after her. Jack's voice sings: "Here we go gathering nuts in May, nuts in May, nuts in May. Here we go gathering nuts in May on a cold and frosty morning." Then he jumps and yells, "Whoops!"

Once again, humor disguises the darker implications. Jack has already harmed society by making it the brunt of his Irresponsible Science. He has defied their "fence of propriety" and now he defies their "fence of authority." That is, he has transgressed social and legal bounds. However, he can defy conventional walls only for so long before the dangers outside those walls catch up to him. At Kemp's house, Flora tries to warn him of the drug: "Father believes the power of it will go, if you know what you're fighting." It appears that awareness of what is on the other side of the fence may enable one to deal with its possible dangers. However, Jack ignores her. Too long outside the walls of convention makes him totally eccentric, completely mad. Society will not let him sustain his nonconformity indefinitely. It will eventually defeat him, surrounding him with a second police cordon and gunning him down *inside* the "fence of authority."

Yet staying within the fence, choosing to follow convention and conform to its standards of ordinariness and mediocrity, is no guarantee of safety. Kemp, Jack's opposite, prefers his "plain, straightforward job" researching food preservatives. He argues for consistency and conservatism. However, his philosophy of avoiding risks by following the safe, marked road cannot protect him from a fatal accident. Jack represents the unforeseen mishap which can affect plans despite every precaution. He diverts Kemp from the safe road and sends him through a fence where the cliff on the other side means death.

In both film and novel, rooms become an important image for suggesting secrecy or openness. The closed or locked room represents the isolated, private place where secret knowledge is hidden. Inside, contained by the four walls, this knowledge remains inert. Outside, exposed to the world, this knowledge becomes volatile, usually with harmful effects because its secretive nature implies evil origins.

Jack pursues his original research in a locked laboratory with its locked cupboards. When he moves to the Lion's Head[9] in Iping, he continues experimenting, cooped up in a private room. Pressured by his landlord's eviction notice, he exposes his invisibility, which leads to panic and anarchy in the normally quiet village.

By contrast, the film's first shots of carefree socializing in the Lion's Head pub and Jenny Hall's unconcern about a lost door key imply easy-going, free-spirited natures. And Dr. Cranley's laboratory, a large, spacious room with easy accessibility, connotes freedom. Cranley enters the room without formality, not locking the door behind him. As he goes about his business experimenting with two test tubes, Flora enters unannounced from the stairway and Kemp comes in moments later through a different door. Cranley's lack of security suggests he is an unsecretive individual.

Kemp's study also suggests this about him, at first. The Invisible Man sneaks in through the French doors while Kemp reads in his armchair, listening to the radio. After this invasion, Kemp learns to be secretive. While Jack sleeps, he locks the study door so he can safely telephone the police and call Cranley for help. Later, the police empty the room of its furniture and run a dragnet across it to make sure the Invisible Man is not there to overhear their plans to trap him. The room, formerly decorated and cozy, now looks barren and bleak, indicating Kemp's state of mind and implying what happens to the person whose life is reduced to locked rooms because of paranoia or guilt.

Like Jack, the albino Griffin works behind locked doors to find the secret he can use for his own selfish purposes. His discovery occurs in his small apartment on Great Portland Street and he continues his experiments in the parlor he usurps at the Coach and Horses. For both of them, locked rooms are a physical separation from society, representing their mental and emotional alienation. Whether intentional or not, their loss of sympathy with humanity, especially in regard to a common moral sensibility, isolates them from the community of humankind. This is what makes them monsters.

A third image, the window, the means of seeing into or out of a room, has a dual significance. The quality of the view outside the window indicates the quality of the perspective of the person inside the room. The visibility of the room from outside relates to the candidness of the person inside. Blinds open or drawn signify the openness or paranoia of the person within the room.

After renting his room at the inn, Jack stands at the window looking out until Mrs. Hall has readied his room and left. Then he quietly draws the shade and curtains. His penchant for secrecy appears an obsession, for Kemp also tells Flora how Jack had kept the blinds drawn in his lab: "Would a man with nothing to hide have need for locked doors and drawn blinds?" And later, when Jack visits Kemp, he makes him draw the blinds.

In contrast, Cranley's lab contains a huge bay window overlooking the table where he carries on his experiments, further connoting his candid, open nature. At Kemp's house, when Flora visits Jack, the blinds on the bedroom windows are suddenly open, for his relationship with her is innocent and open and needs no pretense of mystery.

At the Coach and Horses, after renting his room, Griffin's first act, like Jack's, is to close the curtains. From then on he always keeps the windows blinded. By contrast, Kemp works in a study whose "blinds were up because there was no offence of peering outsiders to require them pulled down" (Ch. 15). One works in the secrecy of guilt and fear; the other is open and candid.

In terms of the window relating to perspective, Griffin and Kemp view the world differently. Kemp, looking out his window, can admire a golden sunset (Ch. 15) or, inspired by the sight of a crowd and a starlit night, can speculate on the direction of society (Ch. 17). When the Invisible Man looks out his window at the nighttime sky, he ruminates on selfish designs (Ch. 19). The two men, in their disparate subjective outlooks, represent the extremes of social- and self-consciousness.

Related to the window are the Invisible Man's goggles. They prevent people from seeing his eyes, the "windows of his soul," but they do not prevent him from seeing theirs. They represent a selfish, one-way vision of the world. At the same time, because the lenses are blue, they distort the true color of the world, so that while wearing them, Griffin cannot see nor appreciate the world as it really is. He is unable to admire golden sunsets or clear nights as Kemp can.

Another important image is that of the house, which, as used here, seems to have its significance rooted in Wells's *The Chronic Argonauts*.[10] After taking possession of a dilapidated, deserted house, Nebogipfel, one night, turns on his Time Machine:

> Suddenly a strange whizzing, buzzing whirr filled the night air. . . . The house no longer loomed a black featureless block but was filled to overflowing with light. From the gaping holes in the roof, from chinks

and fissures amid tiles and brickwork, from every gap
which Nature or man had pierced in the crumbling old
shell, a blinding blue-white glare was streaming. . . .
Then from the gleaming roof-gaps of the house suddenly vomited forth a wondrous swarm of heteronomous living things—swallows, sparrows, martins, owls,
bats, insects in visible multitudes, to hang for many
minutes a noisy, gyrating, spreading cloud over the
black gables and chimneys, . . . and then slowly to thin
out and vanish away in the night.

The scene describes an exorcism, Science purging the house
of Nature. Science's ambiguous value lies in its indiscrimi-
nate eviction of the "heteronomous" creatures, both those
connoting good (swallows, sparrows, martins) and bad (owls,
bats, insects). Adding to the ambiguity, Nebogipfel's intentions for the machine are honorable, but going back in time
he kills a man in self-defense, suggesting unpredictable
dangers in the use of Science.

The Invisible Men are products of an unpredictable,
irresponsible Science. What may have had potential to do
good is used for evil. Being unseen, they become, in effect,
evil spirits or poltergeists. They take over rooms and houses
in what resembles satanic possessions. Ridding them from a
place becomes a ritual of exorcism.

The first scene in the pub room of the Lion's Head Inn
shows two men at the bar talking about a little boy caught in
a snowdrift. The speaker describes the outcome: "Brought
the fire engine round, put the hose pipe in, pumped it
backwards, and sucked him out." This image of exorcism
suggests the weapon Society uses to deal with the Invisible
Men.

When George Hall orders Jack to leave his inn, he is
making a clumsy attempt at exorcism. Jack, instead, orders
him out of his room, and George confronts him: "Look here,
is this my house or yours?" Jack uses his notebook to
bludgeon George, driving him out of the room and down the
stairs. Next, Constable Jaffers enters as a legal exorcist, and
Jack also beats him. When the inn is finally rid of its "evil
spirit," it is not by a successful exorcism. Jack leaves of his

own free will after regaining his notebooks and killing the police chief.

As for Griffin, the attempted eviction at the Coach and Horses has similar ineffective results. Like Jack, he returns later to recover his notebooks. He makes fools of Dr. Cuss and Rev. Bunting, who, along with Kemp, represent the stalwart, upright middle class.[11] Then he escapes in a second chaotic flurry with the villagers.

Wells's Griffin also experiences an earlier exorcism, which he narrates to Kemp. While living in his apartment on Great Portland Street he receives an "ejectment" notice for failing to pay his rent. He eludes the landlord and his sons, but in his paranoia he fears they will discover the purpose of his invention, and so he burns it. The fire grows into a conflagration, a spiteful purging which rids the building of the other tenants as well as himself.

In the film's scene at Kemp's house, where the police close in on Jack, high overhead shots and quick cuts show neat horizontal rows of uniformed police moving in a synchronized pattern, suggesting exorcism refined into a formal ceremony. It fails, but later, in the scene outside the barn, they repeat their ritual, adding fire to drive the "evil spirit" from its possessed "body." This time, the ritual executes a successful purging.

"The Siege of Kemp's House" (Ch. 27) becomes the violent climax in the conflict between possession and exorcism. The "evil spirit," in a mad frenzy, drives Kemp—that is, sanity—from his house. Griffin momentarily takes possession, but in turn is driven from the house by two policemen, symbols of law and order. Kemp's house is left in ruin, signifying the violence inherent in the struggle between good and evil.

When Thomas Marvel inherits the stolen money, he uses it to buy an inn, which he names The Invisible Man. Every night, by himself, he pores over the notebooks he stole from Griffin, hoping one day to decipher their contents. In effect, the inn becomes Griffin's one complete, successful possession, its exterior structure purchased with money he stole and its interior essence alive with his mysterious, illicit knowledge. Kemp and Adye still question Marvel for his part in the affair, but he, like Griffin, hoards his secret, and because he cannot figure out the cyphers, they do him no good.

The final sentence, "none other will know of them [the mysterious cyphers] until he dies," appears ambiguous. It may mean that the secrets of invisibility will die with Marvel, or it may mean that after Marvel dies, the secrets will come to light, having fallen into the hands of another seeker of dangerous unpredictable, secret knowledge.

Besides the conflict of Science against Humanity, the novel and film also include a conflict of Science against Nature. When the noise and light from Nebogipfel's Time Machine expel the creatures from the house, it signifies an incompatibility between Science and Nature, as if certain scientific knowledge contradicts natural law and repulses Nature. This appears to be the case when Moreau's artificial duplication of humans falls short of natural procreation and he creates hideous monsters. In like fashion, the Time Traveller's journey is a physically upsetting experience, and Griffin's process makes him so sick that he would welcome death.

The Invisible Men, to achieve their ends, expect to use Science to circumvent Nature. Instead, Nature restricts them in ways they had not anticipated. Weather can thwart their invisibility, because to remain unseeable they must go about naked, which, as exemplified in the early scenes of both film and novel, is a hardship in cold weather. Despite their invisibility, they occupy physical space, and people, unable to see them, collide with them, leaving them banged and bruised. Food recently eaten remains visible in their stomach until assimilated, making them vulnerable to discovery. Weather, corporeality, and appetite, directly related to the basic necessities of food, clothing, and shelter, expose the monsters' limitations and prove that Science may baffle Nature but cannot totally escape her control.

Whale makes the conflict of Science against Nature more obvious by personifying Nature in the character of Flora. In an early scene, Flora talks with Kemp in a sitting room. He stands to the left, and she, right, poses in front of a bay window. Between them, a vase of long-stemmed flowers rests on a table. The camera cutting back and forth gives the impression that they are talking "through" the flowers, and that the flowers separate them and prevent them from getting close. In one shot, a medium close-up, Flora moves closer to the flowers, and in a second shot, a tight close-up, her head appears just above them, her face merging with the blossoms. Her identification with the flowers is unmistakable, if a bit overstated, her name already bearing that significance.

This is one of a number of "telescopic" montages which appear in the film. The technique focuses attention on a detail possibly obscured in the larger, general picture.[12] This device first appears in the credits, where overblown, blurred titles, extending beyond the boundaries of the frame, suddenly condense within the frame into clear, resolved letters for each reading. This also relates to the image of fences, which, when crossed over, take the trespasser into an unclear, unknown realm, but when heeded, make things appear clear and understandable.

In this scene which parallels her window-seat scene with Jack, Flora sits down on the window box. Kemp walks behind the table and remains standing, partially hidden by the flowers. He reveals his love. He lives within the bounds of propriety and convention and argues that this qualifies him as a stable and therefore desirable man. Yet, his manner is stifled and unromantic, too indifferent to merit Flora's love. Jack, on the other hand, reveals in that later scene a playfulness which, despite his degenerating sanity, makes him appear more human than Kemp. However, his experiment has alienated him from her. Although they profess a love for Flora, both men are associated with Science, a force which corrupts and inhibits a genuine communion with Nature.

Kemp's vision of Science is a conventional, traditional, practical one. It is simply a profession, a means to a living. Yet, as he is physically obscured by the flowers, his personality is overshadowed by what Flora represents, Love and Beauty and Nature. He cannot fully appreciate this, and so must exist alone in his study with only her portrait, her artificial likeness. His door and blinds remain open, but he lacks the depth of character to deserve her.

Jack, meanwhile, has the more charismatic personality. His inventiveness and the uniqueness of his discovery show him to be a man of imagination and determination. However, Science betrays him and he loses touch with Love and Nature. In taking monocaine he has poisoned his mind with a corruptive agent which prevents appreciation of the fine, innocent things of his previous life. Nature becomes obscured and he loses contact with those things which inspire human love and passion.

The distance between Jack as Scientist and Flora as Nature is made apparent by the elaborate camera movement ending her scene with Kemp and by the dissolve into the next scene, Jack's room at Iping. In a medium-close two-shot, Kemp, sitting behind Flora, tells her that Jack never cared for anything but "test tubes and chemicals," that he was inconsiderate to leave without a word, and that she should see how he loves her himself. Flora trembles, cries out, and falls forward on the seat. The camera cuts to a medium-close of Flora sitting forward, sobbing, then tracks left and up as Kemp stands, partly obscured by the flowers. In a dynamic tracking shot, the camera pulls straight back and then diagonally, right to left, from a medium shot of Kemp to a long shot of the two people far in the background of the spacious room, Flora crying on the seat beneath the window.

The scene dissolves into a medium-full shot of Jack in his private room, holding a flask and standing behind a table cluttered with test tubes and chemicals. He turns and retreats diagonally toward the window. He stumbles on a box and kicks it angrily. He holds up the flask to the light, then returns to the table and sets it down. With his arms akimbo, he speaks through his bandages in a muffled angry tone, "There's a way back, you fool. There must be a way back."

Jack's effort to find a "way back" becomes the motif of Restoration, an attempt to redeem the self, to reclaim a former innocent, simpler existence which has been lost through a foolish miscalculation. However, once the apple has been bitten, once Pandora's box has been opened, restoration becomes impossible. In the Flora-Kemp scene, the camera's tracking back from a medium to long shot shows how far away Flora has become for Jack, who appears near the foreground of the next scene. Also, she "dissolves" before he appears, indicating her figurative vanishing for him as his Science has made him literally vanish for her.

Coincidentally, just after Kemp tells Flora that Jack prefers his test tubes and chemicals to her, Jack appears, toying with his test tubes and chemicals. Kemp's accusation seems warranted, yet Jack's obsession with "a way back" indicates his fear and regret, human traits which earn him sympathy.

In a further irony, the restorative elixir which eludes Jack may be present all the time in the Halls' barroom: liquor. Jenny drinks it to restore her composure after Jack frightens her by pushing her out the door and making her drop her tray. And George drinks it after his fall down the stairs, sitting with bandaged head and downing several glasses for medicinal purposes.

In Wells's novel, a similar coincidence occurs between the Invisible Man and the Halls. On the evening Griffin was out robbing the vicar, George and Jenny

> went down into the cellar. Their business there was of a private nature, and had something to do with the specific gravity of their beer. (Ch. 6)

Here, something done illegally and secretively seems acceptable, in one way because it is humorous, but more so because it is familiar. Griffin's crime is not invisibility, as he notes to Jaffers who comes to arrest him, but tampering with secrets which are not common knowledge. Interestingly, another name for "specific gravity" is "relative density," which, compared with "optical density," makes the two "experiments," in their terminology, appear related. The latter, deviating from the known and familiar, becomes offensive to the ordinary layperson.

In his effort to restore himself, Jack appears noble because he is trying to correct his mistake. Griffin also wants to restore himself, but with the evil intention of making his tyranny more efficient, practical, and enjoyable.

Although their two different personalities arouse different sympathies, the two Griffins show how the benefits of

Science are often accompanied by detrimental side effects, so
that they elicit from the audience similar ambivalent responses toward Science. Wells iterates this in his early
scientific romances and Whale imitates him by repeating the
idea in several of his films.

Notes

1. The term "fixed idea" appears here and in other Wells stories.
   It refers to a mental conditioning in which a person becomes
   obsessed with a belief, concept, or objective. Implicitly, the
   fixed idea stifles the flexibility of the imagination, while
   dominating other thoughts, feelings, and actions.

2. Griffin mentions how seeing a former woman friend recalls for
   him a nostalgic past. However, he calls her "ordinary" and
   bluntly dismisses her from his memories to concentrate on his
   present scientific pursuits. Perhaps in the same way, Jack
   momentarily divorces himself from Flora, but his anxiousness
   to find "a way back" shows him not so totally indifferent to his
   human sentiments.

3. This is a classic device, the initial farce giving way to tragedy
   and making death a grimmer reality when contrasted with the
   earlier playful tone. In Wells, the Wicksteed murder, although
   inconclusive, indicates Griffin's potential to carry out his
   threats. In Whale, the starkly brutal murder of the gruff police
   chief (Holmes Herbert) proves Jack a horrible and real
   menace.

4. Whether Griffin's death is tragic or not is debatable. In his
   book *H. G. Wells* (London: MacMillan, 1987), Michael
   Draper gives a concise, insightful analysis of the novel and
   claims that Griffin "does not even manage to die with the
   heroic bearing of a tragic figure" (48). Frank McConnell (*The
   Science Fiction of H. G. Wells*) also presents a well-written
   analysis and notes Griffin's ambiguity as an evil but gifted
   individual suppressed by the masses: "the special individual
   does have his special rights and his special social sanctions"
   (121). My feelings lean toward McConnell's, based on my
   argument above and on the powerful dramatic image drawn by
   Wells, which inspires the sensation of tragedy.

5. It is important to separate the doctor's motives in the film from those in the novel, where his ambition was quite different. In the book, the "good" Jekyll unleashed his Hyde personality with the specific intention of satisfying his base appetites without damaging his upstanding reputation or upsetting his conscience.

6. Benson, p. 44. Originally, the role had been offered to Boris Karloff, but he refused, disapproving of having his face shown only at the end when the Invisible Man materializes in death. In fact, though his friend, Whale was pleased with his decision, feeling him wrong for the part. (For what reason is not clear, but since the voice was crucial to the Invisible Man's personality, Karloff's lisp might have been a drawback.) Instead, Whale pushed for 44-year-old stage actor, Claude Rains. He wanted him for his voice even though he had failed his screen test; the result was that Rains was lifted immediately to stardom.

7. In the Preface to *Seven Famous Novels by H. G. Wells,* (New York: Alfred A. Knopf, 1934), Wells explains his strategy to make the Science plausible.

8. This and other scenes in the story reflect the concerns of the Depression era (money, homelessness, anger at authority). The great artistry in Whale's film is its black comedy. It inserts humor into the morbid issues of the times, providing the audience with a momentary escape from the hardships outside the theater.

9. In Wells, the inn was named the Coach and Horses. The Lion's Head could be another allusion to the griffin, which has the body of a lion but the head of an eagle. If the griffin could acquire the head of a lion, it would establish its integrity as a normal creature instead of being a fantastic monster. Figuratively, Jack comes to Iping to do this. However, his invisible head is the first thing he exposes to the villagers, evidence that he has failed to restore the physicality which would once more make him whole.

10. In fact, this early time-travel story shares more with *The Invisible Man* than it does with *The Time Machine.* Many parallels exist between the protagonists, in the narrative voice, and in the imagery.

11. As in *The Time Machine,* Wells satirizes the middle-class leaders of society. At the same time, Rev. Bunting represents Wells's recurring image of the hypocritical clergy (see p. 145, note 21).

12. Consider also the montage sequence when Jack enters the Lion's Head or when the Iping police chief holds the inquest at the pub.

IV: THE WAR OF THE WORLDS

A: Modernized Martians: Reinventing *The War of the Worlds*

In adapting H. G. Wells's *The War of the Worlds* (1898) to their 1953 film, director Byron Haskin, producer George Pal,[1] and writer Barré Lyndon devised a landmark science-fiction classic. Especially impressive are the special effects, for which Gordon Jennings posthumously won an Oscar. Outstanding, too, are Haskin's pacing and Everett Douglas's editing, which create a taut rhythm of tension and release alternating throughout the story.

In many ways, the film is highly original, borrowing only the bare plot of Wells's novel. A meteor crashes to earth. People, curious to see it, flock to it as if it were a holiday attraction. The meteor turns out to be one of many spaceships from Mars with alien invaders who intend to conquer earth. The Martians prove a juggernaut of ruthless destruction, their war machines so formidable that the world's weapons cannot stop their advance. Their conquest of humanity appears inevitable until an unexpected factor intervenes: earthly bacteria, benign to humans, kill the Martians, who lack immunity to them.

Much of the critical praise for Wells's story concerns an approach which has become a convention for many science-fiction writers ever since. As in his other works, he ingeniously superimposes the strange and paranormal on ordinary existence, disrupting the familiar routine of people's lives and subjecting them to something alien and unfamiliar.[2] In *The Time Machine,* for example, an Englishman, without leaving his home, finds his familiar world altered after transporting himself into a distant future. On the island of Dr. Moreau, Prendick is so affected by his ordeal that when he returns home to England he perceives it an alien environment difficult to reconcile with his feelings. The Invisible Man, an extraordinary monster confronting ordinary people, upsets the English countryside (although his limitations hamper him and he creates only a minimal, isolated disturbance).

As if to rectify the Invisible Man's ineptness, Wells grants his malevolent Martians a superior intelligence and technology which are sure to penetrate humanity's impregnable conceit that it possesses the most advanced mind in the universe and that the present order of things will go on ad infinitum. When the English countryside around London becomes a battlefield, all institutions which have been held dear are destroyed. Routine activity (Londoners waiting for trains, church bells ringing) and common people (cyclists, tobacconists, grocers) contrasted with the devastation wrought by Martian warfare create an extreme shock-effect in the world made alien for humankind.

Because of the effectiveness of Wells's contrast, some sf critics would have preferred a more faithful film adaptation, especially in the use of the original setting, and they see Haskin's moving events to Los Angeles as a major flaw. In his comprehensive book, *Science Fiction in the Cinema* (New York: Paperback Library, 1970), John Baxter writes:

> . . . by setting the story in California rather than Wells's beloved English Home Counties Haskin removed the book's most impressive quality, the horror of death and destruction in familiar surroundings, of a society one has known and loved coming apart before one's eyes (146).

The late Ray Harryhausen, premier special-effects expert, also expresses nostalgia for Wells's story:

> I did a number of drawings and took them all over Hollywood. This was long before George Pal produced it for Paramount. Again Jesse Lasky was interested and he tried to get MGM to do it but nothing happened. I still have the drawings and would like somebody one day to remake *War of the Worlds*—the way Wells wrote it rather than modernizing it as Pal did.[3]

Any disenchantment with the film, outside of minor technical flaws, seems a personal bias. The film critics of 1953 were captivated and gave it extremely favorable reviews. And when it was recently released on videotape, it was among the top twenty best sellers. In a 1975 interview, Haskin addresses one specific criticism:

> A recent writer on science fiction films said it was bad to have removed the story from its identifiable background, but it was identifiable to Americans, and that's who we were making the picture *for*. In making our choice we did as Orson Welles had done. We transposed it to a modern setting, hoping to generate some of the excitement that Welles had with his broadcast.[4]

On Halloween, 1938, Orson Welles produced an American radio broadcast of *The War of the Worlds* using a journalistic format. Instead of crashing in Horsell, England, the Martians first land on a farm near Grovers Mill, New Jersey, and the invasion is depicted in a series of news bulletins, on-the-spot reporting, and interviews with witnesses, scientists, and military personnel. Welles's approach gave a realistic, timely quality to the event, and many listeners, mistaking the fiction for an actuality, exemplified life imitating art when they evacuated their homes in fear of an alien attack.

The effective consequences of the radio broadcast seem to justify Haskin's decision to relocate and update the event. He realized that the impact of the novel depended heavily on the destruction of the familiar by a mysterious, formidable force, and this he painstakingly preserved in his film version. For his primary audience, the crises at Horsell, Woking, and Chobham might as well have occurred on Mars. By switching the action to America, he gave Americans a sense of the familiar and retained the dominant disturbing tone of Wells's story.

In the film, the appearance and nature of the Martians and their machines deviate radically from the Wells account. Some of these refinements may diminish the story's original terror, such as deletion of the Martian enslavement of humans and their vampiric method of nourishing themselves, but despite these changes the film manages to complement most of the novel's intentions.

When Wells's unnamed Narrator sees his first Martian vomited from its spaceship, he describes it in repulsive terms:

> A big greyish rounded bulk, the size, perhaps, of a bear, was rising slowly and painfully out of the cylinder. As it bulged up and caught the light, it glistened like wet leather.
>
> Two-large dark-coloured eyes were regarding me steadfastly. The mass that framed them, the head of the thing, was rounded, and had, one might say, a face. There was a mouth under the eyes, the lipless brim of which quivered and panted, and dropped saliva. The whole creature heaved and pulsated convulsively. A lank tentacular appendage gripped the edge of the cylinder, another swayed in the air.
>
> Those who have never seen a living Martian can scarcely imagine the strange horror of its appearance. The peculiar V-shaped mouth with its pointed upper lip, the absence of brow ridges, the absence of a chin beneath the wedge-like lower lip, the incessant quivering of this mouth, the Gorgon groups of tentacles, the tumultuous breathing of the lungs in a strange atmosphere, the evident heaviness and painfulness of movement due to the greater gravitational energy of the earth—above all, the extraordinary intensity of the immense eyes—were at once vital, intense, inhuman, crippled, and monstrous. There was something fungoid in the oily brown skin, something in the clumsy deliberation of the tedious movements unspeakably nasty. Even at this first encounter, this first glimpse, I was overcome with disgust and dread. (Bk. I: Ch. 4)

Later, he gives a less emotional, more clinical description of the Martians:

> They were huge round bodies—or, rather, heads—about four feet in diameter, each body having in front of it a face. This face had no nostrils—indeed, the Martians do not seem to have had any sense of smell,

but it had a pair of very large dark-coloured eyes, and just beneath this a kind of fleshy beak. In the back of this head or body—I scarcely know how to speak of it—was the single tight tympanic surface, since known to be anatomically an ear, though it must have been almost useless in our dense air. In a group round the mouth were sixteen slender, almost whiplike tentacles, arranged in two bunches of eight each. (Bk. II: Ch. 2)

The contrast in the tonal quality of the two passages is significant. Although the Narrator tells the whole story in flashback, his first description captures the thrill of his initial impression of the Martians, an emotional, jumbled reaction showing revulsion for their unearthly ugliness. The second description seems that of a detached scientist analyzing his subject without being critical of it, stating his hypotheses coldly and without judgment.

Although both descriptions create specific images of the Martian, the first fails to categorize it, making it a kind of chimera (combined bear, snake, and wet leather) and stirring feelings of disgust. The second description, suggesting an octopus, presents a clearer image of the Martian, but the resemblance to a familiar creature sterilizes some of its alien strangeness and the lack of emotional connotations reduces its impact on the audience.

The implication is that, during a crisis, people respond with emotions fueled by desperation. When the crisis passes and they can examine the event in retrospect, they look at it more coolly and analytically. The tonal contrast in the passages reflects the contrast between passion and intellect and raises questions about what it means to be dominated by one or the other, an important difference between Martians and humans.

Considering this, the Narrator of the novel refers to "a certain speculative writer of quasi-scientific repute" who had "forecast for man a final structure not unlike the actual Martian condition." Ironically, that "writer" is Wells himself, who wrote an essay, "The Man of the Year Million," for the *Pall Mall Budget* (1893). In it, he speculates on what man may become if evolution should proceed in a certain direction. His head will grow larger to accommodate a hypertrophied intellect, while his body will atrophy because of diminished carnal needs, except for the hands, which are "the teacher and agent for the brain." The Martians bear out this speculation, coming from an older planet and being further along on the evolutionary scale.

Accompanying an expansion of the intellect is a decrease in the intensity of emotions. The growth of reason and logic is inversely proportional to the development of human sympathies and considerations. *The Time Machine* contains a passage foreshadowing this phenomenon.[5] When the inventor stops in the year 802,701 A.D., his first sight, the colossal white sphinx, inspires him with thoughts of what humans may have become:

> What if cruelty had grown into a common passion? What if in this interval the race had lost its manliness, and had developed into something inhuman, unsympathetic, and overwhelmingly powerful? I might seem some old-world savage animal, only the more dreadful and disgusting for our common likeness—a foul creature to be incontinently slain. (Ch. 3)

The Time Traveller's speculations contain several ideas related to the Martians. First, they are cruel. They kill ruthlessly, as when they ignore the white flag of Professor Ogilvy and his deputation who try to approach them with peaceful intentions. Second, with their enlarged heads and advanced technology, they represent the domination of intellect over emotion, having "developed into something inhuman, unsympathetic, and overwhelmingly powerful." Third is the suggestion that the Martians may have once resembled humans. Their wanton killing may be motivated in part by their dread and disgust for "our common likeness," Man reminding them of their primitive origins and seeming "a foul creature to be incontinently slain."

Compared to Wells's Martians, the film's single representative Martian (Charles Gemora) reveals the aliens as more anthropomorphic but clearly inhuman.[6] It is dwarfish and goes about naked as an animal. It has pink skin, long spindly arms, and three fingers like jointed knitting needles tipped with suction cups. Its head looks like a large misshapen potato, lumpy and flat and horizontally elongated. Predominant on its face is its one circular eye, composed of three rounded triangular lenses, red, green, and blue.

In *Future Tense,* Brosnan disagrees with Haskin's belief that the Martian appearance "was very important":

> . . . even that brief scene was a mistake: it would have been best never to have seen what the Martians looked like, thus maintaining their basic mystery (91).

Brosnan's suggestion may have merit for a different sf story, but in this case he overlooks some things (including its relevance to the film's imagery, discussed below). First, Wells describes his Martians, not with detrimental consequences, but with the effect of intensifying the horror. And this intensification carries over into both Welles's 1938 radio broadcast[7] and the 1953 movie which allows us to see the invaders. The Martian appearance increases our fear and dread because we cringe at the idea of being dominated by creatures which are not only repulsively ugly, but which, despite their superiority, also embody our concept of something inferior.

Second, the Martian's appearance is one of the film's most intense scenes. Trapped in a farmhouse when one of the alien cylinders crashes into it, Clayton Forrester (Gene Barry) and Sylvia Van Buren (Ann Robinson) try to escape.[8] The Martians, however, know they are inside and have pushed dirt against the sides to imprison them. While they look for a way out, Sylvia glances into the next room. In a subjective long shot, we see what she sees: a radiant pink creature glides quickly into and out of view, long bony arms waving above its head.

Startled, Sylvia tells Forrester she saw "one of them." When he asks, "What was it like?" we feel she answers for all of us: "I couldn't see much in the dark, but it was one." This vague glimpse of the alien whets our curiosity and we wait in anxious anticipation for a clearer view.

Forrester discovers an axe. He begins to hack at the debris,

The War of the Worlds (1953, Paramount Pictures): Confronting an Unknown Invader. Trapped in the demolished farmhouse, Forrester (Gene Barry) readies to protect Sylvia (Ann Robinson) from the Martians. The biblical analogy to Adam and Eve harassed by the Serpent is faintly evident and supports Haskin's religious theme.

trying to make an opening. Seconds later, a Martian probe slithers down through a hole in the ceiling. Sylvia turns and comes face to face with it. Forrester, like a knight rescuing a damsel from a dragon, lops the "head" off its long serpentine neck.

The decapitated "neck" recoils into the spaceship and Forrester returns to chopping at the collapsed wall. Sylvia helps remove planks. Behind them, in the dark recesses of the ruined house, shadows move across the wall. The camera tracks to a medium close-up of Sylvia diligently helping Forrester. Quietly, from the right side of the frame, the tendril-fingered hand of the Martian appears and rests on her shoulder. She freezes, then turns, open-mouthed. The camera tracks to the right and down along a skinny, pink arm to the dwarfish, potato-headed Martian touching her. Forrester pulls Sylvia back and holds her. With his free hand he aims his flashlight. The alien raises two bony hands, trying to shade its eye. Forrester pushes Sylvia aside. He hurls his axe at the creature. A shrill squeal sounds. The camera cuts to a quick shot of the Martian fleeing into the shadows, arms flailing, the axe protruding from its chest.

The tension in this sequence builds along with the three graduated Martian encounters: the brief, distant, obscure view of the passing alien, the confrontation with the probe-head, and the physical contact with the alien scout. The film lets Sylvia, rather than Forrester, respond initially to all three encounters, because, in terms of former (now archaic) film conventions, the woman is allowed (in fact, expected) to display her emotions. Her reactions give aural and visual expression to what the audience should be feeling at this moment. Forrester, displaying the former conventional expectations of the man, responds with masculine protectiveness, each time pulling the woman from danger and stepping forward himself to use violence against the foe.[9]

Finally, a third value in showing the Martian is that it complements Wells's intentions in at least two ways. Unlike the novel, the film does not analyze the Martian's appearance. Yet the large head, frail body, and long arms and fingers reflect Wells's evolutionary theory. The grotesque, oversized cranium suggests the expanded intellect and, when considered with the wanton destruction of property and lives, implies that the conflict between emotion and intellect has finally been settled and that sympathy and pity are extinct in these creatures.[10]

In the novel, the Martians' primary motive for their invasion is self-preservation. Their own planet is dying and Earth poses a possible sanctuary for perpetuating their species. A secondary motive is that Earthlings serve as a food source, their blood providing nourishment. Part of the Martian terror lies in their vampirism. The Narrator describes enough of what he sees to suggest the hideousness of their method, but he omits explicit details, letting the reader's imagination invent the possible horrors.

Explained near the beginning of the film by a Narrator (Sir

Cedric Hardwicke),[11] the Martian invasion arises from the same primary motive as in the novel, namely, self-preservation. However, the film offers only a vague idea of what intentions the Martians may have for humanity. While hiding behind a wall in a collapsed farmhouse, Forrester and Sylvia observe the Martian probe-head. Forrester says, "They're looking for us. . . . They could be as curious about us as we are about them." Sylvia suggests, "Maybe they want to take us alive." The implication that the Martians may want live human specimens reveals no purpose beyond satisfying their curiosity. Otherwise, the invading juggernaut seems bent on total annihilation of the human race.

Of all the differences between novel and film, the most striking are the Martian machines. Wells's Martians use three-legged, hundred-foot-high machines, which walk with the "parody of a human stride." The Narrator describes his first glimpse of one:

> A monstrous tripod, higher than many houses, striding over the young pines, and smashing them aside in its career; a walking engine of glittering metal, striding now across the heather; articulate ropes of steel dangling from it, and the clattering tumult of its passage mingling with the riot of the thunder. A flash, and it came out vividly, heeling over one way with two feet in the air, to vanish and reappear, almost instantly as it seemed, with the next flash, a hundred yards nearer. Can you imagine a milking stool tilted and bowled violently along the ground? That was the impression those instant flashes gave. But instead of a milking stool imagine it a great body of machinery on a tripod stand. (Bk. I: Ch. 10)

These machines shoot a terrible heat-ray which burns everything inside its radius (an uncanny anticipation of the modern laser beam). Later, the Martians add a second weapon, black smoke propelled from long black tubes, which asphyxiates all who fall under its cloud. A third device, the flying machine, appears momentarily, but the Martians die before it becomes consequential. These last two inventions forecast the gas bombs and airplanes used for the first time as weapons in World War I.

By contrast, the Martians of the film use streamlined flying machines which glide over the countryside, but do not move as nimbly or swiftly as the giant tripods. They resemble something "between a flying saucer and a manta ray," having a "green frontispiece and wingtips" and "a cobra-like appendage that protruded from the top."[12] The "head" of the cobra contains a single "eye" or lens which serves both as a periscope and as the source of the heat-ray, a splintered beam of yellow-white light comparable to that of Wells's invaders. Haskin's Martians do not spew black smoke, but they, too, have a second weapon, a green solid beam which shoots from the wingtips of their machines and acts as a disintegration ray.

Wells's Martians have invented cyborgs, living machines created by merging organic life with mechanical parts. The tripods become the mobile body, the agile carrying case for the inert Martian head-body which sits in the "cranium" of the machine and functions as its guiding intellect. In the film, the blood from the mechanical-looking probe shows that these Martians, too, have developed a species of cyborg. But whereas Wells's Narrator offers theories on this collaboration between being and machine, especially as an evolutionary advancement, Forrester and his scientists never explain it. Only Sylvia's hysterical screaming expresses some indescribable horror at what this might mean.

As formidable as they appear, the Martians of the novel are not indestructible. A fluke barrage of cannon fire destroys one machine and the ironclad *Thunder Child* destroys two others, one with its guns and one in a head-on collision. On the other hand, the Martians of the film fortify themselves with "some sort of electro-magnetic covering, a protective blister," and are totally impregnable to humanity's most modern weapons, including the atom bomb.

The degree of Martian vulnerability affects the depth of humanity's hope in its struggle for survival. Wells allows for some hope by making the machines at least slightly vulnerable. Haskin, however, encourages total despair by making the machines apparently invincible. And out of this difference in Martian vulnerability and the consequent ability to hope come the main themes of the two stories. Wells is interested in a "secular cooling," Haskin in a "cooling" toward religion.

The Narrator of the novel remarks that "the secular cooling that must someday overtake our planet has already gone far indeed with our neighbor" (Ch. 1). Denotatively, "secular cooling" means the ages-long devolution in a planet's lifetime, while connotatively it suggests the evolutionary "cooling" of passions in the wake of intellectual expansion.

The Martians, like the Morlocks, are the culmination of eons of physical mutations and represent one of man's possible evolutionary destinies. They are the superior beings who have endured in the struggle for survival while inferior ones have become extinct. And since they prove themselves superior to humans, they should be expected to conquer the Earth. However, in respect to Darwinian theory of natural selection, a "joker"[13] emerges from the pack. Certain germs have developed a symbiotic relationship with humans, making Earth a conducive habitat for our species and a noxious place for Martians.

Haskin channels Wells's secular theme into a religious motif. Prominent in the film is the latest technology of modern civilization: automobiles, telephones, watches, hearing aids, microphones, news broadcast equipment, radios, electric lights, movie theaters with electrified marquees, and tape recorders. Especially obvious are the most advanced instruments of science and warfare: Geiger counter, azimuth compass, microscope, epidiascope, biotics, sonic radar, field phones, binoculars, naval destroyers, half-tracks, tanks, field artillery, jeeps, cannon, "high-level bombers," supersonic jets, the Flying Wing, and the A-bomb.

Forrester and his fellow scientists at the Pacific Institute of Science and Technology represent the vanguard of scientific knowledge. Their failure to find a solution against the Martians signifies humanity's intellectual inferiority to them and portends its doom because of its inability to respond effectively in the struggle for survival. In a sequence of scenes heavily laden with religious allegory, the film ultimately suggests that when all our human efforts fail, our faith can expect a spiritual force to save us.

In the scene after the Flying Wings drops the A-bomb on the Martians, General Mann (Les Tremayne), coordinator of America's military force, turns from his observation post, angry that they have failed to stop the machines. On his left cheek, a prominent bloody scratch shaped like a "T" marks "general Man" as a Christ-figure. At the nadir of his existence, his moment "on the cross" when he faces apparent inevitable extinction, General Mann expresses an irrepressible hope to continue the struggle for survival. Expecting Science to solve humanity's dilemma, he tells Forrester, "We'll establish a line and move them all the way back to the mountains. Our best hope lies in what you people can develop to help us."

However, the Pacific Tech scientists and their equipment are waylaid by rampaging mobs. Humankind has become too desperate to wait for Science to find a way out of this peril.

Forrester remembers Sylvia's story, that when she was a child and most afraid she had hidden in a church by the door. Dodging the destructive rays of Martian machines, he winds his way through the ruined streets of Los Angeles, stumbling into several churches where he finds people grouped in prayer. It becomes clear that humanity's physical weapons have failed and its only recourse is a spiritual weapon, a miracle.

Forrester finally spots Sylvia on the far side of a crowded church. With Armageddon almost upon them, they frantically squeeze their way through the congestion of people, trying to reach each other before the end comes. The camera cuts to outside where a Martian machine gliding down the street fires its splintered white ray. A cut to inside the church shows a low-angle shot of a stained-glass window bursting inward. The tall mosaic figure, apparently God the Creator, shatters, spraying glass shards in all directions. The confident alien invaders have blasphemed against God. Plaster and debris bombard the crowd, and after the noise and screams there is a sudden quiet hush.

Out of a billowing cloud of dust appears the intimate medium-close shot of Forrester clutching Sylvia in his arms;

they are the only people left in the world, the Adam and Eve of the new era of humanity.[14] Silently, the camera tracks back. The pair stands alone, until gradually, others crouched in the aisles and pews rise and move in a steady stream toward the back of the church. From the doorway, looking out toward the street, the crowd sees a Martian machine crashed against the buildings opposite.

In a tensely quiet moment, a hatch on the underside of the crashed machine opens and a long emaciated arm drops out, its spindly fingers groping along the door. The pinkish color fades to a blackish green. Forrester steps forward, feels its pulse, and makes the unnecessary announcement: "It's dead." Then he turns toward the crowd: "We were all praying for a miracle." He looks upward at the sky as church bells begin to peal with the vaunting sounds of religion's triumph.

The next sequence of shots shows Martian machines dying all over the world. The Narrator's last words make the religious motif explicit: "After all that men could do had failed, the Martians were destroyed and humanity was saved by the littlest things, which God in His wisdom had put upon this earth."

The penultimate shot shows a multitude of people standing on the slopes of the San Gabriel Hills outside Los Angeles. The setting alludes to Angel Gabriel who will blow the last trumpet on Judgment Day, and the multitudes represent those who gathered to hear Christ preach on the mountainsides around Jordan and will await Him on the Last Day. As the people stand and the Narrator finishes speaking, choral voices rousingly sing the last line of a hymn: "In this world and the next. Amen."[15] "World" contains the ambiguous connotations of planet and after-life, suggesting God's omnipresence and omnipotence on all planets before and after death.

The final shot consists of a wide, high-angle view of ruined and burning buildings of Los Angeles at sunset. In the left foreground, a large church and its spire dominate the frame, appearing to be the guardian of humanity, no matter what harm may threaten it.

As in Wells, people have been put into a predicament

outside their control. Humanity's willful attempt at self-determination through science and technology has been thwarted. Wells resolves the problem physically with a natural phenomenon, the struggle for survival influenced by natural selection. Haskin resolves it spiritually by emphasizing Divine Providence, as if the germs were God's agents, His "angels" protecting His Chosen People from the evil of Sennacherib.[16] The literary convention of "deus ex machina," summoned through faith and trust in the protective power of God, becomes in the film, a literal and practical consideration for humankind.

B: "The Great Disillusionment": Diminishment of the Hero

At the end of the first paragraph of *The War of the Worlds,* Wells's Narrator writes that "early in the twentieth century came the great disillusionment." "The great disillusionment" reflects similar phrases which appear in Wells's later utopian fiction: "the great Change" (*In the Days of the Comet,* 1906) and "the Age of Confusion" (*Men Like Gods,* 1923; *The Dream,* 1924; *The Shape of Things to Come,* 1933). As a "fin de siècle" writer, Wells uses these terms to define a climactic moment in the history of humanity when it realizes, with fear, reluctance, and nostalgia, that its present social order is not efficient enough to be perpetuated in the future. *The War of the Worlds* does not describe that future as Wells's utopian works do, but the story leaves the reader with the feeling that he should reconsider his relationship with the universe in a new and perhaps more "humble" way.

Many of Wells's stories satirize our vain belief that in all creation we possess the superior intelligence. In "The Empire of the Ants" and "The Valley of Spiders," for example, men are overcome by the littlest creatures which, up to now, they believed they dominated. The insect-like Selenites of *The First Men in the Moon* (1901) parallel the octopus-shaped Martians in that while they resemble lower life forms, they possess greater intelligence and have achieved a more advanced civilization than humanity.

Related to *The War of the Worlds,* two significant entries in these superiority-reversal tales are "The Star" (1899) and "The Crystal Egg" (1899). In the former, astronomers (among them, a Dr. Ogilvy, whose name reappears in *War of the Worlds*) observe that the approach of a stray star has deflected Neptune's path around the sun. The event leads to catastrophic upheaval on our own planet, which, seen from the viewpoint of Martian astronomers, appears only a relatively minor disturbance. The limited perspective of the Martians which produces their mistaken conclusion reflects humanity's equally limited vision, which assumes it perceives more than it does.

In "The Crystal Egg," a shopkeeper discovers that a crystal knick-knack on his shelf transmits images from another planet, possibly Mars. Looking into it, he sees the insect-like inhabitants and their cities.[17] Ironically, the egg transmits both ways and the aliens can also see him. The story ends with the suggestion that we are being observed by extraterrestrials who may be trying to decide if they should invade our planet. *The War of the Worlds* confirms their decision.

Besides Byron Haskin's *The War of the Worlds,* there appeared at this time three other important sf films dealing with alien encounters, *The Day the Earth Stood Still* (Robert Wise, 1951), *Invaders from Mars* (William Cameron Menzies, 1953), and *It Came from Outer Space* (Jack Arnold, 1953). While Haskin's aliens carry on an external war, Menzies' invaders attack internally. By inserting electronic implants into the necks of their victims, the aliens deprive them of their individuality, transforming them into uniform, unthinking automatons carrying out the single will of the central alien intelligence.[18] They are justified, however, in that they want to prevent earthlings from developing a technology which would enable them to travel in space, possibly reaching and corrupting their planet.

The Day the Earth Stood Still and *It Came from Outer Space* deal with aliens intending no harm, but possessing a technology so advanced that, if provoked, they could destroy the Earth. Both reveal humanity's penchant for violence and its immaturity in the extraterrestrial community.

The most important idea shared by these films and related to Wells's novel concerns humanity's relationship with the universe, how it figures in the scheme of the cosmos beyond its own limited, vain imaginings of its singular, superior position. And central to this notion is Darwin's theory of evolution. If other planets are part of this theory, each undergoing its own "secular cooling," then some will be further ahead of others on the evolutionary scale.

The theory of evolution includes a number of variable factors, such as the struggle for survival, survival of the fittest, and natural selection. If one accepts Darwin's theories, then humans, as animals, cannot be excluded from them:

> . . . the same unconscious and cosmic force that drives all other seed drives also us. At a stroke, man and his civilization become the products of blind chance and galactic accident. Culture, purpose, consciousness become arbitrary, momentary things: for all the power of reason, reason appears now only a version of survival adaptation, like the scorpion's sting or the rabbit's hind legs. And those massive constructs of human intelligence, art, religion, morality, and ethics, become at once terribly endangered and terribly precious. They, more than anything else, are what make us human. But they, also more than anything else, are what make our treasured humanity appear arbitrary and—in the cosmic context of things—vulnerable.[19]

As simply another animal in the great scheme of creation, Man suffers his "great disillusionment," that is, loses his singular specialness. He achieves a depressing awareness that other creatures in the cosmos may be superior to him, and that because of this, things he once considered extremely important are actually not so. The two versions of *The War of the Worlds* reflect this loss of singular superiority by decentralizing the main characters, Wells's Narrator and Haskin's Clayton Forrester.

In a kind of "literary evolution," the Narrative Voice of Wells's *War of the Worlds* descends directly from the Voice narrating his previous novel, *The Invisible Man*. In that work, the story depends on the Narrator's compilation of information from news sources and interviews. Several times he refers to himself as "I" and "we," suggesting he is one of the villagers who witnesses Griffin's antics, but he remains unidentified and depersonalized, an anonymous voice in the crowd.

The Narrator of *War of the Worlds* is likewise unidentified, but not so obscure. He tells us he is a "speculative philosopher" living in Maybury with his wife, and his account of his personal experiences adds a roundedness to his character. Yet, while he compiles information using methods similar to those of the Narrator of *The Invisible Man,* he presents it in a way that diffuses the focus of attention between himself and the larger situation around him. The most important factors in this respect are his bother's "eyewitness account," his interjected theories of the Artilleryman, and his relationship with the Curate.

The brother, like the Narrator, assumes the role of nameless observer rather than heroic protagonist. At one point he attempts to help two women assaulted by vandals who want to steal their pony-chaise. However, when the "knight in shining armor" suddenly finds himself overcome by the villains, the "damsel in distress" ends up having to rescue him, negating his heroic gesture.

At this point, the Narrator's second-hand account carries a less emotionally involved tone. The Voice shifts focus from one group of people to another, telling the story of anonymous humanity, not of a single, known individual. The main character represents the collective and is embodied in the image of the torrent of people flowing in an exodus from their homes. No one stands out. The brother accompanies the two women, helping them on a limited, personal level, and this seems as much as anyone can do for his neighbor.

The *Thunder Child* episode also reflects this anonymity and collectiveness. In their altercation with the Martians, the mariners represent a body of mankind, not individuals, confronting an enemy. The ship's self-sacrifice in destroying the two Martian machines is more a unified human effort than a single hero rising above common folk to defeat a foe.

The Artilleryman is a deceptive hero-figure. He convinces

the Narrator of the possibility of people living among the Martians like rats, burrowing tunnels and hiding in the underground drains and subways. His speculations show him to be a man of imagination and cunning, another Odysseus eluding the giant Polyphemus, not to defeat the enemy but to gain time so that humans may continue their species in the struggle for survival.

The Narrator is impressed with his rhetoric and logic. In executing the plan, however, the Narrator finds fault with the strategy: the dig starts from an unsuitable spot and manholes giving immediate access to the drains make tunneling unnecessary. Most of all, the Artilleryman prefers talk to action. He would rather "reconnoitre" than spend time on the digging he claimed was so important. The man who appeared a savior of humanity, instead proves himself a false hero.

Telling his story in flashback, the Narrator inserts, at various points, theories about the Martians which were not formulated until after the invaders had been destroyed. These insertions, instead of being obtrusive, create the effect that the Narrator shares the focus of the story with the Martians.[20] This seems appropriate since both represent Everyman in a way related to evolutionary principles. The Narrator is the individual responding predictably to a crisis testing his instinct for survival. His personal, localized conflict is countered by the Martians who, as the culmination of eons of physical development, represent what humans may become in time, since we are subject to the same dynamic evolutionary forces as all animals. As another way of diffusing the image of a hero-figure, this approach emphasizes theories and ideas rather than the single character's conflict.

Yet the Narrator's individuality is clearly defined by his two most important relationships, that with the Artilleryman (already noted) and a second, critical bond with the Curate.[21] The Curate is reminiscent of Prendick's Monkey Man in *The Island of Doctor Moreau,* who believed that impressive words and obscure ideas comprised "big thinks" and separated them from plain, everyday "little thinks" (Ch. 21). The Curate's conversation depends on the high-blown language of biblical quotes, but he jumbles and misquotes the verses, revealing himself devoid of original thinking and only a poor aper of others' "big thinks." In this respect he relates to the Artilleryman, who expresses grandiose designs in idiomatic speech. Both represent men whose pompous rhetoric obscures the ridiculousness and impracticality of their ideas.

The Narrator exposes the Curate as a sniveling, abject coward who behaves deplorably and hinders their efforts to evade the Martians. However, this estimate loses credibility in light of his distorted perception of himself. While fleeing the black smoke, the Narrator and Curate find refuge in a house in Halliford. The Narrator describes his feelings:

> My mind was occupied by anxiety for my wife. I figured her at Leatherhead, terrified, in danger, mourning me already as a dead man. I paced the rooms and cried aloud when I thought of how I was cut off from her, of all that might happen to her in my absence. . . . Such vague anxieties keep the mind sensitive and painful. I grew very weary and irritable with the curate's perpetual ejaculations; I tired of the sight of his selfish despair. After some ineffectual remonstrance I kept away from him, staying in a room—evidently a children's schoolroom. . . . When he followed me thither, I went to a box room at the top of the house and, in order to be alone with my aching miseries, locked myself in. (Bk. II: Ch. 1)

Ironically, the Narrator acts no differently from the Curate. They both suffer "vague anxieties" which "keep the mind sensitive and painful." The Narrator's concern for his wife appears honorable, but is really no less a "selfish despair" than the personal frets of the Curate. His depiction of his companion as an ignorant, spoiled child reflects his own disposition when, trying to escape him, he adopts the same childishness by playing "hide-and-seek" and ends up, appropriately, in the child's schoolroom.

The Narrator lacks the ability to sympathize with his neighbor. Instead of reacting to the Martian invasion as a catastrophe which should unite them, he withdraws into his petty private concerns. His estimate of the Curate may be accurate, but he appears just as guilty in confusing "little thinks" with "big thinks."

Later, trapped together in a house demolished by the crash of the fifth cylinder, the two men continue their childish rivalry. They skirmish for access to the single peephole overlooking the Martian pit, and they bicker over how to distribute the food supply. On the second issue, the Curate favors an unrestricted appetite, but the Narrator argues for strict rationing, trying to have his way by offering the Curate the last bottle of wine as a pitiful bribe. Their inability to compromise appears an analogy of people and governments who debate between prodigality and conservationism. As extremes, both "solutions" are undesirable and irreconcilia- tion can lead to disaster, as it does here.[22]

The two men seem equally stubborn and boorish. The Curate whines loudly, threatening to attract the Martians in what seems a death wish.[23] Still clinging to the will to live, the Narrator clubs him with the handle of a meat chopper:

> With one last touch of humanity I turned the blade back
> and struck him with the butt. (Bk. II: Ch. 4)

The Narrator implies that he possesses sympathetic human feelings, and perhaps his failure to yield to his murderous impulse supports this. However, his reaction to the Curate revolves around a basic animal urge, the instinct for survival. If anything sets him apart from the animal, it is not this last-second change of heart, but the guilt he feels afterward for causing the Curate's capture and death by the Martians. Overall, the Narrator's relationship with the Curate exposes him, not as a noble, self-reliant, industrious being, but as an ordinary human struggling frantically, desperately to survive a life-threatening situation.

In one respect, the Narrator parallels two other Wells characters, Pollock of "Pollock and the Porroh Man" and Edward Ponderevo of *Tono-Bungay*. Each is responsible for the death of another who appears inferior to himself, and each, pursued by guilt, tries to justify his crime by alluding to the dead man's inferior status. However, if, on the evolution- ary scale, humans are considered superior beings, then this conclusion must apply to all humans. It is hypocritical and egocentric for any one person to try to categorize the relative status of another superior being. In *The War of the Worlds,* while the Narrator and Curate engage in a conflict to determine superiority between individuals, the highly advanced Martians wage a similar but broader conflict suggestive of competition for superiority among races and nations. Combined with Wells's allusions to the wanton extinction of the dodo and the Tasmanian civilization, this reveals the story as an analogy concerning humanity's hegemonic practices.

The film replaces the Narrator with Clayton Forrester,[24] a character who has little in common with him. Forrester is a prominent astro-nuclear physicist.[25] Consulted for advice in the war against the Martians, he becomes more actively involved in the larger conflict than does the isolated Narrator struggling for his own survival.

Although married, Wells's Narrator becomes separated from his wife and experiences his ordeal without her. Forrester, on the other hand, pairs off with Sylvia, sharing several crises which contribute to the development of their relationship. As a lover and a character involved in the center of the action, Forrester appears more a hero than the Narrator. However, complementing the novel, the film does several things to compromise that status.

First, in a similar way that the Narrator's heroic position is diluted, the film treats Forrester ambiguously, making him a highly visible figure but undercutting his prominence. When first seen, he sits eating with fellow scientists at their fishing camp, appearing a group member, not an outstanding individual. Of all the scientists, he alone decides to visit the meteor site, but his arrival receives no fanfare. Talking to him, Sylvia betrays her infatuation with "Dr. Forrester,"[26] but does not even recognize him, although she has seen photographs of him and written about him in her college thesis.

After seeing the meteor, he spends that Saturday night at a square dance. The scene starts with a close-up of the bridge and bow of the fiddler's instrument while the square-dance caller drones instructions into his microphone. The camera

cuts to Forrester and Sylvia on the dance floor in the
foreground, romping among the other smiling dancers.
Again he appears part of the crowd, not a distinct individual.

At one point he changes partners. Spinning away from the
second girl, he backs into the camera lens and blots out the
view. The scene fades into a high-angle shot of the crash site
where three men around a campfire guard the smoking
meteor, large and ominous in the upper right corner of the
frame. Forrester has literally turned his back on the meteor,
has put it out of his mind to have fun like any of the other
ordinary people whose dominant concern is diversion
through music, dance, and laughter. His excuse is that no one
can do anything further until the meteor cools off, but this
attitude seems contradictory in a "top-notch scientist" whose
curiosity should have made him one of the three men
watching the meteor.

Cutting from the meteor site, the camera shows Forrester
sidling through a room of crowded tables, his up-raised hands
clutching two Coke bottles. Because he stands and moves
among seated people, he appears a dominant figure, but
when he takes his seat at Sylvia's table he becomes one of
their number.[27]

Forrester tells her, "If we could gather all the energy
expended in just one square dance, we could send that
meteor back to where it came from." This seems more the
trivial joke of a naive layman than the speech of a leading
astro-nuclear physicist who has seen one of the biggest
meteors ever to land on earth. Instead of showing a scientist's
curiosity and excitement by meeting with other experts to
speculate on its puzzling radioactivity and hollowness, he sits
conversing frivolously with common folk. Forrester's reputation gives him status, but his behavior suggests an ordinariness which undercuts his potential hero image.

As another method of modifying his status, the film often
shows him appearing in the background while the foreground
carries the important action. For example, in the scene inside
the tent where Colonel Heffner (Vernon Rich) stands over a
map discussing strategy with his men, Forrester stands to the
rear with Sylvia in an inaudible conversation with a group of
men. The camera follows Heffner to a radio. After he

finishes, Forrester enters the frame, offering him a cup of coffee. In scenes like these, Forrester maintains visibility, but his remoteness suggests a reduced involvement in the action and in the decision-making.

In a related way, group shots are arranged to give him prominence without actual dominance of a scene. He may appear the largest figure or be positioned in the center (often with Sylvia at his side), although another character controls the moment. For example, when Dr. Duprey (Ann Codee), centered amid the scientists, sits at her microscope and discloses the Martians' anemia, Forrester stands directly behind her. And when another scientist demonstrates the Martian lens by projecting an image of the group on a wall, Forrester, although at the rear, stands tallest.

Shifting the focus of attention to various authority figures keeps Forrester from appearing as the central coordinator of the effort to save humanity. At different times, Sheriff Bogany (Walter Sande), Pastor Matthew Collins (Lewis Martin), Colonel Heffner and General Mann, among others, step forward to dictate the action.

A final consideration of the diminished hero role concerns the central character's ultimate failure to conquer the enemy. In the farmhouse, Forrester, rescuing Sylvia from the Martian, attains a limited victory, but cannot rescue humankind. In a similar way, the novel's Narrator, hiding in the collapsed house, becomes a passive reporter of events rather than an active deterrent of the invader. Both characters are overshadowed by an alien threat greater than themselves and by a solution intervening from an external source (whether Natural Selection or Divine Providence). As a result, they are reduced from heroic to common status, their ordinariness exposed especially because the force which saves humanity (germs or God) must also rescue them.

Notes

1. Pal had already established himself as a noted producer of sf films with *Destination Moon* (1950) and *When Worlds Collide* (1951). Although not immune to criticism, both were highly

praised for their intricate and extraordinary special-effects which imparted a sense of realism to the adventures. In 1960, he directed *The Time Machine,* again receiving critical acclaim for its effects depicting the hero's journey through time.

2. In addition, Wells borrows from the surge of popular "invasion stories" of the late 19th Century which dealt with England under siege from some foreign country, such as France or Germany. Sir George Chesney's *The Battle of Dorking* (1871) and Sir William Butler's *The Invasion of England* (1882) are among the best known.

3. Brosnan, p. 96.

4. *Ibid.*, p. 90.

5. Anthony West, *H. G. Wells: Aspects of a Life* (New York: Meridian, 1985), p. 232.

6. Gemora took six months to build the Martian from a design by art director Albert Nozaki. Because of his small stature, he could manipulate it from inside, moving arms, head, and eyes, and making its veins throb. Their concept seems a prototype for similar-looking aliens used by Steven Spielberg in *Close Encounters of the Third Kind* (1977) and *E.T.: The Extraterrestrial* (1982).

7. Welles retains H. G. Wells's image of the Martian, which an amazed radio announcer, broadcasting "live" to his listeners, describes in an eyewitness account of the first Martian emerging from its cylinder.

8. That the names of the two main characters are associated with a forest seems significant. Perhaps the film is implying one idea from the novel, namely, that on the evolutionary scale humans still have strong connections to nature, while the Martians, with their highly developed intellects, are more removed from it.

9. Since sf often emphasizes technology over character, Haskin's use of elaborate and fascinating special effects at the expense of interesting, rounded personalities seems excusable. Yet, while appearing cardboard stereotypes, many of his characters have important allegorical relationships to the story, such as

General Mann, who signifies humanity's determination and resilience in the face of catastrophe.

Gene Barry's Clayton Forrester is dull and flaccid, but made so with the deliberate intention of suppressing his potential heroic status (see Section B). Ann Robinson has been criticized for her performance as a teary-eyed hysteric. This seems unfair in respect to what she represents, the abandoned child. First orphaned by her parents and then her uncle, and now caught in a crisis without benefit of familial protection, she displays emotional outbursts which express the childlike fears every person has of total and hopeless abandonment. Robinson capably plays the part of the pitiful, forsaken child.

10. In "Filming *War of the Worlds*," an article he wrote for *Astounding Science Fiction* (October 1953, pp. 100–111), George Pal says, "In one respect we hewed right to the Wells original. That was in his conception of a Martian being." He must be aware of his alien's physical differences. What he probably means is that they made an adaptation which captures Wells's primary intent.

11. There are actually two Narrators in the film. The first, Paul Frees, speaks before the titles appear. The timbre of his voice sounds remarkably like that of Orson Welles, probably a deliberate allusion to the man who masterminded the unforgettable radio version. His tone is firm and intense, complementing documentary footage of World Wars I and II and creating an emotional crescendo leading into the title, *The War of the Worlds*. He appears later in the film as a commentator strolling about a military fortification. Unable to transmit his reports, he records his observations on a portable tape player.

The second Narrator, Sir Cedric Hardwicke, speaks immediately after the titles in a smoother, less emotional tone. He narrates the story proper, borrowing much of his dialogue from Wells's text. He intervenes three times: he presents the initial situation, later describes the Martian onslaught during a montage sequence of disaster and devastation, and finally explains the outcome.

12. Brosnan, p. 91.

13. The "joker" appears in the card games the Narrator plays with the Artilleryman and foreshadows the "joker-germs" which upset the "play" of the Martians (Bk. II: Ch. 7).

14. Reinforcing the Adam and Eve image, this shot mirrors the earlier one where Forrester embraces Ann in the dilapidated farmhouse. There, they stand together, fearing discovery by the Martian probe, its snakelike cord making it suggestive of the corrupting Serpent.

15. These are the final words to the second verse of "Now Thank We All Our God," a hymn of thanks and praise for God's infinite kindness toward humanity—a theme appropriate to Haskin's purpose.

16. This allusion belongs to Wells, along with his original quote that the Martians were "slain, after all man's devices had failed, by the humblest things that God, in his wisdom, has put upon this earth" (Bk. II: Ch. 8). Like Haskin, his references to God and prayer give his story religious implications, but these receive secondary attention, compared to evolutionary principles which he stresses as the dominant forces defying humanity's effort to control its destiny.

17. Because the creatures appear insect-like, it seems more likely that they relate to the Selenites of *The First Men in the Moon*. That novel also involves a transmission (by radio) and insinuates an alien intention to attack Earth.

18. Wells's *Star-Begotten: A Biological Fantasia* (1937) speculates on Martians affecting human evolution by bombarding Earth with cosmic particles, gradually mutating our genetic makeup. His consequences, however, are more optimistic in that the change produces superior humans with greater awareness of what they have to do to transform the world into Utopia.

19. McConnell, *The Science Fiction of H. G. Wells,* p. 59.

20. As a comparison, Melville's *Moby Dick* (1850) interrupts the flow of the fictional narrative with factual commentary. This device, in addition to shifting the focus among several characters, produces a similar effect of obscuring the designated protagonist as Ishmael, Queequeg, Ahab, or even the Whale.

21. In many of Wells's works, a curate or vicar appears as a satirical clown-figure representing the inflexible, narrow-minded, pretentious views of organized religion (for other

examples of such characters, see *The Wonderful Visit, The Invisible Man,* and *The Food of the Gods*). The film's Rev. Matthew Collins (Lewis Martin), as a noble, self-sacrificing (although foolishly sentimental) character fits in with Haskin's religious motif, but drifts considerably from Wells's portrayal of the inept clergy.

22. This is another example of Wells's playing antithetical concepts against each other. (Compare the scientific positions of Griffin and Kemp in *The Invisible Man,* the attitudes of the Time Traveller and Frame Narrator expressed at the end of *The Time Machine,* and the metaphorical images of the giants and little people in *The Food of the Gods.*)

23. The Narrator again shows he is not above the level of the Curate when, later, despondency erodes his will to live and he tries to commit suicide by directly confronting a Martian machine. He is spared only because, by coincidence, bacteria have finally stopped the invaders.

24. For the Mercury theater's 1938 radio broadcast, writer Howard Koch created his main character by combining Wells's Narrator and Dr. Ogilvy in the person of a Princeton astronomy professor, Dr. Richard Pierson (Orson Welles). Screenwriter Barré Lyndon borrows something of Koch's idea in creating Clayton Forrester.

25. An ironic similarity exists in that, although a "speculative philosopher" seems less credible than a physicist, both are theoreticians making qualified guesses based on empirical information. Perhaps the former has a fictional reputation because his forecasts about the future seem remote, while the scientist's concern with immediate answers makes him appear more factual and practical. As additional ironies, Forrester's field, astro-nuclear physics, is a title suggesting interest in extremes of size, and his expertise, related to inanimate matter, lacks knowledge of the biology important in the final "war" between the Martians and Earth's bacteria.

26. From here on, despite what seems a developing romance, she calls him "Dr. Forrester," and he says nothing to change the way she addresses him. One implication is that Forrester

becomes a father-figure replacing her Uncle Matthew, another surrogate father.

27. Forrester's sidling through the crowd and advancing to the foreground to be with Sylvia is imitated by the Martian scout who sidles past the opening in the collapsed farmhouse and sneaks into the foreground to touch Sylvia. For both, the movement suggests the diminishment of status, distance and isolation imparting a mysterious quality but proximity and involvement reducing that mystique. The parallel maneuver also links the alien to Forrester, implying he is a rival "suitor" to be contended with.

V: THE FIRST MEN IN THE MOON

A: Juran's Reasonable Facsimile

H. G. Wells's *The First Men in the Moon* (1901) has been adapted for film several times. Georges Méliès[1] combined Wells's novel and Jules Verne's *From the Earth to the Moon* (1865) to produce an innovative fourteen-minute silent film, *La voyage dans la lune* (*A Trip to the Moon,* 1902). Another silent version using Wells's title appeared in 1919, a full-length feature directed by J. V. Leigh.[2] In this chapter, however, the discussion focuses on one film deserving the most consideration for comparison with Wells's novel, Nathan Juran's ambitious production of 1964.

Some reviews of Juran's *First Men in the Moon* give it conditional approval. *Leonard Maltin's TV Movies and Video Guide* (New York: Signet, 1989), for example, rates it three-stars (four stars means "the very best") and describes it as follows:

> Lavish adaptation of H. G. Wells novel is heavy-handed at times, overloaded with comic relief, but still worthwhile.

Others see it as puerile entertainment, like John Brosnan, who, in *Future Tense,* says the film

> hasn't much to commend it apart from Harryhausen's impressive special effects. . . . it was played strictly for laughs and obviously aimed at the juvenile market (158).

Most critics agree that special effects director Ray Harryhausen deserves singular credit for the convincing artistic illusions he creates for this film.[3] He simulates an imaginative underground lunar world populated by insect-like creatures, even if that world does not completely adopt Wells's concept. The mammoth labyrinthine chambers and colossal structures, because of their concrete visual impact, evoke an awe greater than that aroused by Wells's descriptions of the Selenites' huge machinery. Gargantuan caterpillars, a bottomless prism-tunnel, and a monstrous golden stairway leading up to the sphere-encased throne of the Grand Lunar make astounding impressions which draw the audience into a totally new and alien world.[4]

The film's humor, at time farcical, receives most of the criticism, although in this regard it actually mimics the novel (in much the same way that James Whale imitates Wells's slapstick in *The Invisible Man*). Wells's Cavor blown into the mud and he and Bedford colliding and tumbling together in the wind after the furnace of cavorite explodes (Ch. 2) fit in the same category as Juran's Arnold Bedford floating up to the ceiling in a chair while Cavor, screaming for his worker Gibbs to bring a ladder, frantically gropes to pull him down. The important thing is that, underlying the humor, the film recaptures many of the more serious themes of the novel. In this respect, it was not "played strictly for laughs and obviously aimed at the juvenile market."

In addition, the actors, whether in a starring or supporting role, perform credibly and admirably. Of the three main actors, Lionel Jeffries, portraying the inventor Joseph Cavor, shows exceptional flexibility. Early in the story he is convincing and funny as the typical absent-minded scientist. Yet later, he reverses his character, appearing more genuinely passionate in his concern for the Selenites and sentimental in his tenderness toward Kate. In the end there seems to be an attempt to make him a sympathetic, tragic figure, and while this may not fully succeed, it is due to the abrupt change in his character, not to his performance.

Martha Hyer, as Katherine Callendor, supplies the romantic love interest. She is beautiful but not fragile, important for her role as a strong, liberated woman who still retains feminine charm. Edward Judd portrays Arnold Bedford with the same smug, pretentious air inherent in the original character. He adeptly personifies the debonair deceiver who would use both lover and friend for his personal gain.

The film's plot imitates the original, although the screenplay, co-written by Nigel Kneale[5] and Jan Read, includes several deviations, such as a modern-day frame story and the character Kate as a romantic love interest. The inserted opening frame, set in 1964, shows a United Nations team of astronauts making the first lunar landing. On the moon, they discover a Union Jack and a sheet of paper, indicating that some visitor had preceded them. On one side of the paper are the handwritten words, "Claimed for her majesty, Queen Victoria, in the year of Our Lord, 1899." On the other side appears a legal summons for Katherine Callendor of Dymchurch, England. A delegation from the U.N. races to the small town's municipal building where the registrar (Miles Malleson ably personifying the stalwart British bureaucracy) informs them that, ironically, he had been married to her, but she died ten years ago and cannot corroborate how the Union Jack had come to be on the moon. Her former address, Cherry Cottage, leads them to Arnold Bedford, an aged man living in the Lime Nursing Home outside Dymchurch. Arnold's explanation becomes the inset story of how he, Katherine, and Cavor made their earlier trip to the moon.

Like Wells's Narrator (simply called Bedford), Arnold tells how, after failing at some unnamed business venture, he retires to the country to escape his creditors and write a play. (Unlike Bedford, who lacks a love interest, Arnold has the added intention of seducing Kate). There, he meets Professor Cavor, an absent-minded scientist working on an anti-gravity material called cavorite. In manufacturing his liquid substance, Cavor plans to coat it on a sphere in order to travel to the moon.[6]

Arnold finagles a partnership with Cavor, seeing profit potential in cavorite. He rejects Cavor's offer to fly to the moon, but changes his mind when the scientist tells him the lunar landscape is rich in minerals, including gold. They launch the sphere (Kate being pulled in at the last second) and eventually reach the moon.[7]

They encounter unexpected beings, whale-sized "moon-calves" (giant caterpillars in the film) and dwarfish insect-like Selenites. After their adventures among the moon creatures, Arnold and Kate regain the sphere to return to earth, but the curious scientist, intrigued by his discoveries, orders them to leave without him so that he can remain and study the Selenites.

Wells's Bedford, on the other hand, after becoming separated from Cavor, is forced to leave the moon without him. He implies that the scientist, curious to learn about the Selenites, has allowed himself to be captured. Cavor later radios information to earth about the Selenite society, which he gathers from living among them.[8] In a final transmission, Cavor attempts to reveal his formula for cavorite, but is abruptly cut off. Bedford assumes that the Selenites have killed him to quash his secret and prevent other humans from invading their world.

The film has a quite different ending. In the closing frame, a television set is wheeled into Arnold Bedford's room where a crowd of U.N. delegates, reporters, and nursing home staff witnesses the lunar astronauts discovering the Selenites' underground chambers. All is deserted and in a state of decay. Suddenly, the vaults collapse around the explorers, and the commentator offers several theories for the deterioration, one of which is that the race had been wiped out by "some all-conquering virus." Obviously, the film makes an ironic allusion to Wells's *War of the Worlds:* here men are taking their germs to the aliens instead of waiting for the aliens to come to them.

In retaining most of Wells's narrative structure, the film borrows many of his images but varies them in original ways. Some are reduced in significance, while others have been altered to expand the novel's ideas. The central images of the sphere, cavorite, the foot (shoe or boot), the window, and movements of ascent and descent are interwoven to connote antithetical concepts of death and rebirth, restriction and freedom, knowledge and ignorance, struggle and submission.[9]

A tomb/womb image in the two versions, the sphere, like the Time Traveller's machine, becomes associated with death and rebirth.[10] After Bedford and Cavor entomb themselves in it, they "die" to all they had known on earth. On the moon, the sphere becomes an egg birthing the two space travelers to a new existence.[11] Like infants, they have to learn to walk. And once they do, their gait, limited on earth, becomes almost unbounded flight on the moon. As Cavor says, "We are out of Mother Earth's leading-strings now" (Ch. 8).

The sphere becomes a third orb between the earth and the moon, mirroring the hollow moon as a shell masking life inside. In the novel, after hearing strange sounds emanating from below the surface, Bedford asks, "Was this arid desolation . . . only the outer rind and mask of some subterranean world?" (Ch. 9). Observations restricted to surface appearances can only attain limited information. To dispel incomplete truths and false assumptions one must penetrate the mask[12] and probe the deepest limits, which is why Cavor, a dedicated scientist, remains behind to research as far as possible into the moon.

Movements of ascent and descent become related approaches in the search for knowledge. To learn about the moon, Bedford and Cavor leave the earth, ascending in their sphere. However, as they travel closer to the moon, their movement becomes a descent. Bedford notes this sensation:

> . . . the moon was "down" under my feet, and . . . the earth was somewhere away on the level of the horizon, the earth that had been "down" to me and my kindred since the beginning of things. (Ch. 5)

To acquire more knowledge, they must descend even farther into a subterranean world. Cavor eventually reaches the ultimate source when he gains access to the Grand Lunar's central vault.

In the film, Arnold and Cavor literally penetrate the mask when they crash through the prism dome and descend into the interior caverns. However, when Cavor later enters the Grand Lunar's throne room, he makes a long ascent up a wide golden staircase lined with crystal stalagmites. The Grand Lunar's hall is brightly lit, signifying Cavor's upward climb from the dark recesses as a movement from ignorance to knowledge. The Grand Lunar, although below the surface, still occupies a position above the common Selenites, suggesting his relative superiority to them.

Windows represent several things. Related to the rebirth concept, they offer access to new information and knowledge, although their restrictive frames limit the scope of that new knowledge. In the novel, Bedford first sees Cavor from his bungalow window; his impressions are limited to the scientist's eccentric appearance. Afterwards, Cavor and Bedford discover that the moon sustains life when, looking through the portholes, they see the desolate terrain become transformed into a thick lunar garden, the image itself related to rebirth. Yet their discovery is restricted to vegetation. Not until they go beyond the limits of the sphere, to the world outside the window,[13] do they learn the deeper secrets of lunar life.

Bedford's view of the garden is also imperfect because the portholes, while clear in the center, create distortion around the edges. The film repeats this idea several times. When the travelers land on the moon and peer out the small porthole, they see a circular-framed portion of the moon. Arnold asks, "What now?" and Cavor yells, "Explore!" The only way to see more of that limited area is to get outside the window and into open space.

Captured by the Selenites, Kate is put inside a glass cell with a large round window that acts like an X-ray machine. The Selenites watch her skeleton hammering on the glass with her shoe. They observe only a limited portion of her, the physical skeletal part. They neglect the emotional, psychological side. This idea occurs again later when the Grand Lunar interviews Cavor. In the discussion of war, the Grand Lunar reduces violence to illogical behavior, ignoring variable human situations which might require it, such as a position of self-defense.

Ultimately, windows represent nearly any "outlook" which becomes a narrow view restricted and distorted by personal evaluation. And this extends to the novel's double narration. When Cavor transmits his portion of the story,

some of his observations portray Bedford as less capable than
Bedford had made himself appear. Bedford comments on
such disparaging remarks:

> "Poor Bedford," he says of me, . . . and he blames
> himself for inducing a young man "by no means well
> equipped for such adventures. . . . " I think he
> underrates the part of my energy and practical capacity
> played in bringing about the realisation of his theoreti-
> cal sphere. "We arrived," he says, with no more
> account of our passage through space than if we had
> made a journey in a railway train.
>   . . . I must insist that I have been altogether juster to
> Cavor than he has been to me. I have extenuated little
> and suppressed nothing. But his account is:
>   "It speedily became apparent that the entire strange-
> ness of our circumstances and surroundings . . . was
> exciting my companion unduly. On the moon his
> character seemed to deteriorate. He became impulsive,
> rash, and quarrelsome. . . . "
>   . . . I dislike the idea of seeming to use my position
> as his editor to deflect his story in our own interest, but
> I am obliged to protest here against the turn he gives
> these occurrences. (Ch. 22)

Cavor's criticism becomes a self-reflexive comment on the
Narrative Voice. By offering an alternate, disparate perspective of the same situation, it sets up a dialectic between Cavor
and Bedford, separating them both from the supposedly
all-knowing Author and giving them the semblance of real
persons with human foibles and inconsistencies.[14]
The film might have used a voice-over to recapture the
original dramatic irony, Arnold describing things differently
from their actual presentation on the screen. Such a device,
however, might have been too obtrusive. Instead, Bedford's
unintentional contradictions are replaced with dramatic and
situational irony in the visible actions of the characters,
which may explain why farce appears so prevalent in the film.
The foot/shoe/boot image is linked to ideas of struggle
versus submission, restriction versus freedom, although
applied in different ways in the novel and film. In Wells, the

image appears early when Bedford seeks his "pied-à-terre" at Lympne. A "foot to the ground" denotes his temporary lodgings, while also implying that the play he expects to write should give him a solid "footing" in his struggle to succeed.

Lympne is "in the clay part of Kent." The postman sometimes walks his route "with boards upon his feet" and the neighbors have on their doorsteps "big birch besoms . . . to wipe off the worst of the clay" (Ch. 1). In addition, when Cavor first appears he is distinguished by his feet, which, already large, "were . . . grotesquely exaggerated in size by adhesive clay." These images recall the expression, "feet of clay," implications of humanity's evolutionary origins and of its earth-bound gravitational imprisonment, both of which it cannot easily escape.

On the moon, Cavor wants to surrender peacefully to the Selenites in order to communicate with them, but Bedford argues, "They are a different clay" (Ch. 12). Because moon soil differs from that of earth, the Selenites would have evolved into something inhuman. And like the Time Traveller, who felt repulsion toward the ugly Morlocks, Bedford feels an alienation which compels him to rebel against them. He yields to his instinct to survive and resorts to violence. Cavor, on the other hand, lets scientific reason override this urge and submits to the moon creatures without a struggle. He suppresses his revulsion, hoping to exchange ideas with them (although in his transmission he admits disgust for some of them and their habits).

Cavorite relates to the foot imagery. It frees the two men from the restraints of gravity, enabling them to break with their earth-bound heritage ("the earth that had been 'down' to me and my kindred since the beginning of things") and to discover a new way of walking on the moon. However, such liberation tempts them to jump about carelessly, with near injuries in some nasty falls. Cavor notes, "This moon has no discipline. She'll let us smash ourselves" (Ch. 8). Like the Invisible Man, they acquire a power which appears an asset, but contains inherent dangers if not regulated properly. Freedom and restriction become relative to circumstance.

In the film, foot imagery is not connected with evolution. Instead, it relates to a number of different ideas, including stability and practicality and situations involving union versus repulsion, often with the implication of violence.

In the opening frame's lunar landing, for instance, as the jettisoned pod descends toward the moon's surface, it extends its "legs" for touch-down. One leg, shown close-up, frames the lunar landscape in the background. Then the camera cuts to a close-up of one of the leg's "shoes" touching the ground and sinking into the soft ooze. Minutes later, an astronaut dangling from a trapeze descends from the belly of the pod (another birth image). The camera shows an isolated close-up of the ground. The astronaut's boots enter the top of the frame and drop onto the gray soil.

The "feet" in this scene make the first contact which unites ship, then man, with a totally alien world. At the same time, the sinking of the pod shoe into the soft goo suggests a kind of violation of "Selene's" pristine land. Ironically, she has already been abused by previous trespassers (that is, not only by Cavor, but by his germs which may have obliterated the Selenites, the "owners" of the moon), and earth's international celebration of the present landing appears ironic and invalid.

Arnold's attempt to take advantage of Kate parallels the astronauts' landing on virgin soil. Letting her believe he has intentions of marriage, but planning only a brief affair, he has invited her to visit him at Cherry Cottage (the name, of course, suggestive of her maiden status). The rented cottage overlooks a canal and has a narrow footbridge leading up to it.[15] When Kate arrives, he guides her across, telling her to "watch her step." Later, he starts to carry her bag up the stairs, but she takes it from him: "I can manage quite well alone." In crossing the bridge, she has agreed to a union with him. However, unlike the moon with its passive reception of the astronauts, she is more sure-footed and independent than he had expected.

When Arnold visits Cavor in his laboratory, he sits in a chair coated with cavorite and ends up floating against the ceiling. Shots taken from angles above and below him and from outside the lab door emphasize his boots dangling around the legs of the chair. Originally, he had come to refuse Cavor's offer to buy Cherry Cottage, but now he gleefully rambles on about forming a partnership. He talks of the profit-potential of cavorite and how it can make them rich. As an after-thought, he asks, "What ideas did you have for it?" Cavor answers, "Nothing practical . . . a trip to the moon." The shock of the suggestion unseats Arnold and sends him crashing through the lab table and to the ground.

Suspended off his feet, Arnold's imagination runs wild with extravagant plans and unrealistic expectations for their collaboration. When hit with a more outrageously impractical idea than his own, he returns to his senses, that is, he plummets back to earth where he can ground his feet in reality. His violent fall suggests the risk of dwelling too long on impractical dreams.

When Cavor climbs the great golden stairway up to the Grand Lunar's throne-room, the bottom of his knickers are slightly pulled up, exposing part of his calf and making his shoes more prominent. (Faulty editing during his ascent first shows both legs exposed, then one, then both again.) The exposed calves above the plodding feet make Cavor a ludicrous figure, but they also suggest a vulnerable innocence as he attempts to make contact with the ruler of the Selenites.

In contrast to its association with union, the foot also relates to rejection or repulsion, especially of a violent kind. After her capture by the Selenites, Kate, appearing as a skeleton on an X-ray screen, pounds her shoe on the glass while a creature examines her second shoe. Kate hollers, "You'd better give it back to me or I'll let you have the other one." Later, when Arnold fights the Selenites, he has a gun, but instead of shooting it, he uses it like a club, hitting them with the butt end, that is, with the heel and toe of the stock. And before he and Kate are finally about to escape in the sphere, he sits in the open hatch, one leg and foot dangling outside, while he tries to convince Cavor to return with them. The Selenites attack him, but he boots them away.

A key image of violent repulsion occurs when Arnold and Cavor first confront the Selenites. Like Wells's characters who are goaded to cross a plank into dark obscurity, Arnold and Cavor are prodded to cross a narrow stone bridge over a deep chasm. In a scene mirroring the frame story's lunar landing when the pod leg in the foreground frames a long shot of the moon's terrain behind it, the camera shoots a close-up of Arnold's boots from a low angle, showing them large in the foreground, shuffling backwards along the precarious bridge, while the Selenites appear small in the background behind the over-sized boots.

Arnold could submit to their prods, as Cavor, the scientist anxious to make contact with this new life form, is willing to do. Instead, Arnold rebels, swinging out with his diving helmet. His violent outburst rejects contact with this mysterious and intimidating race. However, in the struggle for survival, Arnold's violence seems rational and Cavor's submissiveness foolish. What appears a negative display of belligerence is actually a justifiable, practical response to an ominous threat.

B: Juran's Film: The Wedding as the Unifying Motif

Union or Fusion, symbolized in one respect by foot imagery, becomes the film's central concept and is signified by a more all-encompassing pattern, the Wedding. In the opening frame story, a commission from the U.N. Space Agency rushes to Dymchurch, England to verify the existence of Katherine Callendor, the name on the legal summons found on the moon by the lunar astronauts. At the entrance to the municipal building, the delegation is held up by a wedding party celebrating on the way out. Inside, the registrar, covered with confetti and streamers, greets Richard Challis (Hugh McDermott) and his people. He asks, "Is this in regard to a birth, wedding . . . or death?" His question suggests that within the limits of a person's life, the only event worth recording is marriage.

Intending to pull out the book of births, he accidentally grabs the book of deaths. He excuses himself: "Weddings, weddings, weddings"—pulling off the streamers—"they've always affected me, even now." Margaret Hoy (Betty McDowall) says in an aside to Challis, "They've never affected me, much to my regret." Weddings become associated with human emotions, especially sentimentality, establishing a contrast with the Selenites, who seem to lack such feelings.

The Wedding Motif appears early as an important image in the film, and when expanded through connotation, relates to most of the film's ideas, some positive (international cooperation), others negative (imperialism). Significant is the emphasis on the wedding itself, the celebration of the union, which contains idealistic implications beyond those associated with marriage in general. Related images of bonding, cooperation, and communication are often played against the antithetical concepts of separation, repulsion, and competition.

Besides its references to literal weddings, the frame story also contains figurative weddings. The lunar landing, a joint space venture by a United Nations team of astronauts, suggests a "wedding" of countries, especially of the United States and Russia whose representative astronauts co-pilot the manned capsule. When the first astronaut is lowered, the camera takes a tight close-up of his boots dropping onto the lunar soil. An abrupt cut leads to superimposed shots of the people on earth celebrating the achievement, the "wedding" of man and moon. In a series of cuts, commentators reporting in English, Russian, and Japanese contrast with the U.N. astronauts, who speak English. On earth, language still divides nations, although the lunar mission seems a beginning to breaking down barriers to international cooperation.

Cooperation, an extension of the wedding motif, is suggested in the opening credits. With few exceptions, the titles accompany sectors or divided sections of the moon, implying partial contributions to the film. Because the director coordinates and unifies all individual efforts, his name appears with a full moon. In the inset story, Cavor's submissiveness to the Selenites indicates a willingness to cooperate, while Arnold's and Kate's resistance shows their refusal to work agreeably with them.

Communication, too, suggests a form of wedding, contact made between different sources with the intention of achieving understanding and sharing ideas. The U.N. astronauts conversing in English, contrasted with the newsmen commentating in different national languages, emphasizes one hindrance to international unity. However, the newsmen broadcast during a brief montage sequence of superimposed shots showing the whole world celebrating the lunar landing. Where language divides people, a cooperative achievement unites them.

The Selenites, using some kind of crystal translating device, are able to learn English while Kate and Cavor talk in the glass cell. Their learning the language makes it possible later for Cavor to communicate with the Grand Lunar. In one of the most eerie, intriguing moments of the film, the Grand Lunar, enthroned within a large sphere filled with a swirling blue haze, whispers his questions to Cavor who readily answers him. The communication, however, does not involve an exchange. The Grand Lunar learns about humans, but Cavor gains no knowledge about the Selenites.[16] Arnold, hidden among the stalagmites, abruptly ends the interview when he bounds into the chamber and yells, "Cavor, this is not an audience. You're on trial!"

In this communication, the sharing becomes lopsided, the man giving while the alien takes. Arnold recognizes the danger in this. Cavor, bent on making contact and engrossed in the presence of this new life form, overlooks it or dismisses it. When Arnold and Kate finally ready the sphere for their escape, Cavor remains behind, hoping to mend his relationship with the Selenites and reestablish communication with them, even if it means risking his life.

Another important theme categorized under the wedding motif is imperialism, the idea of one territory uniting another to itself in a kind of shotgun wedding. Cavor's claiming the moon for Queen Victoria and Bedford's remark that the moon is "an empire Caesar never dreamed of" are obvious references to this. And when the U.N. delegation enters the registrar's office to verify how a Union Jack might have got on the moon, one of them says, "This will take the frosting off the U.N. [wedding?] cake—Mother Empire still waving the flag." The comment ironically weds the mother image with imperialism while referring to an independent aggressive act that undermines international unity.

When the delegation's car pulls up to the municipal building, all but the Indian representative, Doctor Tok (Marne Maitland), get out. As Margaret Hoy closes the door, Tok sneezes into a handkerchief.[17] Reporters approach Tok, but still coughing, he rolls up the window.

The incident combines the concept of communication with imperialism. Tok, of course, reminds us of India, a one-time subject of England's empire but now a free, independent state. While he cooperates in the joint space effort, his rude cutting off of the reporters shows a reluctance to share in total communication. He is a cool, abrupt character, curt towards Arnold when later he shows him pictures of the discovered lunar artifacts. International cooperation and communication are important, but in practice, the degree to which nations embrace them becomes a subjective matter.

For the film's three main characters, explicit references to marriage reveal their literal connection to the wedding motif. Cavor rants over Kate's leaving open the greenhouse doors, which, by lowering the temperature of the cavorite on the sphere, could ruin the experiment.[18] Thinking her Arnold's wife, he yells, "Thank the Lord I never got married. My mother warned me. She was right. My goodness, she was right." His farcical tirade evokes laughter from the audience, but if marriage is a positive venture (as the film generally implies) his vehemence against it becomes pitiful. Isolation with his research and an obsessive devotion to Science seem a trivial, lonely thing next to sharing a nurturing relationship with a woman.

Arnold, too, remains unmarried. His attempt to seduce Kate without intending to marry her incurs the "punishment" of his spending his final days as a lonely old man in a nursing home, a reputed senile crackpot with a "lunatic obsession."[19] The ironic coincidence of the sentimental registrar having married Kate, suggests that, if marriage is a blessing, his sentimentality rewards him with the wife denied to the isolated Cavor and the conniving Arnold.

C: Arnold/Bedford, Joseph/Cavor: Parallels and Divergences

An examination of the Bedfords and Cavors in both versions shows how the union motif is important to their

respective relationships. The three-way "wedding" of the
film characters automatically carries deviations from the
novel's treatment of the simpler Bedford-Cavor bonding, but
the film borrows enough from the original to make Arnold
and Joseph clear imitations of their counterparts.

Wells's Bedford, like Arnold, is a corrupt ne'er-do-well
opportunist hoping to make money without having to work
for it. After failing at a business venture, he retires to the
seclusion of the country, planning to write a play to repay his
remaining creditor:

> He ran me hard. It seemed to me at last that there was
> nothing for it but to write a play, unless I wanted to
> drudge for my living as a clerk. I have a certain
> imagination, and luxurious tastes, and I meant to make
> a vigorous fight for it before that fate overtook me.
> . . . I knew there was nothing a man can do outside
> legitimate business transactions that has such opulent
> possibilities. . . . (Ch. 1)

While he confesses a noble determination to succeed and
claims to control his situation, dramatic irony exposes his
distorted view of himself. His expectation to complete a play
in ten days, praising his own cooking because "you know, it
had a flavor," boasting over the purchase of a cask of beer on
credit, and taking advantage of a "trustful baker," all depict
him as a self-centered, self-deceiving fool and petty swindler.

Arnold, beginning his inset narrative, defines a similar
situation for himself:

> I'd been engaged in an unsuccessful business specula-
> tion. To be frank, my creditors were pressing me hard.
> You see, I'd always had the idea I could write a play,
> wonderful financial possibilities in a successful play. So
> I looked around for somewhere secluded where I could
> write. In the end, I rented a cottage near Dymchurch. I
> remember because it was along an abandoned canal. (A
> rippling effect across the screen indicates the end of the
> opening frame and the start of the inset story.)

By comparison, Arnold's words lack the dramatic irony
implicit in Bedford's narration and fail to suggest anything

significant about his character. However, as the story continues, his lying and conniving are wrapped in dramatic irony, deceiving the other characters but never the audience, something Bedford tries to do. Ultimately, both expose themselves as the same kind of selfish hypocrite and petty cheat.

Bedford, struggling to write his play, becomes distracted by this "oddest little figure," dressed in "cricket cap, an overcoat, and cycling knickerbockers and stockings," who walks past his window[20] at the same time every day for two weeks. By introducing himself, he makes Cavor self-conscious about his habit, and now, knowing Bedford is watching him, the scientist cannot concentrate during his walks. He offers to buy Bedford's bungalow. Bedford, although he rents, considers "selling" to the naive scientist, but stalls to learn more about his research.

Bedford offers himself as a sounding-board for Cavor's ideas. The scientist trusts him, and Bedford learns enough to realize he should attach himself to Cavor as his practical business partner:

> I tried to make him understand his duties and responsibilities in the matter—*our* duties and responsibilities in the matter. . . . I stuck like a leech to the "we"—"you" and "I" didn't exist for me. (Ch. 1)

The partnership solidified, Cavor proposes a trip to the moon. Bedford declines until he is attracted by the possibility of discovering minerals, especially gold. More important to him, however, is the idea of the "rights of pre-emption," a monopoly granted them on the basis of their being the first ones there: "This is imperial! I haven't been dreaming of this sort of thing" (Ch. 3).

In the film, the word "imperial" becomes associated with Cavor. He says it several times, once just before claiming the moon for Queen Victoria and again in the Selenite translation cell when one of his interpreters mimics him by using the word. It serves as an obvious reminder of imperialism, a suggested theme in both film and novel, and an important motif coming out of Wells's earlier work, *The War of the Worlds*.

The film alters the way the men meet, but many similarities in the relationship remain. Arnold tells Kate he owns Cherry Cottage (inherited from an aunt who considered him her favorite nephew) when in fact he rents it. Cavor, after discovering the cottage inhabited, fears his experiments might endanger them and he attempts to buy it. With Arnold absent, Kate consents to sell. Later, Arnold confronts Cavor to cancel the sale, but when he learns of cavorite and considers its profit potential, he, like Bedford, connives to deceive the business-ignorant scientist.

To complete the sale, Arnold, committing one of his most despicable deeds, suborns Kate to act as the owner of Cherry Cottage and sign the property over to Cavor. She assumes the money will enable them to get married, but after she signs, Arnold explains that the money is for investing in Cavor's research and that their marriage will have to wait. Later, a warrant officer serves Kate a summons for her crime. This same summons becomes the sheet on which Cavor writes his claim for the moon. Thus, the single paper refers to two illegal transfers of property, one through insidious deceit, the other by an overt act of imperialism.

Avarice instigates Arnold's and Bedford's whim to attach themselves like parasites to their respective Cavors. On the other end, a naive trust and a desire for companionship motivates the scientists to bond themselves unwittingly to the con-men.

Joseph Cavor's first appearance suggests a parallel with his original counterpart. A long shot shows him riding a bicycle up the tow path along the canal, wearing the same clothes described by Wells's Bedford. His nervous, spastic mannerisms reflect the foppishness of the original character, whom Bedford had thought "to use . . . as a central figure in a good farce" (Ch. 1), which, ironically, *The First Men in the Moon* becomes.

Joseph Cavor differs from Wells's Cavor in his compassion and considerateness. His concern for the welfare of his neighbors in light of his dangerous research suggests he assumes responsibility for his actions. On the other hand, Wells's Cavor is far from considerate and responsible. In the experiment where the furnace explodes and destroys the house, he appears apathetic to the death of his three assistants (who, unknown to him, had neglected the furnace and were safe at the local pub). Furthermore, he hopes the explosion, which damaged neighboring houses, will be blamed on a cyclone and not traced to him. In that case, if public assistance should be handed out, he would appear eligible for compensation which he could apply to more research. His response to this incident reveals him as no less selfish and irresponsible than Bedford.

The film presents the scientist as eccentric but not exceptionally dangerous, the farce nullifying the seriousness of the violence. The novel makes a more ominous statement. For Wells, as iterated throughout his scientific romances, this becomes the critical paradox of the scientist: he subordinates and endangers human life while pursuing some discovery that is supposed to benefit the common good. Cavor's attitude, at least in part, shows him to be of the same ilk as Moreau and Griffin.

Wells's Bedford and Cavor do not develop or change during their experiences. Introducing his story as a flashback, Bedford says he has aged from his ordeals, but "whether they have brought any wisdom to light below it, is a more doubtful matter." At the end of the story, he appears no more productive than before he met Cavor. He has become a vagabond in Europe, capitalizing on his adventures by writing about them, his easiest route to some degree of financial success.

Whether Cavor dies is not clearly determined (although Bedford believes so). In any case, his final radio messages depict him as unchanged, ever devoted to the pursuit of knowledge and thrilled by what he learns while living among the Selenites. And he still appears the absent-minded fool. Naively trusting the Grand Lunar, he expounds on humanity's inclination for violence and confesses that he is the sole inventor of cavorite, two foolish admissions which make him responsible for Selenite fears of an invasion from earth.

In contrast, the film's Arnold and Joseph, after landing on the moon, undergo apparent changes which consequently alter the tone of the story. (The tonal change seems a substitution for the novel's change in narrative viewpoint, and similarly divides the story into two parts.) Where previously they had shared the buffoonery, Cavor for a time continues the farce and Arnold becomes more sober.

Outside the sphere for the first time, Cavor, getting too much oxygen, becomes giddy with his new power to jump freely about the landscape. He leaps from rock to rock, falls down, then somersaults and becomes wedged in a rock "throne," the imperialist imprisoned by the rocks he has claimed. And later, during their frantic escape from the giant caterpillar, Cavor, who has been gradually disrobing, appears a ludicrous clown when his pants drop around his feet. He trips and is unable to climb up the precipice to safety. Arnold saves him by throwing his helmet at the monster, distracting it.

In time, however, farce disappears completely. Captured by Selenites, Cavor is put into Kate's glass cell. They hug. After the Selenite learns their language, they are released. They walk about the huge caverns, hand-in-hand (like two lovers or two lost children wandering in an amusement park or fantasy land). When Kate appears tired, Cavor gently seats her on the step of the glass cell and rolls up his jacket like a pillow for her.

This seems an odd change in his behavior, not clearly growth or "development," but more like a side of him not shown before. His kindness and soft words fall short of romantic implication, but they suddenly change our attitude toward him. He becomes more real than the farcical figure he has appeared to be until now.[21]

On the moon, Arnold seems to grow more belligerent and domineering. Already during their journey to the moon he had begun to give curt orders to Kate. His abruptness continues later when, pressing Cavor against a cavern wall with the gun, he demands that he help him and Kate escape. Cavor, by now a more serious character than before, wants time to communicate with the Selenites. The elements of farce have disappeared and the scene, more tense than before, appears a life-threatening conflict between the characters, not a light-hearted burlesque.

While Cavor visits the Grand Lunar, Arnold and Kate ready the sphere for their escape. At one point, he curtly orders her to stop what she is doing and to help him, as if his job were more important. Then, when one blind on the porthole fails to work, he becomes ill-tempered. To fix it, he retrieves Cavor from the Grand Lunar's chamber, shooting out the main light-crystal and violently beating the Selenites. Cavor whimpers, "Why couldn't you have left me?" Arnold snarls, "Don't flatter yourself. I didn't risk my neck to save you," and gruffly pushes him ahead. The serious, realistic behavior of the two men erases the farce while revealing the strain on their relationship.

Cavor helps Arnold and Kate repair the blind and makes them leave without him. He backs through a door into the next room. Turning, he falls forward, his arms spread out on a table fitted with a small sink containing the imitation cavorite the Selenites had tried, but failed, to duplicate. Behind Cavor, through the zigzag opening of the giant valves, appears the sphere, rumbling and kicking up smoke and dust. In the foreground, Selenites appear right and left of the cringing scientist, each seeming to press slowly upon him. The farcical figure has been transformed into a pathetic martyr for the cause of Science.[22]

Notes

1. In *A History of Narrative Film* (New York: Norton, 1981), David A. Cook discusses a number of Méliès's contributions to film, including "increasing the standard length of fiction films" (16). From Verne, Méliès takes the idea of shooting the astronauts' projectile from a canon. Copying Wells, he has them actually land on the moon and descend into it in a confrontation with the Selenites. An interesting variation occurs at the beginning when the magician-astronomers disrobe to transform themselves into scientists. Their change reflects the way Wells uses Science as a substitute for Magic: ". . . by the end of last century it had become difficult to squeeze even a momentary belief out of magic any longer. It occurred to me that instead of the usual interview with the devil or a magician, an ingenious use of scientific patter might with advantage be substituted. That was no great discovery. I simply brought the fetish stuff up to date, and made it as near

actual theory as possible" (Preface to *Seven Famous Novels by H. G. Wells*).

2. This film is difficult to locate. John Baxter, in his *Science Fiction in the Cinema,* relies on a second-hand account for his brief comment: " . . . a triangle love story was introduced for greater effect. Unfortunately this did not divert attention from the lunar scenes, described by an observer as 'inadequate' " (18). This is enough to suggest a partial relevance to Juran's 1964 film which also incorporates an "eternal triangle" in its story.

3. Juran and Harryhausen collaborated earlier on *20 Million Miles to Earth* (1957) and the adventure-fantasy *The 7th Voyage of Sinbad* (1958), both films depending on elaborate special effects for their dominant impact. Juran also worked under the pseudonym Nathan Hertz, directing such infamous films as *Attack of the 50-Foot Woman* (1958).

4. Size and scale, important metaphors for Wells, appear in many films for the same reasons he had used them, to create a sense of other-worldness and to indicate intellectual and technological advancement. *First Men,* among other films like *Metropolis* (Fritz Lang, 1926), *Things to Come* (William Cameron Menzies, 1936), and *Forbidden Planet* (Fred McLeod Wilson, 1956), immediately imparts sensations of wonder when its colossal images appear on the screen.

5. Kneale is best known for his authorship of the Quatermass series.

6. In one experiment where Cavor's three incompetent and unreliable assistants neglect the furnace, the concoction explodes, destroying the house. The incident appears in both versions, but while for Wells it contrasts with the efficiency of the division of labor in the Selenite society, in the film it merely contributes to the farce.

7. Omitted from the film, a lunar garden blooms before Bedford's and Cavor's eyes. Juran avoids Wells's faulty assumption that the lunar atmosphere contains breathable oxygen. At the same time, he ignores certain scientific principles, such as the effects of weightlessness on the space

travelers and the proper suits needed for walking on the moon. Because he takes such literary license with these "facts," he might have remained faithful to the novel and allowed for a garden on the moon.

8. The film leaves out Cavor's transmission and, instead, integrates part of his lengthy message into Arnold's on-going narrative, such as his meeting with the Grand Lunar (a discrepancy, since Arnold is not present to record their discussion. Otherwise, he witnesses most of the events or can learn them second-hand from Kate, who saw things he did not).

   The film reveals some aspects of Selenite society, but not to the same extent as the novel, and usually by altering the original ideas in some way (such as mummification of an unemployed Selenite instead of drugging him). In Wells's version, Bedford's story concerns their journey to the moon, their capture, and his escape and return. Cavor's subsequent transmission deals with the Selenite society, giving the novel a dichotomy based on changed perspective.

   Many critics find the change creates some unevenness, although without being actually disruptive or incongruous to the story. In *The Early H. G. Wells,* Bergonzi notes ambiguity in Wells's intention for the satire of Cavor's section. Whether he expects serious consideration of the Selenites' ideas or uses their behavior to mock human institutions, is at times unclear and inconsistent. On the other hand, John Huntington, in *The Logic of Fantasy: H. G. Wells and Science Fiction* (New York: Columbia, 1982), defends such ambiguity as part of Wells's method of using contradictions to display irresolvable paradoxes. Cavor's description of the Selenite society, which, from birth, treats and conditions each creature to specialize in one particular task that will contribute to the function of the whole, serves as a source for Aldous Huxley's *Brave New World* (1932).

9. Huntington discusses the extensive use of "opposition" in Wells's presentation of social and scientific paradoxes.

10. In the film, the initial image, a large, bright sector of the moon against a black void, dissolves into a darkened sector with a spaceship orbiting it. The spaceship then ejects a smaller pod (symbolically named Early Child) containing the men who will

land on the moon. Although not strictly a sphere, the "Mother-ship" relates to the birth image and also introduces a mother motif which recurs throughout the film.

11. Bedford and Cavor exemplify the double, an image appearing frequently in Wells's stories. However, here the image is not as defined as between other doubles, such as the Time Traveller and Frame Narrator, or Griffin and Kemp. Bedford and Cavor may be "twins" whose rivalries arise from different motives and attitudes, but their contrast is not clearly antithetical.

12. False assumptions and re-evaluated theories are prevalent in many of Wells's works. Consider the amended speculations of the Time Traveller or Prendick's inferences about the relationship between Moreau and the Beast People (see note 13).

13. The window is a prominent image in Wells. Consider the scenes in *The War of the Worlds* when the Narrator has a limited view of events from his study window and in *The Invisible Man* when Kemp, also from his study window, forms his narrow opinion of Thomas Marvel, seen running outside.

14. The technique of setting an outsider's voice against an insider's appears in Wells's first serious work, *The Chronic Argonauts,* as the "exoteric" and "esoteric" views. It recurs in many of his short stories and in most of his sf novels from *The Time Machine* to *The First Men in the Moon.* Usually, it takes the form of a layman narrating the story, with a scientist allowed an inset opinion that raises much of the controversy. Often, contradictions are implied by the Narrator himself.

15. Bridges and staircases, images which, like the foot, suggest linkage or union, appear more extensively in the film than in the novel. Wells's Bedford and Cavor cannot cross the Selenite bridge enshrouded in darkness, signifying the gap between the two species, which cannot be reconciled and joined. In the film, a similar incident occurs (discussed below), and additional bridges and staircases suggest various kinds of unions.

16. Cavor's interview here deviates considerably from Wells's version. In the original, separated from Cavor and unable to find him, Bedford returns to earth. Cavor then lives for a time alone among the Selenites before meeting the moon's absolute

ruler (Ch. 24). Their discussion becomes more an exchange than it is in the film. For instance, instead of Cavor giving one-way information about how the iris protects the human eye from excessive light, he, in turn, learns that the Selenite eye, though more sensitive to light, can see heat.

17. Tok's head cold foreshadows one of the theories about the demise of the Selenite civilization. In the closing frame, with the crowd gathered around Arnold's television witnessing the crumbling of the underground lunar city, the commentator says, "There seems every evidence of some kind of contamination. . . . Did they take off for another planet? Or were they wiped out by some all-conquering virus . . . as deadly as a plague or as infectious as an ordinary common cold in the head?"

Arnold, amused, turns from the TV to look through his telescope at the moon: "Poor Cavor . . . he did have such a terrible cold." However, Cavor had wiped his nose only a couple of times before sending Arnold and Kate off in the sphere, no obvious indication of "such a terrible cold."

If meant to indicate the cause of the Selenite doom, the head cold appears a weak device. However, it contributes to a more interesting, more ambiguous ending when coupled with the commentator's theories and other possible inferences. For instance, when Arnold and Kate escape from the moon, their sphere flies up the central shaft and shatters the prism which feeds sunlight to power the Crystal Dynamo. If this could not have been repaired in time, the Selenites (and Cavor) would have died.

Then again, the Grand Lunar feared another invasion from "imperfect" earthmen and intended to restrict Cavor's secret by keeping him on the moon. Because Bedford escaped with the sphere, it meant he had the power to return (although the Grand Lunar could not know that on its earth landing, the sphere sank into the ocean). To preserve their race, the Selenites might have fled to another planet as the commentator suggests, especially since they have Cavor, who could make cavorite for them. (In the novel, cavorite requires helium, an element lacking on the moon. The film, however, omits this point not to discourage Cavor's potential to recreate his formula.)

18. Kate becomes a Pandora-figure, opening up several literal and figurative doors that disrupt the plans of both men. Her

intrusions, countered by her considerateness (she stocks the sphere with food, covers a sleeping Cavor with a blanket), imply the ambivalences in any marriage, whether between man and woman, among the international astronauts, or between Cavor and the Selenites.

19. "Dymchurch," the setting for Arnold's cottage and Cavor's house, suggests a "dim church," a vague, obscure place whose light is too weak to guide them to the wedding altar.

20. See Note 12.

21. *The Eternal Triangle,* the title of Arnold's unwritten play, suggests a rivalry with Cavor for Kate. However, a romantic relationship between Kate and Cavor never develops and the suggestion becomes tenuous.

22. The initials "J.C." mark Cavor as a Christ-figure, a weak implication until this ending. However, the final shot of him cringing pitifully, a "sacrifice" on the "altar" next to the reconstructed cavorite, contains an interesting allusion to the Mass as a duplication of the Last Supper and Christ's offering of bread and wine—and of Himself.

VI: THE FOOD OF THE GODS AND HOW IT CAME TO EARTH

A: Gordon's Treasonable Facsimiles

Director Bert I. Gordon credits H. G. Wells's *The Food of the Gods and How It Came to Earth*[1] (1904) as the source of his films, *The Village of the Giants* (1965) and *The Food of the Gods* (1976). However, as adaptations, the two works are extremely remote analogies.[2] In both cases, Gordon ignores the original plot, theme, setting, and characters, and bases his stories on only a few isolated ideas from the original. This in itself is not a faulty approach to filmmaking, but his slipshod, amateurish results, filled with incoherences and trivialities, make them works of inferior quality.

In *Future Tense*, John Brosnan describes Gordon as

> a film-maker so determinedly crass in his work that he makes Roger Corman[3] look by comparison like the genius many people say he is (Gordon is currently enjoying a comeback, thanks to the sf boom, and is doing his best to destroy the reputation of H. G. Wells with such films as *Food of the Gods* and *Empire of the Ants*).

Gordon tries to justify his approach to filmmaking:

> In the first place, you've got to understand that the movie audience today consists almost entirely of teen-agers. Either they're naive and go to get scared, or they're sophisticated and enjoy scoffing at the pictures. There isn't much a teenager can scoff at these days, you know.[4]

With this narrow estimate of the American teenager's mentality, he deliberately flaunts trite dialogue, sloppy special effects, imprecise editing, and weak acting in order to encourage ridicule of his films and create entertainment out of ineptitude. Economically, this may be a legitimate approach, but technically, his films are wasteful excursions into pettiness. His posture seems a masochist's excuse for neglecting craftsmanship—or for coping with the fear of failure.[5]

Gordon's shallowness is further reinforced by his reliance on a single, repeated allegorical device to express his theme, namely, scale. *The Amazing Colossal Man* (1957), *Beginning of the End* (1957), *War of the Colossal Beast* (1958), *Empire of the Ants* (1977),[6] and the two films discussed here exemplify this limited idea: the giant (whether man, ant, or grasshopper), in the film tradition of James Whale's *Frankenstein,* personifies Irresponsible Science or Rebellious Nature. It emerges as a backlash to Science's mishandling of its discoveries and metes out swift, uncompromising punishment. (Gordon's initials, B.I.G., blatantly stand for his persistent adherence to the size motif.)

Because Gordon's two "Food" films are tangential to Wells's original work, few corresponding details exist between them. A synopsis of Wells's story will substantiate the extent of Gordon's deviations.

The Food of the Gods is not among Wells's best novels. Written near the end of his most imaginative cycle of stories, it contains elements which foreshadow his transition to a more explicit, less ambiguous (and so, less poetic) approach to his themes. He often resorts to a journalistic, essay-like style,[7] whereby the narrator's voice becomes difficult to separate from that of the author's.[8]

The story begins with two scientists, Redwood, a physiologist, and Bensington, a chemist, collaborating on the discovery of a new food which increases growth. They debate the name, finally settling on Herakleophorbia, "Food of Herakles," connoting its ability to increase strength.[9] It affects the growth pattern of infants but not of adults who have completed their growing cycle. In the clandestine way that most of Wells's scientists operate, they secretly buy an experimental farm to conduct their initial research on chickens. They hire an elderly couple, the Skinners, to tend the farm and record the daily progress of the chickens' growth.

The Skinners are careless, slovenly people. They keep the Food uncovered and accidentally spill it on the vegetation. Thistles, nettles, and a canary creeper grow beyond normal size and turn the surrounding property into a jungle. Wasps, earwigs, and rats get into the Food, and in time, become a menace to the countryside. The chickens run rampant in nearby Hickleybrow before they are killed by the townspeople or captured by a circus owner. A wasp kills a grocer. Rats attack a doctor returning from an evening housecall. The doctor escapes, but his horse falls prey to the ravenous monsters. Irresponsible Science, the Science of Moreau and Griffin, once more endangers life in its reckless pursuit of knowledge.

Redwood and Bensington enlist the help of Cossar, a civil engineer whose practical methods are in contrast to their theoretical science. Under his leadership, they blow up the wasp nest and ferret out and shoot the rats. Then they burn the experimental farm and the surrounding hypertrophied vegetation.

Mr. Skinner, returning to the farm, disappears into the "Incognito," an ambiguous fate already shared by the Time Traveller and Professor Cavor. Mrs. Skinner flees the farm to live with her daughter, expecting to give to her infant grandson, Caddles, the same Food that nourished the chickens. In the meantime, with the help of Winkles, the family physician, Redwood has been secretly giving the Food to his own son, Edward, who grows beyond the normal rate. Redwood's impatience to try the untested Food on a human iterates how Science unconscionably seeks its own ends while jeopardizing life.

With the elimination of the threat at the experimental farm, the "public mind" momentarily decides the Food is a great innovation. Bensington receives accolades for the discovery, until Caterham, a charismatic politician, begins pointing out the dangers of having a few superhumans among normal men. Bensington questions himself and considers scrapping the project, but Cossar badgers him: "Go on with it! . . . What do you think you were made for? Just to loaf about between meal-times?" (Bk. I: Ch. 4). Individual purpose and initiative become important issues, countering the "public mind" and bureaucratic morass that hinders efficiency and accomplishment.

Although Cossar has successfully defeated the wasps and rats at the experimental farm, the Food, once released, cannot be contained. Outbreaks of hypertrophy occur in many isolated areas, and the new supernormal growths begin to compete seriously with the previous normal standards. Along with the animals and foliage, many children, including the three sons of Cossar, have received the Food and giganticism has developed into a more commonplace occurrence. However, although tolerated, there is strong popular resistance to continued use of the Food.

This competition between innovation and custom becomes the pivotal conflict. The initial attitude toward Science appears simple and obvious: it is a reckless and life-threatening occupation of irresponsible men. Halfway through the story, however, this attitude shifts to something more complex: Science may pose serious dangers with its new discoveries, but these should be tolerated as minor inconveniences in light of what it contributes to humanity's advancement and growth. Science requires a trial-and-error period, which, while sometimes producing detrimental side-effects, is a necessary first step toward "progress."[10]

Ultimately, the story becomes a heavy-handed allegory. The giants stand for progress, men who benefited from Science and plan to continue its application to initiate reforms and renovations for society. The "little people" who resist any change stand for stasis and conservatism, a kind of mental and physical stagnation. Led by Caterham, a vocal but shallow-minded politician, they cling to their customary routines, petty habits, and "fixed ideas,"[11] which limit their imagination and prevent expansion and growth.

The giant Caddles appears an attempt by Wells to create a tragic figure, but he falls short. His education is limited to biblical precepts by his mother and the Vicar who, afraid of him, try to instill him with fear and guilt in order to control and manipulate him. His illiteracy and ignorance lead directly to his death.

Confined to working in a chalk pit (ironically mining the material a teacher uses as an educational tool), he grows lonesome and disgusted. One day he rebels, wrecking the pit and walking to London to find his proper place in the world. Unable to read, he ignores the signs forbidding the giants to enter restricted areas. Seeing the city people meandering about, he echoes Cossar's earlier remark to Bensington about purpose: "What are ye for, ye swarming little people? What are ye all doing—what are ye for? . . . What are all you people doing with yourselves? . . . What is it all for and where do I come in?" (Bk. III: Ch. 3).

Feeling hungry, he "commenced robbery" on a bakery truck. He walks across several lawns, ruining the turf and knocking down the fences around them. When the police insist that he return home, he "wrenched up the standard of a tall arc light, a formidable mace for him." Finally, men with rifles, wearing the "uniforms of the rat police," confront him. Caddles kills one officer with his "mace" before he is shot dead.

Caddles appears a victim of ignorance. He robs and kills out of basic animal instincts, appetite and self-preservation, which, if the implication is valid, could have been controlled if his rational side had been nurtured, that is, if he had received the proper education. Instead, his mind and body, destined for great things, are stifled by small-thinking people who more fittingly deserve the doom he receives.

Suggesting an approach to education, Wells describes Redwood's construction of Edward's nursery (plenty of paper and crayons to let the imagination run free, blocks for building, etc.). However, the effect of education on the ability to control emotional and physiological needs and desires seems strained, and the idea that this would have saved Caddles is remote. His death does inspire sadness, and maybe pity, but it is not genuinely tragic.

Young Redwood falls in love with the Princess of Weser Dreiberg, defying the "little people" who fear procreation among the giants. These two, together with Cossar's three sons, form the nucleus of the race of Giants. They represent the future of humanity, a world where changes are accepted because change means progress and beneficial improvements for society. The story ends with the giants preparing for a final confrontation with the "little people," the outcome left undetermined. The suggestion is that such a conflict always has been and will continue to be an on-going struggle between visionary "giants," that is, the people of imagination, and the common folk, those who resist beneficial change. Growth and change are inevitable in any case, a natural function of evolution, which must occur with or without the approval of the masses.[12]

B: Gordon's *The Village of the Giants:* Sincere Silliness

In making *The Village of the Giants,* Bert I. Gordon merely extracts the germinal idea of giganticism from Wells's novel and uses it to devise his own story addressed to a teenage audience. A child prodigy invents a growth food. A group of rebellious teenagers steals the food, expecting to use it to take over the village. However, the boy-scientist concocts an antidote, a smoke which counters giganticism. He releases the fumes near the gang of giants. They shrink back to normal size and are run out of town, humiliated.

Part of the story's sterility comes from reducing Wells's multiple conflicts (Stasis versus Progress, Beneficial Science versus Harmful Science, Imagination versus Fixed Idea, etc.) to a single simple conflict of Teenager versus authority (especially Adult Authority). The conflict is represented by two teenage factions, the eight Rebels led by Fred (Beau Bridges) and the Village Teens led by Mike (Tommy Kirk). Their rivalry is established in the early scenes and reinforced throughout the film in a series of altercations.

The Redwood and Bensington characters are replaced with a precocious ten-year-old chemist named Genius (Ron Howard), who invents the "Goo"[13] that increases growth. The boy-figure reduces the scientist to a puerile level, which suggests his work is child's play and contributes to the farcical tone of the story.

When Genius first appears, he emerges from the basement

and enters his parents' living room where he interrupts his sister Nancy (Charla Doherty) necking with Mike on the couch. He carries a beaker of smoking liquid, rattles off the names of several obscure chemicals, and declares his surprise: "They're not compatible. This stuff is supposed to blow up." Nancy chases him away: "You and I aren't going to be very compatible either, Genius, if you don't get out of here." Compatibility becomes the main issue of the film, particularly in the way the two teenage factions respond to authority (the "establishment," the adults).

After Genius leaves, the two lovers resume their kissing. Seconds later, an explosion from the basement interrupts them. They run down into the smoking lab where the young scientist emerges from behind a table, his glasses coated with a red film: "I put an electric charge to that stuff I was mixing, and then Bam! the whole place blew up." The electric charge acts as catalyst upsetting the balance of a potentially volatile mixture. In the same way, the Rebels are an alien force which enters Hainesville and disrupts the stable situation existing between adults and teenagers.

The Village Teens are compatible with adults. When the Sheriff (Joseph Turkel) eventually confronts the giant Rebels, Mike stands alongside him, supporting his position as the lawful adult authority. Yet the Village Teens are not totally submissive. Nancy's parents are spending the night in Los Angeles because a mudslide has blocked the road into town. While the two lovers neck on the couch, soft music plays on the phonograph and they talk of doing what many normal teens might do with such an opportunity. Still, this seems innocent and tolerable when contrasted with the initial appearance of the Rebels.

The first shot of the film is a close-up of a smashed road barrier, its "CLOSED" sign broken in half. The camera tracks along the muddy ground, showing raindrops plopping in the puddles and an automobile tire lying on the ground. Then it tracks up to the tail-end of a blue Thunderbird crashed into an embankment, a telephone pole angled across its hood. A cut to the passenger side of the car shows the door suddenly flung open. A girl, Merrie (Joy Harmon), pokes out her head, screams, then opens her mouth to catch raindrops on her tongue. She strokes her hair and face and steps out into the rain. The other passengers follow her out. With the car radio blaring rock music ("Woman" by the Beau Brummels), all begin dancing wildly, frenetically in the rain and mud, finally ending in a mud-wrestling orgy. They find a fallen road sign, "Hainesville, 3 miles," and decide to go there to see what trouble they might cause.

The broken "closed" sign and road barrier signify the Rebels' penchant for disobedience, their defiance of authority, and their willful trespassing of restricted areas (they move into the village's abandoned theater and then try to take over the town). In contrast, Genius's lab door and walls are covered with warning and off-limit signs. He can expect them to be obeyed because local mores have fostered an attitude in the Village Teens that respects the voice of authority.

The loud raucous music fueling the Rebels' frenzied dancing contrasts the romantic guitar music heard during the lovers' quiet interlude. Both are examples of rock music, teen music, but the former seems a flagrant rejection of adult sensibility, while the latter appears a compromise with it. Complementing this, the Rebels' car, a Thunderbird, signifies their motto, "thunderbirds"—who plan to make a big noise in the small town. At the same time, their casual concern for their own wrecked vehicle indicates the unlikelihood that they will respect the property of others.

Like the novel's wasps, rats, and pond beetles, various creatures eat Genius's Goo. A cat laps up the food and grows giant-sized, giving Mike the money-making idea to feed the formula to livestock to increase the food supply. He succeeds in trying out the Goo on two ducks (substitutes for Bensington's chickens). He intends to keep his plan a secret, but the ducks escape and end up dancing among the teenagers at a no-liquor night club.[14] Like Winkles, Redwood's family doctor, the Rebels become curious and want to learn about the growth food for selfish purposes.

While feeding the ducks, Mike had dropped some of the Goo on the ground. Genius's dog Wolf eats it and becomes giant-sized.[15] Mike tells Genius to make some more Goo, a task which becomes the film's running joke. Brief scenes showing his exploding mistakes and grotesque results from faulty concoctions are inserted intermittently into the main story.

A fourth giant creature, a spider, appears in the basement when Mike and Nancy return to hide the secret formula. Mike electrocutes it by bursting a water pipe and throwing a live light-bulb socket onto the floor. In a paltry special effect, the spider glows red, turns into a black silhouette, and sinks out of sight below the bottom of the frame.

Seconds later, Mike and Nancy leave the house. The Rebel Pete (Tim Rooney) sneaks into the lab through the basement window. As he snoops around looking for the food, the floor appears dry and no dead spider is evident. Like the cat, which ran out the door when Genius's dog barked at it, the spider's remains disappear from the story without explanation. Pete has no idea what the Goo looks like, yet after a brief search, he goes directly to the cabinet where Mike has hidden the formula and brings it to the waiting rebels outside.

Although a few of the Rebels, including Fred, are reluctant to eat the Goo, all take it on a dare, accusing each other of cowardice if anyone refuses. The episode suggests how peer pressure forces individuals to take drugs (which the Goo is) if they are to remain a part of the group. In this, a parallel exists with the novel's message concerning conformity. Wells's common folk, like any social group such as the Rebels, expect conformity and condemn those (the Giants) who deviate from their strictures. Ironically, taking the Goo also means rebellion against adult standards, in a similar way to Wells's Giants' resistance to adherence to the mediocre standards of the little people. The Rebels, then, mirror Wells's Giants in that taking the Goo represents both an act of conformity (within the group) and nonconformity (with "The Establishment").

After becoming giants, the Rebels kidnap the Sheriff's young daughter to insure their protection and strengthen their demand that all the guns be confiscated. Mike leads one bungled attempt to capture Fred as a reciprocal hostage, and in the melee Nancy becomes a prisoner of the Rebels.

In a second plan, Horsey (Johnny Crawford) leads two

others into the theater to rescue the girls, while Mike, outside, distracts the Rebels by attacking them. He hurls stones from a sling.[16] Each missile sails directly across the screen, arching left to right instead of toward the giants, and they bend backward in a delayed, slow-motion reaction (the stone having already disappeared out of the frame).

Fred effeminately throws a makeshift spear at Mike. Several missed tosses force Mike to retreat toward the steps of city hall. He becomes trapped on the landing (although the front door is open and he could have run inside), and Fred threatens to club him with a light-post (Caddles' mace?). Meanwhile, Genius has discovered the antidote. He ties the fuming mixture on the back of his bicycle, races to city hall, and weaves between and around the feet of the giants until the cloud of smoke engulfs them. They shrink. Mike struts stiffly down the steps and punches Fred to the ground. The Rebels, their over-sized clothes draped around their bodies,[17] retreat to the taunts of the crowd ("Well, back down to size, huh?" "Who's your tailor, Freddy?").

The Rebels return to their wrecked T-bird, taking the story full circle. Fred leads them forward and past the car on their hike to the next town. Suddenly, they halt, interrupted by the deep bass voice of a man off-camera: "I beg your pardon. Are you people coming from Hainesville?"

In a bored echo, Fred answers the unseen gentleman: "Yes, we're coming from Hainesville."

"Is that the place where they have the Goo?"

"Yes, that's the place where they have the Goo."

A dwarf (the deep-voiced speaker) enters the frame and passes in front of Fred and the other Rebels, followed by a single-file parade of short people who wend their way into the background toward Hainesville. Fred and the Rebels, disinterested and unsurprised,[18] exit the frame, left, as the title "The End" appears over the scene.

The dwarfs' interest in the Goo reopens the closed circle, creating a parallel with Wells's undetermined conclusion. In this case, however, the ambiguous "End" emphasizes the farce rather than some meaningful, thought-provoking implication.

C: Gordon's *The Food of the Gods:* Anemic Gore

Bert I. Gordon's film *The Food of the Gods* limits itself to
the first third of the novel, using the giant wasps and rats as
the main conflict of the story. Compared to the farcical
nature of *The Village of the Giants, The Food* seems a more
serious attempt at filmmaking, and most of the gory special
effects are successful in exciting feelings of dread and disgust.
However, once again, the dialogue fizzles into inane irrelevancies, reducing the story to an inconsistent blend of
horror and triviality.[19]
Morgan (Marjoe Gortner), a football player invited by his
friend Davis (Chuck Courtney) to visit him on a remote
island, brings along his public relations agent, Brian (John
Cypher). While crossing on the ferry, Morgan, in a voice-
over, recalls his father's warning. One day, he predicted,
Nature will rebel against Man for polluting the environment
and upsetting the ecological balance. An obvious statement
of the theme, it echoes Wells's initial concept of the dangers
of reckless Science, but ignores the counter-theme of
tolerating these dangers if humanity is to progress and
improve its condition. For Gordon's purpose, it may not be
necessary, but its omission narrows and simplifies the
implications of the film.
Supporting Morgan's monologue, a montage sequence of
isolated spots on the island shows a dam and various fences
set into the landscape, as if these man-made artifices were
built to restrain and control Nature. The giant wasps and rats
become Nature's agents, revolting against abuse and re-
straint.
Davis takes Morgan and Brian on a deer hunt, displaying
his lack of sportsmanship by using dogs and riding on
horseback. The dogs corner a deer. Morgan arrives first and,
compassionate toward living things, shoos the deer away.
Davis rides up, angry that the animal escaped. He continues
the pursuit, getting ahead of the other men. Alone in a
circular clearing, he is attacked by giant wasps descending
from the sky.[20] He dies, his face horribly distended—
punishment for his cruelty to animals.

Morgan runs to a nearby farm for help. It belongs to the
Skinners, who, unlike the original elderly couple, own the
property. Morgan calls out, but gets no response. He enters
the barn and runs into a bevy of giant chickens. One nearly
pecks him to death until he kills it with a pitchfork. Mrs.
Skinner (Ida Lupino) greets him with a shotgun, then asks
him in to see something that scares her. He is reluctant: "Hey
look, lady, I've already seen your chickens."

Gnawed holes in the wall confirm that rats have got into
the Food. She points to a kettle of slop: "This is the way it
comes to us from the Lord." And even as she speaks, a wasp
perches on the lip of a jar marked "F.O.T.G."

The Skinners are as careless with the Food as their original
counterparts. Her explanation that the Food bubbles out of
the ground, however, is a significant deviation from the
novel. Instead of a scientific invention, the Food originates in
Nature ("from the Lord") in a kind of spontaneous genera-
tion. A realization of Morgan's father's prediction, the Food
represents Nature's reaction to environmental pollution,
and, similar to Wells's suggestion, acts as the backlash to
reckless and irresponsible Science. However, the Food's
coming from an obscure "natural" source, not from Science,
relegates the film to the horror genre, not sf.

Mr. Skinner (John McLiam), absent from the farm while
trying to sell the Food to Jack Bensington in the city, returns
via the ferry. He drives a red Volkswagen (the color
foreboding his violent death) which, as cars will do in such
situations, stalls on a deserted road. In a gruesome scene, the
giant rats surround the car, break in through the windows
and doors, and drag his body into the woods. Skinner's
certain fate differs from that of Wells's character, whose
disappearance can only be explained by speculation. The
lisping language of the original Skinner makes him more
humorous and interesting than his flat film counterpart. And
his glass eye, the indifferent evil eye, contrasted with his
human sympathetic one, seems more significant in that he,
who appears torn between ambivalent natures, might have
been torn apart by the effects of an ambiguous Science.

The rats' breaking into Skinner's car signifies Nature's
contempt for human technology. Related to the fences

shown earlier, the automobile gives a person a sense of power. It acts like a mobile fortress, protecting him from the elements while enabling him to trespass on Nature. Nature continues its defiance, however, when the rats later overrun the mobile home of a young couple (Tom Stovall and Belinda Balaski).

Bensington's[21] car, a big brown Plymouth, appears before he does. Close-up shots of the front end show it plowing ahead like a juggernaut through grass and mudholes. Aloof and indifferent, it whizzes past the remains of Skinner's abandoned VW and ignores the waving pleas of the couple with the disabled mobile home. In a long shot of a tranquil lake, the car suddenly enters the frame, speeding along and billowing exhaust fumes.

Confident in the impregnability of his car, Jack Bensington (Ralph Meeker) later suggests that they use it to forge through the rats and escape to the ferry. Morgan disapproves and wins support from the others. When the rats later surround the house, Morgan, unable to know for certain if Bensington was wrong, second-guesses himself. The audience, however, knows what happened to Skinner and that, ultimately, Nature is more powerful than a mere human invention.

Morgan and Brian easily destroy the giant wasps, as Cossar had done, except that they use dynamite, an explosion more dramatic for the film than a simple smoking and burning of the nest. In dealing with the rats, however, the film greatly expands their role.

Wells's giant rats create panic, killing sheep and horses, but never killing a human. In a terrifying episode, their attack on the country doctor almost succeeds, but he escapes. He runs to a bakery shop where the baker's cautious delay in opening the door is a great suspenseful touch and reflects Wells's insight into human nature. The film, on the other hand, because it depends on the rats for its primary effect, repeatedly shows them mauling and dismembering the cast for the sake of repulsive horror.[22]

In the book, Cossar's final confrontation with the rats contains some tense moments, but the episode is never drawn explicitly enough to provoke genuine thrills. Even his ferreting through the rat tunnels, which could have been described more vividly for drama's sake, ends abruptly when, with only one rat left, "Cossar and the lantern went in again and slew it." In contrast, the film ends with a lengthy, tense confrontation at the Skinners' farm, where all the characters have congregated. Bensington and Mrs. Skinner become rat food, and Brian gets dissected trying to help Morgan electrify a fence.

Morgan finally dynamites the dam. The ensuing flood swirls about the house, while from the second-floor balcony, the four survivors watch the waters drown the rats. As an anticlimax, a giant white rat, the supposed intelligent leader of the pack, steps from behind the roof and attacks the little group. Morgan's gun clicks empty. He turns it around and clubs the rodent with the butt. The bloodied creature falls into the water and sinks to the bottom.

After the flooding subsides, Morgan and Tom gather the dead rats into a heap. In a kind of baptismal ritual, Lorna pours the last bottle of the Food on them and throws away the jar. Morgan douses the pile with gasoline and sets it on fire. The water and fire act as purifying agents, cleansing the ill effects of a human mistake. The two couples who leave the island become Adams and Eves going out to try anew to correct the errors of the past.

The film then presents an epilogue. While Morgan narrates how his father had accurately predicted Nature's rebellion against humanity's environmental abuse, two jars that had contained the Food are washed away by a rivulet and eventually carried into a stream where dairy cows are watering. One cow eats the residue inside the jar. The scene cuts to a schoolroom, where on the wall a picture of a milk bottle is captioned, "Our most nearly perfect food." The camera shows children holding their milk cartons, then tracks to a single boy seated, sipping his milk from a straw.

This scene makes *The Food* a "prequel" leading back into Gordon's earlier *Village of the Giants*. One weakness in the ending is that, while it suggests something threatening, it lacks any clear indication of what effect, good or bad, the Food will have on humans. For Wells, expanded size means expanded intellect, something he claims is desirable and beneficial. In the film, only physical growth is evident. Perhaps, like the Goo in *The Village,* its ethical application would depend on the individual who takes it.

Notes

1. Wells's novel is known more familiarly by the first half of this long title.

2. See Wagner's definition of analogy in the Introduction, p. 12.

3. Roger Corman produced and directed the leading low-budget sf-horror films of the fifties and sixties, setting trends with early fluff like *The Day the World Ended* (1955) and *It Conquered the World* (1956).

4. Douglas Menville, *A Historical and Critical Survey of the Science-Fiction Film* (New York: Arno Press, 1975), p. 151. (Reprinted from Hollis Alpert and Charles Beaumont, "The Horror of It All," *Playboy,* March, 1959, p. 88.)

5. An argument might be made that Gordon had the potential to make a good film. He controls many aspects of his projects, directing, writing, and special effects, and in all these his capabilities at times are apparent. If his slipshod finished products are intentional, as he says, it suggests that, with more serious attention to detail, he might have constructed better films.

6. This is another film based on an H. G. Wells story and having nothing in common with it.

7. Despite this change in style and the fact that his subsequent works fall into a predictive pattern of promoting utopian ideals in a futuristic society, Wells's skills as a gifted writer remain evident. He admits in his *Experiment in Autobiography* that he altered his style purposely, deserting his literary approach for something he thought more important, a clear, straightforward message.

8. An important earlier novel to compare in this case is *The Invisible Man,* where the Narrator seems a member of the

village and has compiled information from interviews and news accounts to write his story. The Narrator of *The Food* plays a similar role, but unlike the former's less obtrusive comments, his explicit assertions, such as the "futility" of opposing the "public mind," sound too often like authorial intervention. Henry James, originally an avid Wells fan, called this device intrusive, and his criticism led to a rift between the two contemporaries.

9. The alternative name, Titanophorbia, seems more fitting in terms of the Food's most obvious effect, hypertrophy. The debate over the name suggests the inability of the scientists to predict the exact consequences of their experiment. At the same time, neither name accurately reflects Wells's intention, which is to have an expanded intellect accompany the increase in size.

10. All of Wells's early scientific romances propound this paradox of Science, that it endangers life in order to enrich it with greater knowledge. However, the tendency is to stress the negative, that Science courts a Forbidden Knowledge which harms more than helps. *The Food* is among the first of his writings to toll the virtues of Science so explicitly. Scientific development, along with education and the nurturing of the imagination, becomes part of the cornerstone for Wells's utopian theories.

11. See Chapter III, p. 142, note 1.

12. In Wells's later works, this becomes his central debate between high-minded, imaginative thinkers and shallow-minded common folk. Consider the central ideas in the two films discussed in the Appendices, *Things to Come* and *The Man Who Could Work Miracles*.

13. The term "Goo" replaces Wells's "Food." This suits Gordon's attempt to use juvenile jargon to differentiate the two teenage groups. Words and phrases like "groovy" and "dig that nitty-gritty" become associated more with the Rebels than with the Village Teens, who tend to talk with less slang and appear in greater harmony with the adults. Despite this meaningful consideration of language, however, most of it is trite, collapsing into numerous clichés ("turn the tables,"

"back to the drawing board," "we'll just have to live with it"). The extravagant repetition of the word "just" is a good barometer of the fatuous dialogue.

14. This scene exemplified several of the faults of the film. In a matte shot, the ducks appear gigantic, dancing side-by-side with the teens. However, at times, their tails, when crossing the matte border, appear truncated, and the strings, which force them to bounce in time with the music, are visible. Using the ducks as puppets is a cruel, inhumane act, the more so considering the senselessness of it.

    This scene, like many others, becomes too drawn out, belaboring a joke that was not funny to begin with. At the same time, the camera cuts repeatedly to close-ups of the women's shaking breasts, hips, and derrières, a pointless sexual exploitation which recurs throughout the film.

15. Already noted, Redwood's Herakleophorbia works only on creatures whose growing cycle is not over. Genius's Goo works on any animal who takes it.

16. Mike plays David trying to get the better of the Goliaths. (In this way, he vaguely corresponds to Wells's Caterham, who was dubbed "Jack the Giant-Killer.") In retaliation, Freddy throws a spear at Mike. He says to Merrie, "I'm gonna give you his head on a silver platter." The Rebel Harry (Kevin O'Neal) smiles, "That was Samson and Delilah." Actually, it was Herod and Salome, but even if corrected, the allusion is irrelevant.

17. When the Rebels first grow to giant-size, their bodies rip through their clothes. In a parody of Adam and Eve suddenly finding themselves naked, they use the theater's props and curtains to hide behind. Now, after shrinking, the Rebels' clothes should be extremely large. Instead, they are just a bit baggy, not an accurate rendering of the proper relative scale.

18. Under-reaction is an important comic device for Gordon, who uses it frequently in *The Village*. People show little or no response to unusual events, as when first seeing the giants (except in the case of the spider, which is downplayed by feeble, meaningless dialogue after Mike kills it). The ducks' appearance at the night-club provokes no more than mild

amusement from the teens, who continue to dance. The giant cat is simply chased away by Genius's dog. And Genius is never surprised by the amazing odd results of his several failed experiments to recreate the Goo.

These incongruous lackadaisical responses to unusual situations become mere silliness, not humor. However, one scene does come off as genuinely funny, when the giant Rebels first appear at the teen dance in the park. The Sheriff drives up to tell the youngsters to stop making so much noise. The deputy, having spotted the giants, finally gets the Sheriff to look upward. With hardly more than a dry, crotchety reaction to an inconvenient prank, the Sheriff remarks, "For crying out loud, now what's this?" After an awkwardly drawn-out pause, he adds, "Listen, I don't pretend to know what's going on around here, but it's just been brought to my attention that the theater's been broken into last night and I've got a pretty good idea who did it. Now I want you to go back to the theater and wait there."

For all the times this device is used, it has to succeed at least once.

19. One example should suffice. When Morgan, the hero, is about to set out to destroy the giant wasps' nest, Lorna, his potential love interest, nonchalantly says, "You don't like women around when you're doing your thing, do you?"

"What's my thing?"

"Facing danger."

"I don't mind."

"Are you sure?"

"What's there to mind?"

"Oh, can I come along?"

"Why not?"

"It won't be easy, but I think I can learn to like you. You're the first man I've met who was bold enough to beat Bensington on the one-upmanship."

"Really? You're nice yourself."

If written in earnest, this shows Gordon's glaring ineptitude for dialogue (he wrote the screenplay). If written to give teenagers something to "enjoy scoffing at," it works, but contradicts the more serious, horrible, gory scenes, and creates a discrepancy which hinders the audience's involvement with the film. (*The Village*, though nonsensical, is at least consistently nonsensical.)

20. Looking like blue cut-outs vibrating on stiff wires, the flying wasps are the clumsiest of the special effects. The two times a wasp attaches itself to a person's back, the person looks as if he is being attacked by a child's knapsack. The giant rats which appear later are more convincing.

21. Jack Bensington, a businessman, replaces Dr. Bensington the scientist. He is accompanied by his assistant, Lorna Scott (Pamela Franklin), a bacteriologist whose scientific knowledge means nothing since it never plays a part in the story.

22. *The Empire of the Ants,* made a year after *The Food,* uses the same kind of special effects to arouse the same emotions. In fact, it is exactly the same story, except that instead of rats, ants, made gigantic after eating radioactive waste, do the slashing and tearing apart of their victims.

CONCLUSION

As adaptations of H. G. Wells's scientific romances, the films discussed above all incorporate two similar narrative elements. First, deviating from their sources, they unanimously include a love interest which Wells omits (at least literally) in these novels (with one exception, *The Food of the Gods*). Second, paralleling Wells, they imitate his ambiguous sense of closure.

A practical explanation for the filmmakers' obsession with a romantic intrigue appears in a scene from *King Kong* (Cooper and Schoedsack, 1933). Carl Denham (Robert Armstrong), a director of wild animal films, becomes riled when Weston (Sam Hardy), a theatrical agent, questions his needing a girl for the first time in one of his projects:

> "Holy Mackerel, do you think I wanna haul a woman around?"
> "Then, why?"
> "Because the public—bless 'em—must have a pretty face to look at."
> "Sure. Everybody likes romance."

Denham's inserting a love affair into the unlikely context of a wildlife documentary shows what absurd irrelevancies a filmmaker will exploit to insure financial success.

Weston not only understands, but agrees with the tactic. His approval validates the filmmakers' opinion of what the general public wants and justifies the rationale for the introduction into all the adaptations of a love interest not included in the original stories. It becomes a filmmaker's convention, a necessity (whether real or perceived) for attracting an audience.[1] Wells was deliberate in his omission. He kept the romance in the thrill of the experience, not in the boy-girl relationship, something suggested in Denham's lament to Weston: "Isn't there any romance or adventure in the world without having a flapper in it?"[2]

As if to subordinate the function of the love interest, most of the films contain ambiguities which counter the potential fairy-tale quality of the romance. The time-traveling George and the Martian-hunting Clayton Forrester appear more like father-figures than heroic lovers. A peck on the forehead is the most passionate George gets with Weena, and his return to her is merely Filby's romantic presumption. Forrester never kisses Ann, and at the end of the film she stands apart from him in the consoling arms of a clergyman, still another father-figure in her life. In the television remake of *The Time Machine*, however, and in Meyer's *Time After Time*, the romantic outcome appears more conclusive.

In *Island of Lost Souls*, Edward Parker leaves Moreau's island with Ruth, but has lost the more passionate "animal" love of Lota. Don Taylor's version of *Moreau* offers a strong suggestion that Maria, in leaving the island, may revert to a previous feline form. Jack Griffin as the Invisible Man finds that his reckless experiment, instead of uniting him with Flora, deprives him of her. And in *The First Men in the Moon*, romance is totally undermined. In the opening frame story, we learn that the late Katherine had married a dull, homely clerk who barely remembers she had been his wife. In the inset story, Bedford would have seemed her likely lover, but his callous, devious behavior ruins his candidacy as romantic hero. Even Cavor appears a potential suitor, but his dedication to science and penchant for closed doors foils his chances to win her.

Both of Bert I. Gordon's versions of *The Food of the Gods* contain the cliché formulaic romance. In fact, they are obvious to the point of ludicrousness. In the 1977 film, for example, during their frightening battle with the giant rats, the heroine tells the hero she would like to make love to him. He kisses her: "The first thing we'll do when we get back to the mainland is continue this conversation." And when they finally defeat the rats, we automatically assume that that is what they do.

The second common feature in most of the adaptations is

their retention of Wells's ambiguous sense of closure. Wells's stories conclude open-ended: the Time Traveller may return someday; the Invisible Man's notes may fall into the hands of someone who can decipher their mysteries; if Martians have attacked us, other aliens may exist to repeat the invasion;[3] the outcome of the battle between the giants of the Food and the little people is left undetermined.

The films adopt similar ambiguities. At first, they may seem to conclude with a feeling of finality, but closer examination shows it to be only the illusion of an "end." Filby surmises where George ultimately disappears to on his Time Machine, but while his romantic speculation appeals to our sentimentality, it is only an unsubstantiated guess. In the 1933 version of *Moreau,* the Beast Men gain revenge by torturing the doctor on his surgical table, although we do not see him finally killed. The Invisible Man dies on a hospital bed, but the main ingredient for his serum is known to other scientists, which means that someone may later duplicate it (and several do, in numerous sequels). The questions raised by the television announcer in *First Men* become arguable, unanswerable riddles. These ambiguities enrich the films, making them more complementary to the novels, at least in approach, if not in substance.

Finally, the ultimate indication of Wells's link to film is found in the ironic self-reflexive nature of *The Time Machine.* The story begins with Wells's inventor arguing with his dinner guests about a hypothetical fourth dimension. He claims that everything which exists in the three dimensions of Space must also exist in a fourth plane which he calls the "Time-Dimension." At one point, the Medical Man refutes him:

> . . . why cannot we move about in Time as we move about in the other dimensions of Space? . . . you cannot move at all in Time, you cannot get away from the present moment.

The inventor answers:

> My dear sir, that is just where you are wrong. . . . We are always getting away from the present moment. Our

mental existences, which are immaterial and have no
dimensions, are passing along the Time-Dimension
with a uniform velocity from the cradle to the grave. . . .
if I am recalling an incident very vividly I go back to the
instant of its occurrence: I become absent-minded, as
you say. I jump back for a moment. Of course, we have
no means of staying back for any length of time. . . .
why should [a man] not hope that ultimately he may be
able to stop or accelerate his drift along the Time-
Dimension, or even turn about and travel the other
way? (Ch. 1)

What the inventor has described is the nature and power of
storytelling, a notion made more obvious when he flippantly
dismisses his tale (and by implication, his machine) as
something he "dreamed . . . in the workshop." And while it
relates to oral and written stories, the term "Time Machine"
has an even more literal relevance toward film. Stories
stimulate the imagination, a figurative "machine," causing it
to invent mental pictures which shift us from our "present
moment" to some other imagined time frame. By analogy,
the film projector becomes an actual Time Machine, supply-
ing external pictures which lead us from our "present
moment" to another "projected" time (and place).

It seems fitting that this man with a highly visual style of
writing should write a story which suggests the nature of film.
And it also seems appropriate that with his prolific output of
ideas, he should be the prime source of a new literary genre.
The extent to which Wells has influenced science fiction goes
beyond the six books already discussed and appears too
widespread to define within any limits.

Besides the obvious adaptations of his most famous
novels, many films appear to have been influenced by his
various works, either directly or indirectly. *Metropolis* (Fritz
Lang, 1926) and *Sleeper* (Woody Allen, 1973), tonal extremes as they are, owe something to *When the Sleeper
Wakes* (1899) for their themes of revolt against dystopia. *In
the Days of the Comet* (1906) and the short story "The Star,"
(1899), about the disruptive effects on humankind from a
comet grazing earth's orbit, seem sources for the cataclysmic

events in *When Worlds Collide* (Pal, 1951), and *The Day of the Triffids* (Steve Sekely, 1963), the latter also a derivative of *The War of the Worlds*. *Star-Begotten* contains the seeds for *Village of the Damned* (Wolf Rilla, 1960) and *Invasion of the Body Snatchers* (Don Siegel, 1956; remake, Philip Kaufman, 1978), where extraterrestrial life implants itself into humans, mutating them into its alien species. And if *The Sea Lady* (1902) is considered biological sf, the story of a mermaid persuading a human to follow a different, happier dream occurs in *Mr. Peabody and the Mermaid* (Irving Pichel, 1948) and *Splash* (Ron Howard, 1984).

Many of Wells's short stories also serve as apparent sources for filmmakers. "The Flowering of the Strange Orchid" (1895), where the discovery of a rare plant, the object of a man's quest for fame, nearly proves fatal when it turns out to be carnivorous, bears resemblance to *The Little Shop of Horrors* (Roger Corman, 1960; readapted by Frank Oz from a Broadway musical version, 1986). "In the Abyss" (1897) presents the sea as an unexplored frontier and introduces a sea-alien which prefigures innumerable monsters such as those found in *The Creature from the Black Lagoon* (Jack Arnold, 1954), *Deep-Star-Six* (Sean S. Cunningham, 1989), and *The Abyss* (James Cameron, 1989). "The New Accelerator" (1903) is a drug which, by speeding up the metabolism, enables a person to move about invisibly while others appear to move in slow motion around him. The television movie, *The Girl, the Gold Watch and Everything* (William Wiard, 1980) is based on this concept, the same effect achieved when the wearer presses a switch on a watch. And in a Star Trek episode, the phenomenon reoccurs in aliens who attempt to take over the Enterprise.

Since sf depends on concept more than on character, Wells's science fiction seems the likely source of ideas for writers in this genre. And since his external conflicts and visualized fantastic images are realized in his descriptive powers, his works also serve as a valuable source for film, the visual medium. As implied by Jorge Louis Borges, his timeless themes and mythical concepts contain a layered, multi-dimensional quality, and his stories, which carry the illusion of concreteness, often present paradoxes and unfeasible situations. This slippery definiteness becomes his greatest virtue, for it allows writers and filmmakers to reconceptualize and reshape his ideas for their own purpose. Reading his works, one sees that his reservoir of ideas has not been, and may never be, depleted.

Notes

1. In his article "Filming *War of the Worlds*," Pal reveals the filmmakers' attitude toward this subject as an unquestionable requirement:

> . . . in the film business you have to be practical. No one is less interested in doing routine boy meets girl stories than I. But a boy-and-girl theme is necessary even in a science-fiction film of the scope of *War of the Worlds*. Audiences want it. (*Astounding Science Fiction,* October 1953, p. 102.)

2. Ironically, two of Wells's early scientific romances which do contain a love interest have not been adapted directly for film. *When the Sleeper Wakes* (1899) includes a contrived, syrupy love affair between Graham and Helen Wotton, a flaw Wells recognized when he revised the novel in 1910 and deleted the maudlin relationship. *In the Days of the Comet* (1906) starts out as rivalry in a love triangle and ends as socially-acceptable free love.

3. Also consider the Narrator's last sentence in *The War of the Worlds:* "And strangest of all is it to hold my wife's hand again, and to think that I have counted her, and that she has counted me, among the dead." The use of the present perfect tense instead of the past perfect connotes something dark and ominous. What this might be exactly is not clear, as is typical in Wells's ambiguous endings. One possibility is that, while they "had" thought each other dead, they still do so. The Martian invasion proves humans not the superior race but one small species in a universal scheme. The awareness has left them with morbid feelings about the human condition and its relative insignificance in the greater cosmic design.

APPENDIX A:
THE SHAPE OF THINGS TO COME

A: Futuristic History Lesson

H. G. Wells's *The Shape of Things to Come* (1933)[1] combines historical fact with speculative fancy to produce an "Outline of the Future," an apparent fictional sequel to his 1920 opus, *The Outline of History*. The story covers over 200 years. After cataloging events of the previous and present century which have led to the prevailing conditions of 1933, it cites immediate circumstances as the reason for what happens next. In 1940, a great war engulfs the world, followed by widespread pestilence in the late Twentieth Century. Gradually, an experimental Modern State emerges and evolves into a utopia by the year 2104. Humankind finally embraces the attitudes which stabilize its existence: removal of sexual taboos, eradication of jealousy, and adherence to a "confluent" social mind.

The text reads like a history book, a dry, indifferent narrative relating a series of significant episodes in a cause-effect sequence. It lacks empathetic characters and a centralized conflict, and as such is less a story than a fantastic "essay" forecasting a utopian World State. A Frame Narrator ("H.G.W.") introduces the book, explaining it as his transcription of a manuscript given him by a deceased colleague, Dr. Phillip Raven. Raven had dreamt of an opened tome which, as the pages turned, enabled him to read the recorded events of the future. On waking, he made notes of his vision, and the result is this volume.

Things to Come (1936, London Films): Science as the Foundation for Utopia. In this futuristic image of Everytown, people dwarfed by their architectural superstructures and advanced transit system suggests how technology must dominate lives to provide social stability while fostering progress.

B: The Film's Improvement on the Novel

Wells's film, *Things to Come* (1936),[2] born out of the novel, is a visual representation of the original's abstract proposals. It condenses the expansive scope of the novel, omitting the historical perspective and limiting the span of time to about 100 years (1940 to 2036). It contains five sections comparable to the present-to-future portion of the novel: Present Indifference to World Events, Degeneration (World War and Pestilence), Political Reform, Urban Reconstruction, and the World State.

As a more concrete presentation, the film transforms the original's general descriptions into more localized characters and events. Several characters, appearing at the beginning, reappear at the end as descendants of the earlier families. The main character, John Cabal[3] (Raymond Massey), after his role in the first four sections, is reborn in the final section as his grandson, Oswald Cabal, political leader of the new Modern State. Producing a contrast from the indifferent tone and episodic quality of the original, this device makes the story more personal and gives it more continuity and coherence. The audience follows events by seeing definite effects on visible characters rather than by reading a distant, generalized report. The result is a greater arousal of audience empathy.

The story takes place in an English city called Everytown, a localized setting which represents what is happening in all the cities of the world. It undergoes demolishment in the war and rebirth in the period of reconstruction, an example of humankind's irrepressible potential for industry.

While the novel broods on contrived hypothetical reasons for the world's finally coming around to Wells's "saner" way of thinking, the film signifies a return to the allegorical mode of Wells's earlier scientific romances. It may appear heavy-handed and overly explicit at times, but the film possesses the visual quality of his former descriptive style. Perhaps his ability to contribute to the screenplay indicates that that power had never really left him.

C: A Mosaic of the Scientific Romances

During his writing career, Wells's concrete descriptions, paradoxical concepts, and allegorical stories may have yielded to a more direct and less ambiguous message, but *Things to Come* embodies many of the central concepts of his earlier scientific romances.[4]

The vision of *The Time Machine,* for instance, pits predestination against will, as voiced by the two Narrators with their different attitudes toward the future. The visual impact of *Things to Come,* the whole story taking place in a near-to-distant future, presents a schematic of one possible destiny for humanity. In the conclusion, Passworthy (Edward Chapman) tells Cabal that "we're such little creatures . . . little animals." Cabal rejects the analogy, and when he offers humanity's choices, "all the universe or nothingness," he echoes *The Time Machine's* debate over succumbing to an unchangeable fate or, by an act of will, persisting in the struggle for survival.

Prendick's final thoughts in *The Island of Doctor Moreau* also have significant bearing on the conclusion of the film. The doctor's island ultimately represents a microcosm of life, and while observing the interrelationships of himself, Moreau, Montgomery, and the Beast People, Prendick despairs, feeling "a blind fate, a vast pitiless mechanism, seemed to cut and shape the fabric of existence . . . " (Ch. 16). After arriving in England, he still cannot overcome his disturbing fixation that random chance governs life. Seeking some kind of escape, he takes to star-gazing and finds "a sense of infinite peace and protection in the glittering hosts of heaven" (Ch. 22). He concludes, "There it must be . . . in the vast and eternal laws of matter, and not in the daily cares and sins and troubles of men, that whatever is more than animal within us must find its solace and hope."

Things to Come repeats this idea but in expanded, more optimistic terms. In the final section, the Modern World State has achieved security and stability. Cabal and others, motivated by a relentless quest for progress, propose to increase their (that is, humanity's) knowledge by sending two persons into space, Cabal's daughter Catherine (Pearl Argyle) and Passworthy's son Maurice (Kenneth Villiers). Opposing them is Theotocopulos (Cedric Hardwicke), an artist who incites the masses to rebel against the pursuit of progress and to remain content with their present achievements which have assured them stability and happiness.

To launch the spaceship, scientists have erected a giant Space Gun, which, as a metaphor for Science, signifies a recurring motif for Wells. A "gun," like Science, has power both to destroy and to serve humankind. In competent hands, such as Cabal's, the space launch becomes a meaningful, positive venture. For Prendick, the heavens represent an escape from the routine trivialities of life, a new perspective from which humanity may learn to appreciate itself as more than animal. For Cabal, the heavens represent not escape but direction toward the illimitable potentials for expansion, the endless progress that humans must pursue to prove they are more than animal.

The War of the Worlds and *The Invisible Man* share the motif of the alien invasion that disrupts order and forces society to examine and reorganize itself. *The War of the Worlds* presents a catastrophic invasion, while *The Invisible Man* is a more restricted, localized scare. By destroying complacency and routine, both try to awaken humanity's vain estimate of itself.

Things to Come is filled with "invasions" that disrupt social order. The attack on England is the first and marks the beginning of a war that creates total world upheaval. The drawn-out conflict ends but is followed by the disease known as the Wandering Sickness, a restlessness that drives the infected outdoors to be shot by those fearing their contagiousness. After the Boss establishes his dictatorship in Everytown, Cabal arrives to assert the "sanity" of his "Wings over the World" federation. And later, in the Everytown of 2036, Theotocopulos leads the masses in an attempt to wreck the Space Gun and subdue the restless spirit of progress (from his point of view, a kind of "wandering sickness").

Every instance of disruption requires a period of reorganization, for better (Wings over the World) or worse (the Boss's dictatorship), until, by trial and error, society must finally choose the most efficient, beneficial means of government (that is, according to Wells's causal theory, a chain of "accidents," which lead inevitably to his concept of utopia).

Of all the early scientific romances, *The Food of the Gods,* stressing the idea that progress, at all costs, must override stasis and complacency, has the strongest relationship to *Things to Come.* In the early Christmas scene at Cabal's house, Passworthy claims that war "stimulates progress." Cabal argues that "you can overdo a stimulant."

In the next scene, the world plunges into war, and the effects on civilization bear out both predictions. Post-war Everytown looks like a desolate, primitive encampment. The dictatorial Boss wears a furry animal pelt, suggesting a regression to the barbaric rule of prehistoric times. By contrast, Cabal's Wings over the World, at the same time, has made extensive advancement in air technology, the power that enables them to subdue the world under the rule of "common sense" and "sanity."

After the reconstruction, civilization reaches a magnificent peak. Theotocopulos argues that since order and happiness have been attained, humankind has no further need to pursue progress at the risk of disturbing the status quo. Cabal, however, claims that this is what differentiates human from animal, the unceasing quest to learn more about ourself and our relationship with the universe:

> [There is] rest enough for the individual man. Too much and too soon, and we call it death. But for Man no rest and no ending. He must go on. Conquest beyond conquest. . . . And if we're no more than animals we must snatch each little scrap of happiness and live and suffer and pass, mattering no more than all the other animals do or have done. It is this or that. All the universe or nothingness.

The Food of the Gods ends with the Children of the Food preparing to battle the little people. The giants represent the literal and figurative growth produced by Science, while the little people signify the little minds that adhere to tradition and fixed ideas. The outcome of the confrontation is omitted and presages Cabal's final unanswerable question to Passworthy, a question indirectly posed to the audience as to their choice of progress or stasis: "Which will it be, Passworthy? Which will it be?"

Various accounts of the making of this film point to the main contributors as Wells, producer Alexander Korda, and director William Cameron Menzies. However, Wells's influence on everything from music (he insisted on composer Arthur Bliss) to costumes (his Samurai designs) to script suggests the work is predominantly his. Despite his contesting the final product, the film vividly reflects his personal vision of humankind and its potential for accomplishment.

Notes

1. *The Shape* has obvious predecessors in Wells's *The World Set Free* (1914), *Men Like Gods* (1923), and *The Dream* (1924). All share vaguely similar narrative structures and attempt to awaken humanity's potential to create a utopian society for itself.

2. A 1979 film entitled *H. G. Wells' "The Shape of Things to Come"* (George McCowan, director) gives credence to Gene Phillips's argument that, when a film adapts from literature, its primary title, and especially the author's name attached to it, misleads the public into believing this mediocre film is associated with Wells's work. The dialogue is trite, the plot borrows heavily from several "Star Trek" episodes, and the special effects, although well-executed, appear imitations of George Lucas's *Star Wars*. The only relationship between the film and the title is the gratuitous insertion of John Caball (spelled differently from the original and played by Barry Morse).

3. The initials J.C. automatically suggest him a Christ-figure, and in a limited way he is. He is prepared to make a literal self-sacrifice by accosting the dictatorial Boss (energetically portrayed by Ralph Richardson), interceding for peaceful universal reconciliation. Without having to lose his life, he

triumphs over the Boss and leads the airmen's group, Wings Over the World, in redeeming civilization.

4. Although only the film is discussed here, the novel incorporates many of these same themes but in a more direct, abstract manner. Raven's story ends with a confirmation of humanity's triumph, as opposed to Cabal's question. And the Frame narrator closes with remarks that negate the ambiguousness of Raven's dream, saying explicitly that whether true or not, the only hope for humankind is to make that dream reality.

APPENDIX B:
THE MAN WHO COULD WORK MIRACLES

A: Wells's Original Story: Schematic for a Thing to Come

Although more a fantasy than science fiction, H. G. Wells's "The Man Who Could Work Miracles" (1897) deserves attention in this study for its connection with film and for its thematic relevance to Wells's early works. As in many of his scientific romances, this short story exploits a wishful fantasy common to most people. Like the ability to travel through time or to move about invisibly, the power to materialize objects and to manipulate people at will has universal appeal. Also, as in those other stories, he treats his subject in a satirical way: the marvelous discovery leads to an ambiguous outcome, exposing the negative and positive aspects of human nature and society.

Before examining the film adaptation (directed by Lothar Mendes, 1937), it is necessary to present a lengthy synopsis of the original. The short story is divided into several distinct sections which are later transferred to the film in a parallel but expanded treatment. They may be labeled as follows: Introduction; Discovery of the "Gift"; Fotheringay's Workplace; The Constable Winch Dilemma; Meeting with Maydig; World Catastrophe; and Restoration of Normalcy.

In the Introduction, we realize that the Narrative voice assumes an omniscient viewpoint from some place outside this world. The reason for such a position becomes evident when, halfway through the story, it tells us that although we do not remember, "the reader was killed in a violent and unprecedented manner a year ago." At the end of the story we learn of the cataclysm which, if not for a miracle, would have annihilated us. The Narrator, however, immune to the effects of the calamity, is able to tell us what happened. As with a number of Wells's stories, the tale becomes self-reflexive in that here the nature of a miracle reinforces the plausibility of the story.

The Narrator introduces us to an ordinary, simple-minded clerk named George McWhirter Fotheringay, a "sceptic . . . addicted to assertive argument," who suddenly and inexplicably acquires the ability to perform miracles. Drinking with his cronies at the Long Dragon, he refutes the possibility of miracles, defining them as "something contrariwise to the course of nature done by power of Will. . . . " He attempts to prove his point, but ironically contradicts himself when he commands a ceiling lamp to turn upside down and keep burning—and it does. His will falters and the lamp crashes to the floor.

Ejected from the tavern, he returns to his flat. He lacks the imagination to try anything astounding or original, and he performs a series of familiar, trivial conjuring tricks to convince himself of the reality of his new gift. The next day at Gomshott's, where he works, he produces a pair of diamond cuff links for himself, but makes them disappear when he thinks the boss's son may see them and question him.

That evening, on his way home, George inadvertently blocks the road by transforming his walking stick into a large rose tree. Constable Winch approaches. George again fears discovery and tells the tree, "Go back." The inappropriate command, meant as "Change back," drives the tree into Winch, who promptly accuses him of assault. George, too unimaginative to invent an excuse, admits that he was "working a miracle." An argument ensues, and George, indignant, shouts the euphemism, "Go to Hades!" Winch promptly disappears. George realizes what he has done and alters his command by transferring the constable to San Francisco. From then on, to protect himself against Winch's retaliation, he intermittently wills the officer back in San Francisco. He often refers to the incident, but paralyzed between guilt and fear of punishment, remains totally indecisive on how to resolve it. He can only regret his momentary lapse in self-control.

On Sunday evening, George makes a rare visit to chapel

services where, moved by Mr. Maydig's sermon, he approaches the minister for advice. With a few trivial miracles—changing a tobacco jar into a bowl of violets, then into a goldfish bowl, and finally into a pigeon—he convinces Maydig of his power. Maydig expresses reservation: "It's incredible. You are either a most extraordinary . . . But no—." Even when finally persuaded, he cannot quite reconcile his belief and his feelings: "The power to work miracles is a gift . . . hitherto it has come very rarely and to exceptional people. But in this case—." Maydig's hesitancy to believe stems from George's ordinary demeanor. Yet he cannot deny the visible proof.

Maydig invites George to dine with him. The unappetizing meal leads to a discussion of Mrs. Minchin, Maydig's housekeeper, who is asleep upstairs. George offers to "make her a better woman" and utters a brief incantation. Maydig steps upstairs to inspect the change. He returns, marveling that she has renounced her alcoholic ways for the path of temperance. This inspires him to conduct George in a night of general reformation of London.

After changing all the beer and alcohol to water and making other "needed" renovations and transformations of the area, George realizes it is three a.m. and that he should return home to sleep. Maydig reminds him of his power to control everything and suggests he stop time by stopping the rotation of the world. George does so. The result is a worldwide cataclysm, for the suddenly halted rotation leads to the destruction of the earth.

Fortunately, George thinks quickly enough to will himself invulnerable. Floating in the whirlwind of Chaos, he collects his wits and commands two final miracles: " . . . let me lose my miraculous power, let my will become just like anybody else's will, and all these dangerous miracles stopped. . . . And the second is—let me be back just before the miracles begin; . . . everything as it was—me back in the Long Dragon just before I drank my half-pint. . . . "

In the final section, the world returns to its previous state of normalcy, George forgetting his former power: " . . . his mind and memory therefore were now just as they had been at the time when this story began. . . . And among other things, of course, he still did not believe in miracles." The story ends with George in the pub proposing his definition of a miracle: "It's something contrariwise to the course of nature done by power of Will. . . . "

The last line, coupled with the sequence of events, bears out the epigram of the story: "A Pantoum in Prose." Reflecting the rhyme scheme of a pantoum (abab, bcbc, cdcd . . . xaxa), this story unfolds slowly, reaches its climax, and ends with a return to the initial key words that precipitated the events. Like the pantoum, then, where no matter how far the rhyme scheme travels from the original quatrain and its first rhymed words, the story must find its way back to its source in a predetermined cyclical structure.

The Man Who Could Work Miracles (1937, London Films): Trivial Pursuits. Fotheringay (Roland Young), performing one of his first miracles, upends his candle, precursing his eventual upending of the world. The trite experiment belies the enormity of his power and signifies how humanity's limited imagination inhibits its ability to make use of its fullest potential.

Thematically, the story raises the same two questions posed by the Frame Narrator at the end of *The Time Machine*. The Time Traveller's discovery suggests that if humanity is governed by laws of predestination, it need not make any effort to change things or to resist Fate. However, Human Will urges us to defy disagreeable laws of Nature (especially, for Wells, Darwinian theories of evolution), to struggle against what appears our intended doom. Faced with Oedipus's dilemma, we may choose to be like the unimaginative Fotheringay, lacking the vision to use our opportunities effectively and surrendering to our allotted Fate. Or we may choose to be more like the inventive Time Traveller, applying our imagination productively and seeking a way out of our bounded field of existence.

B: Wells's Film: An Expanded View

Considering that forty years elapse before Wells adapts his story to film, it seems remarkable how faithful the film is to the original. His attitude toward Science, progress, and human nature has changed so much by this time that one expects to see the adaptation revised to fit his new conceptions and new purposes in writing. Yet, although some of the themes are revised, much of the original structure remains. The chief differences concern additional motifs and characters which increase the complications. As a result, the film appears more as a complex rendering of the short story than as something deviating from it.

In its Introduction, the film transforms the Narrator's omniscient perspective into a framing device. Three youthful giants, titanic phantom-gods who roam the stars and to whom the earth appears like a golf ball suspended in the void, debate the worth of humans in the universe. Two of them argue that they are "nasty little animals," "little creatures swarming and crawling." The third giant, more compassionate, intends to bestow on them all his power, though he admits he has a limit:

> That bit of gritty stuff at the heart of every individual no
> power can touch. The soul, the individuality—that

> ultimate mystery—only the Master can control. Their
> Wills, such as they are, are free. But all else, every
> position, every circumstance, is mine.

This describes the extent of the power he finally grants
George McWhirter Fotheringay (Roland Young). The
milquetoast clerk can control movement and circumstance,
but cannot command another to act against his or her Will.
The most poignant example of this restriction occurs when he
tries and fails to make Ada Price (Joan Gardner) forsake Bill
Stoker (Robert Cochran) and be in love with him.

One of the antagonistic gods convinces the Power-Giver to
alter his plan by experimenting first with a single subject:
"Just try one and see what there is in the human heart." The
Power-Giver assents: "Why not? . . . Just any little fellow.
They are all very much alike. I'll take one haphazard." His
assessment of human uniformity implies Fotheringay is
Everyman. However, George more accurately represents
the Common Man, the majority who live under the domination of the authoritative few, the political bosses, suppressive
employers, and social institutions such as banks and
churches.

The Power-Giver extends his hand toward the suspended
orb. The scene cuts to a long shot of Fotheringay walking
toward the Long Dragon. He is smoking a cigarette. He
pauses in the open gate of the fence surrounding the pub.
Above him appears the gigantic clenched hand of the god, its
index finger pointing downward at the little man. The
fingertip emits a cloud of smoke which envelops George just
as he takes a final puff on his cigarette and flicks it away.

This scene exemplifies how the film imagery generates
more thematic possibilities than the short story. First,
George's smoking establishes a motif which recurs throughout the film. Nearly all the principle characters smoke
cigarettes, pipes, or cigars. Reminiscent of the Time Traveller's pipe, smoking relates to pipe dreams, which suggests,
by the extent of the habit, that many people live with private
fanciful whims they will never act on. George is one of these
people. However, he discards his cigarette at the moment the
cloud engulfs him, indicating that this is a turning point for

him. It takes a while, but his suppressed emotions, ferment-
ing gradually, finally burst out when he realizes that his
power gives him the ability to make those pipe dreams—or
most of them—come true.

The fence symbolizes the many restrictive frames of life
which people accept for themselves. The gate allows escape
from or entrance into that restrictive frame. In his social life,
George crosses the threshold to spend time inside the pub.
After breaking the lamp, he is thrown out for neglecting the
proprieties necessary for acceptance in such a circle. At
Grigsby and Blott, where he works, the names of the
partners are enclosed in a circle on the front door. Later,
after seeing profit potential in Fotheringay's miraculous
powers, Grigsby offers him a partnership, his name to appear
in that circle with the other two men. If George accepted
such a partnership, he would limit his miracles to Grigsby's
dictates for the good of the store and lose his freedom to
execute them according to his own Will.

In the next section, the Discovery of the "Gift," the film
transfers the scene almost literally from the short story.
While George argues with the patron Beamish about the
existence of miracles, a variety of camera angles, close-ups,
and medium and long shots of him and all the customers
suggests he is an ordinary, common man indistinguishable
from them. After his proposition that "a miracle . . . is
something contrariwise to the usual course of nature, done
by an act of Will," he upsets the ceiling lamp and is kicked
out by the proprietor (that is, the director of "proprieties").

At his apartment, as in the original, George experiments
with unimaginative conjuring tricks to convince himself that
he has such power. Here, he materializes fruit, flowers, and
small animals, like cats and rabbits, which later causes Bill
Stoker to label him as "the spirit of Nature." This suggests
that the innocent, naive Fotheringay still has some instinctive
ties to Nature. Gradually, however, he strays from harmless,
localized miracles to miracles with more serious widespread
effects, such as the tiger in Maydig's study.

Fotheringay's Workplace, limited in the short story to an
implication about his fear and caution in working the tritest
of miracles, becomes in the film an arena which greatly

expands on and departs from the original. Besides the new name of the store and George's revised position as draper's assistant,[1] the most critical changes include the addition of several key characters and a romantic entanglement.

Unlike Fotheringay of the short story, who hides his power, George of the film openly performs miracles for his co-workers and talks with them about his gift's mysterious origin ("Maybe it's willpower."). He sees little use for his "gift" except as a possible act in music halls. The other clerks offer more imaginative alternatives. The materialistic vamp Ada Price says he could own and be anything he pleases. Kind-hearted Maggie Hooper (Sophie Stewart) warns him that the gift comes from God and should be used for humanitarian purposes. Bill Stoker makes a seemingly selfish proposal: "Do yourself well. Don't give your gift away to anybody."

Ultimately, it is Stoker's suggestion that is most practical and has the most merit. Grigsby (Edward Chapman) and the banker Bamfylde (Lawrence Hanray) would exploit George's ability to insure their standings in the business and financial worlds. Reverend Maydig would direct the miracle-working to make changes according to his notion of a peaceful "golden age." Colonel Winstanley (Ralph Richardson) would suppress George's power to preserve his routine existence. No matter how logical, noble, and selfless the intention, a person must always act from a subjective point of view, and therefore, since George's viewpoint is as justifiable as anyone's, he might as well make his own decisions on how to apply the power he possesses. This same idea appears in the short story as well, but the film develops and iterates it more fully.

In the film, the Workplace fosters a romantic complication not present in the original. George feels torn between two co-workers, Ada and Maggie, who represent polar qualities of feminine attractiveness: the sexual and the wholesome.[2] George describes his dilemma to Maydig: "Maggie is perfectly lovely when she's sewing on my buttons and mending my sox. But there's a come-and-take-me about Ada Price."

Ada already enjoys a love affair with Bill Stoker and has

no romantic interest in George. He tries to use his powers to appeal to her materialistic desires, but fails to sway her. Twice, he plays Pygmalion, adorning her with tiara and necklace and changing her drab black dress to a sultry silken outfit befitting Cleopatra. However, both times her first response is to ask for Bill, suggesting she is impressed by the merchandise but not by the deliverer.

Maggie Hooper is the charming, attractive girl-next-door. When George cures her hurt arm, she encourages him to use his power for healing. Later, George takes control of the world and makes her his queen, but only after he has been rejected by Ada Price. That is, he first responds to his sexual fantasies before he makes the more substantial, rational choice of a mate. He realizes Maggie's importance in his life, but such an awareness cannot quell that singular, overwhelming, innate drive.[3]

Regarding the Constable Winch Dilemma, the film modifies the short story's ideas and greatly expands on the incident. In the original, George's frequent remorseful bouts remind us of humanity's paralysis between fear and desire. He regrets his action, coming as it did from an uncontrolled outburst, but he cannot resolve it because of the threat of punishment. The episode also shows how a lapse in the responsible application of power (both for Science and Authority) can have disastrous consequences. In the film, George's remorse over Winch (Wallace Lupino) appears minimal; his dilemma seems more a question of how to resolve it than of personal anguish. The second issue, the misuse of power, still appears relevant to the film.

The film enlarges on the Winch episode, showing him transported from the fires of hell to the streets of San Francisco. Away from London, Winch becomes an alien, a man inserted into an unfamiliar environment, much as George with his newfound power becomes an eccentric. The familiar, the banner of Colonel Winstanley, Grigsby, and Bamfylde, marks the steadfast traditional way of life, but it also retards progress. Humanity must accept moments of discomforting alienation if it is to grow and expand with the contributions of innovative discoveries, a lesson similar to that proposed in *The Food of the Gods*.

Later, at a hospital where Winch recuperates from shock, three American reporters interview him. One says of his story,

> Just because it doesn't fit in with any of the stock stories, we've gotta cut it out, just the same as we'd a hadda cut out any stories about flying or submarines or radio fifty years ago. It's new news, and the truth is, we mustn't have new news in the newspaper.

Although these appear weak examples of items the news media might censor, Wells makes the legitimate point that authority often suppresses information it believes the public (the ordinary people like Fotheringay) should not or do not need to know. This scene reinforces the theme of suppression of the common majority by the few who wield the power of control.

George's meeting with Maydig[4] (Ernest Thesiger) occurs at Maggie's urging. George sits cringing in a chair while Maydig stands at the hearth. Behind Maydig, above the mantel, a painting of a beam of light identifies him as the source of knowledge and inspiration. (Maydig has chosen this pose deliberately before George enters the room.) To demonstrate his abilities, George materializes a tiger on the hearth rug, then quickly makes it disappear. This is the first time he performs a miracle that produces something life-threatening. Maydig, impressed, shouts, "It's power! . . . Power, power!" The figure of authority revels in the possibilities of unlimited control. He proposes that they reform the world, creating a "golden age" for humanity and offers to guide George in this undertaking.

Maydig asks George to change his neighbor Colonel Winstanley's whiskey into "some simple non-intoxicating fluid" and his weapon collection into "plowshares and reaping hooks." The transformation angers the Colonel, a proponent of smoking, drinking, and war. He learns from Fotheringay of their intention to reform the world, and representing those who wish to perpetuate routine, tradition, and the status quo, he takes it on himself to try to shoot George.

Winstanley's shot misses, but inspires George to make himself invulnerable. In anger, he ignores Maydig's pleading and sets out to transform the planet into "the world of George McWhirter Fotheringay, according to his dreams." His first act is to change the Colonel's house into a gigantic edifice with a Great Hall from which he will rule. He makes Maydig and Bamfylde his counselors. Then he materializes segments of society before him, summoning all the world leaders and demanding that they come to an agreement on how best to run the world. Maydig pleads for time, but George insists he has waited long enough and they must reach a decision now.

Unlike in the short story, where Maydig's foolish advice causes George to stop the earth's rotation, George makes this decision himself. Maydig warns him of "inertia," but now headstrong with power, George refuses to listen. He stops the rotation and inertia sends everything on the earth's surface into turbulent chaos.

The double meaning of the term "inertia" relates to the paradox of tradition versus progress. "The tendency of a body at rest to remain at rest" describes the Winstanley position, which argues for perpetuating routine and constancy. As George tells him, that works for people contented with the status quo, but not for those like himself, who desire change. The second aspect to inertia, "the tendency of a body in motion to remain in motion," refers to those forces (especially the Sciences) which foster continuous change. George, with his limited imagination, sees only the first definition of inertia, the one he scorned. He fails to see the second definition, the natural one which governs time, and his ignorance causes disaster.

Fortunately, George's invulnerability preserves him, and like his original counterpart he makes the two final wishes that everything return as it was before the miracles started and that he lose his power. Once again in the Long Dragon, he demonstrates with the ceiling lamp the impossibility of miracles, and this time the lamp does not turn upside down. If he had the power, he says there are a few things he would like to do. However, when Beamish tells him that, miracles being an absurdity, "you won't ever have the chance," George responds pitifully, "No, I won't ever have the chance—now." This differs from the original because it suggests that Fotheringay remembers his lost powers. His regret that he had the power to change the world but not the imagination necessary to use it effectively gives the ending a more pathetic and tragic tone.

The Fotheringay of the film is far more rounded than his short story counterpart. In the latter, he begins and remains a cautious, passive character totally swayed and influenced by his superiors. In the film, he has more facets to his personality and he undergoes a change. Roland Young, with his soft, whiny, monotone voice and his stifled gestures, excellently portrays the development of the frustrated milquetoast into a domineering authority figure. His jealous rivalry with Bill for Ada and his confusion over his love affairs make him more interesting than the short story character.[5]

One example of the film's imagery reflecting his character development occurs in a series of scenes where Fotheringay meets with his superiors. Conferring with Grigsby in his office and then with Grigsby and Bamfylde at the bank, George sits shrivelled in a chair, hat in hand, displaying a pitiful, cringing demeanor, while his interviewers, symbols of authority, stand in a dominant position over him. He initially adopts this same pose in his meeting with Maydig, but after making the tiger appear, his first miracle connoting aggression, he rises into a standing position making him equal to the minister. The next day, as they stroll near a river, preparing to create a "golden age" for humanity, it is Maydig who sits cringing on a log while Fotheringay stands above him. George has at last assumed the authoritative position matching the scope of his power. From here on he takes control and uses his miracles aggressively and with determination.

Just before George enters the Long Dragon for the story's conclusion, the film returns one last time to the frame story where the three gods discuss their perception of the events. One of the antagonistic gods (George Sanders) foresees nothing for humanity with its "egotism and elementary lust, a little vindictive indignation." The Power-Giver, however, expresses hope:

"They were apes only yesterday. Give them time. . . .
There is something in every one of those creatures more
than that. Like a little grain of gold glittering in sand,
lost in sand, a flash of indignation when they think
things are false or wrong. That's god-like. . . . What if
I give them power . . . bit by bit. If I stir thought and
wisdom into the mess to keep pace with the growth of
power, broaden slowly age by age, give the grains of
gold time to get together. . . . "
"And in the end it will be the same."
"No, it will be different. . . . Come here in an age or
so and you shall see."

The original theme of predestination played against willful
control of one's destiny is still apparent, but revised according to Wells's later thinking, which inclines more toward
hope for humanity and echoes John Cabal's final exhortation
in *Things to Come.* Also, if a miracle may signify Science,
which in its way often appears a miracle, Wells again suggests
the importance of Science in humanity's future. Fotheringay's misuse of his power reflects dangers inherent in the
misuse of Science, but at the same time, "thought and
wisdom" in its imaginative application may save humankind.
The Power-Giver's plan, to give earthlings power bit by
bit, indicates the Darwinian influence on Wells, with the
hopeful prognosis that humans will develop in time. It also
tends to bode something negative, that humans cannot
realize their potential on their own but need the impetus
from some external force to alter their present faulty
attitudes and poor state of affairs.
The idea of a catastrophic event or an alien intervention to
instigate necessary change appears in many of Wells's works:
"The Star," *In the Days of the Comet, The War of the Worlds,
Star-Begotten,* among others. So too, both the short story and
film versions of "The Man Who Could Work Miracles" imply
that there exists some larger invisible force, incomprehensi-
ble to the human mind—God, Nature, "The Master"—
which maintains order in the universe. The Human Will
aspires to god-like status, but is too feeble, too unimaginative, too limited, to compete with such a force. Maybe in
time, if evolution contributes to mental expansion (as

Herakleophorbia does in *The Food of the Gods*), we may attain equality with the gods. Until then, we had better realize our limitations and restrict our interference with Nature to the trivial, harmless tamperings of Fotheringay's initial cautious experiments.

Notes

1. Early in his life, Wells, groping for a choice of career, apprenticed twice as a draper's assistant. These experiences are most vividly reflected in his semi-autobiographical novel, *Kipps*.

2. Wells expressed a dislike for Erle C. Kenton's 1933 film treatment of *The Island of Doctor Moreau* (renamed *Island of Lost Souls*). However, he seems to have borrowed Kenton's concept of the dual nature of woman, the sensuous female embodied in the panther-woman Lota (Kathleen Burke) and the loyal helpmate personified by Ruth Thomas (Leila Hyams).

3. This seems a personal dilemma of Wells, whose own sexual appetite was notoriously insatiable.

4. Once again, the minister or vicar, as a stock character for Wells, appears the symbol of religious hypocrisy and clerical impracticality and foolishness. (See p. 176, Note 19.)

5. Contradictions within a character usually enhance his or her roundedness. The romantic entanglement, by playing George's common sense against his sexual impulses, creates ambiguities which bring out added dimensions in his personality. This becomes apparent in his lust for Ada, jealousy toward Bill, and tenderness with Maggie.

SELECTED WORKS OF H. G. WELLS

1895: *The Time Machine*

1895: *The Wonderful Visit*

1896: *The Island of Doctor Moreau*

1897: *The Invisible Man*

1898: *The War of the Worlds*

1899: *When the Sleeper Wakes*

1901: *The First Men in the Moon*

1902: *The Sea Lady: A Tissue of Moonshine*

1904: *The Food of the Gods and How It Came to Earth*

1906: *In the Days of the Comet*

1909: *Tono-Bungay*

1914: *The World Set Free: A Story of Mankind*

1923: *Men Like Gods*

1924: *The Dream*

1927: *The Complete Short Stories of H. G. Wells*

1929: *The King Who Was a King*

1933: *The Shape of Things to Come*

1934: *Experiment in Autobiography*

1936: *Things to Come* (film)

1936: *The Croquet Player*

1937: *Star-Begotten*

1937: *The Man Who Could Work Miracles* (film)

BIBLIOGRAPHY

Aldiss, Brian, and David Wingrove. *Trillion Year Spree: The History of Science Fiction*. New York: Atheneum, 1986.

Baxter, John. *Science Fiction in the Cinema*. New York: Paperback Library, 1970.

Benson, Michael. *Vintage Science Fiction Films, 1896–1949*. Jefferson, N.C.: McFarland, 1985.

Bergonzi, Bernard. *The Early H. G. Wells: A Study of the Scientific Romances*. Manchester: Manchester University Press, 1961.

———, ed. *H. G. Wells: A Collection of Critical Essays*. Englewood Cliffs, N.J.: Prentice-Hall, 1976.

Bluestone, George. *Novels into Film*. Berkeley: University of California Press, 1957.

Brosnan, John. *Future Tense: The Cinema of Science Fiction*. New York: St. Martin's Press, 1978.

Cook, David A. *A History of Narrative Film*. New York: W. W. Norton, 1981.

Curtis, James. *James Whale*. Metuchen, N.J.: Scarecrow, 1982.

DeNitto, Dennis. *Film: Form and Feeling*. New York: Harper and Row, 1985.

Draper, Michael. *H. G. Wells*. London: Macmillan, 1987.

Geduld, Harry M. *The Definitive Time Machine*. Indianapolis: Indiana University Press, 1987.

Glut, Donald F. *Classic Movie Monsters*. Metuchen, N.J.: Scarecrow, 1978.

Gunn, James. *Alternate Worlds: The Illustrated History of Science Fiction*. Englewood Cliffs, N.J.: Prentice-Hall, 1975.

Hammond, J. R. *Herbert George Wells: An Annotated Bibliography of His Works*. New York: Garland, 1977.

Huntington, John. *The Logic of Fantasy: H. G. Wells and Science Fiction*. New York: Columbia University Press, 1982.

Johnson, William, ed. *Focus on the Science Fiction Film*. Englewood Cliffs, N.J.: Prentice-Hall, 1972.

Klein, Michael, and Gillian Parker, eds. *The English Novel and the Movies*. New York: Ungar, 1981.

Kulik, Karol. *Alexander Korda: The Man Who Could Work Miracles*. London: W. H. Allen, 1975.

McConnell, Frank, ed. *H. G. Wells: The Time Machine/The War of the Worlds*. New York: Oxford University Press, 1977.

————. *The Science Fiction of H. G. Wells*. New York: Oxford University Press, 1981.

MacKenzie, Norman and Jeanne. *H. G. Wells*. New York: Simon and Schuster, 1973.

Maltin, Leonard, ed. *Leonard Maltin's TV Movies and Video Guide*. 1989 ed. New York: Signet, 1988.

Menville, Douglas. *A Historical and Critical Survey of the Science-Fiction Film*. New York: Arno, 1975.

Miller, Gabriel. *Screening the Novel: Rediscovered American Fiction in Film*. New York: Ungar, 1980.

Nichols, Peter. *The World of Fantastic Films*. New York: Dodd, Mead, 1984.

Pal, George. "Filming *War of the Worlds*." *Astounding Science Fiction,* October 1953, 100–111.

Parish, James Robert, and Michael R. Pitts. *The Great Science Fiction Pictures*. Metuchen, N.J.: Scarecrow, 1977.

Parrinder, Patrick, ed. *H. G. Wells: The Critical Heritage*. London: Routledge and Kegan Paul, 1972.

———, and Robert M. Philmus, eds. *H. G. Wells's Literary Criticism*. Brighton, England: Harvester, 1980.

———. *Science Fiction: Its Criticism and Teaching*. London: Methuen, 1980.

Phillips, Gene D., S.J. *Fiction, Film, and F. Scott Fitzgerald*. Chicago: Loyola University Press, 1986.

———. *Fiction, Film, and Faulkner: The Art of Adaptation*. Knoxville: University of Tennessee Press, 1988.

Philmus, Robert M. *Into the Unknown: The Evolution of Science Fiction from Francis Godwin to H. G. Wells*. Berkeley: University of California Press, 1970.

———, and David Y. Hughes, eds. *H. G. Wells: Early Writings in Science and Science Fiction*. Berkeley: University of California Press, 1975.

Rose, Mark, ed. *Science Fiction: A Collection of Critical Essays*. Englewood Cliffs, N.J.: Prentice-Hall, 1976.

Scholes, Robert, and Eric S. Rabkin. *Science Fiction: History, Science, Vision.* New York: Oxford University Press, 1977.

Scot, Darrin. "Filming *The Time Machine.*" *American Cinematographer,* 41, August 1960, 490–498.

Sinyard, Neil. *Filming Literature: The Art of Screen Adaptation.* London: Croom Helm, 1986.

Slusser, George, and Eric S. Rabkin, eds. *Shadows of the Magic Lamp: Fantasy and Science Fiction in Film.* Carbondale: Southern Illinois University Press, 1985.

Sobchack, Vivian Carol. *The Limits of Infinity: The American Science Fiction Film 1950–75.* South Brunswick, N.J.: A. S. Barnes, 1980.

Stover, Leon. *The Prophetic Soul: A Reading of H. G. Wells's "Things to Come."* Jefferson, N.C.: McFarland, 1987.

Suvin, Darko, and Robert M. Philmus, eds. *H. G. Wells and Modern Science Fiction.* Lewisburg, Pa.: Bucknell University Press, 1977.

Tabori, Paul. *Alexander Korda.* New York: Living Books, 1966.

Wagner, Geoffrey. *The Novel and the Cinema.* Rutherford, N.J.: Fairleigh Dickinson University Press, 1975.

West, Anthony. *H. G. Wells: Aspects of a Life.* New York: Meridian, 1985.

INDEX

Italicized numbers indicate pages with photographs; boldfaced numbers indicate pages where Wells's works and their film adaptations are discussed at length.

INDEX

ABOUT THE AUTHOR

Thomas C. Renzi (B.F.A., Ph.D., State University of New York at Buffalo) has had a lifelong interest in film. While in graduate school, he discovered the entertainment and social values of science fiction and became especially enthralled by H.G. Wells. He is presently working on a second book of film adaptations of science fiction literature and is nearing completion of his first novel.